From Sarees To Stripes

From Sarees To Stripes

True Stories of Commercial Women Pilots of India

Captain
Manisha M. Puri

AMARYLLIS

AMARYLLIS

An imprint of Manjul Publishing House Pvt. Ltd.
•C-16, Sector 3, Noida, Uttar Pradesh 201301, India
Website: www.manjulindia.com
Registered Office:
•10, Nishat Colony, Bhopal 462 003 – India
Distribution Centres
Ahmedabad, Bengaluru, Bhopal, Kolkata, Chennai,
Hyderabad, Mumbai, New Delhi, Pune

This edition first published in India in 2022

ISBN 978-93-90924-75-2

Cover Design: Medha Sharma

Printed and bound in India by Parksons Graphics Pvt. Ltd., Mumbai

I dedicate this book to all those who believe in the 'Never say die' attitude – the ones who take all challenges in their life as encouragement, and reach for the skies.

*My dearest and most brave daughters,
Taranee and Anchita, are among them.*

Contents

Different Flaps of the Wing
(The Mid- to Late-1990s)

Generation-Next

Conclusion

राजीव बसंल
अध्यक्ष एवं प्रबंध निदेशक
Rajiv Bansal
Chairman & Managing Director

एअर इंडिया
AIR INDIA

Foreword

I feel proud to introduce Capt. Manisha Puri's book *From Sarees to Stripes*, which showcases the inspiring saga of women pilots since the early days of aviation in India in 1930 till date. The book focuses on the challenges and stress faced by women pilots flying passenger aircraft. The élan with which Capt. Manisha has navigated the skies to compile the book, showing the achievements of her contemporaries and predecessors – makes for both exciting, wonderful reading.

Air India has been soaring high on its accomplished workforce equally represented by women and men employees. Our women colleagues have, for generations, done us proud by excelling in their respective areas of specialization, leaving their mark on the annals of the aviation sector on a global scale.

I understand Capt. Sarla Sharma Thukral was the first woman to fly in India as early as 1935, while Capt. Prem Mathur was the first woman to get a commercial pilot licence in India in 1955. Capt. Durba Banerjee was the first woman to join the then Indian Airlines, the only domestic airline in India in 1966, while Capt. Saudamini Deshmukh was the first woman Commander in India and Asia who operated an all-women flight in 1985. These and many similar stories of women pilots, including that of Capt. Nivedita Jain Bhasin, the youngest woman to get command on Boeing 737 in 1989 at the age of twenty-six, find pride of place in the book.

Our women pilots have helped Air India spread its wings to connect homes and hearts over the last eight decades. Some of them have left indelible impressions with their achievements in the sky. Capt. Manisha has done a commendable job by unfolding some of the lesser-known stories of excellence scripted by these women brave hearts, who would have braved every odd to fulfil their dream of becoming accomplished women commercial pilots on sheer merit and hard work sans any gender consideration.

Our women pilots have grown from strength to strength shattering every myth around flying being a men's preserve. They not only flew state-of-the-art aircraft across continents but created history by operating all-women crew flights over some of the longest and most challenging navigational paths, including the Polar route.

Fuelled by their indomitable spirit to excel, women pilots and employees of Air India have been excelling in their field from the cockpit to the boardroom and in every area of Air India's activities. I am sure the book will not only make for enjoyable reading but will also motivate more and more women to scale new heights in the flying profession.

(Rajiv Bansal)

अर इंडिया लिमिटेड, एअरलाइन्स हाउस, 113, गुरुद्वारा रकाबगंज रोड, नई दिल्ली–110001. फोन : 23422000
Air India Limited, Airlines House, 113, Gurudwara Rakabganj Road, New Delhi - 110001. Tel. : 23422000
वेबसाईट Website : www.airindia.in

Introduction

Some Heroes Wear Wings

As the flight took off from Visakhapatnam Airport, she noticed the engine oil temperature rising. Before her co-pilot could announce this, she monitored the engine parameters, giving the standard call-out. Simultaneously, she steered the aircraft on the prescribed departure track, knowing fully well the limitations of the critical airfield. The aircraft was the Boeing 737, and she had got her command barely a year ago. Within 13 seconds she took action, shutting the engine down (the time limit for this being 15 seconds). Left with a single engine, she informed the Air Traffic Control (ATC) of her decision to return, calmly carried out a single engine and overweight checklist, and executed a safe landing. She was later appreciated for her prompt, correct action that saved the airline some major engine repair work.

On another occasion, after take-off from Aurangabad on a sweltering afternoon with temperatures touching 49°C, the wheel of the B-737 aircraft had, on lift-off, collided with a truck parked outside the airport boundary on a road that was declared a clearway in the prescribed charts. An obstacle on the take-off path changes the actual weight/load that can be carried on any particular day. About 7 seconds had elapsed between lift-off and collision with the obstacle that was about 22 ft high. The left engine of the aircraft stopped working and she made the standard callout of 'Engine One Failed'. As a fairly new co-pilot, she then carried out the prescribed seat-oriented checklist. The aircraft was losing height, drifting to the left, unable to make the necessary almost-360-degree turn to head back to the airfield. So, on instructions from the commander, she located the best possible barren patch of land to make an emergency landing, giving the 'Mayday, Mayday, Mayday!' call and providing the heading, the compass direction in which the aircraft nose was pointed. The impact on landing damaged the aircraft, triggering it to go up in flames, as it carried about 8 tonnes of fuel.

Having survived this accident, she faced the fact-finding body nominated by the Government of India where the contents of the Cockpit Voice Recorder (CVR) and Digital Flight Data Recorder (DFDR) were decoded for over a year. As she had done everything possible under the circumstances, she was exonerated. After this incident, she came back to command the Airbus and flew successfully for more than twenty years.

In yet another episode, on the B-787, about one hour short of landing, she got a message from the airline. 'Captain, FYI, we have just received a warning that there could be a bomb on board your flight, and the bomb explosion time is—.' She read the message twice over and made her co-pilot read it too, before springing into action. Her landing time was 7 minutes after the explosion time mentioned. She took corrective action, asking her co-pilot to perform the 'Bomb on Board' checklist. She increased air speed to the maximum permissible limit and maintained it, trying to reduce the time for her landing. Using all available means of aid, be it the ATC, the crew, or the satellite phone, she informed everyone concerned about her intention to land before the forewarned explosion time and asked for all assistance on landing. Keeping her speed in check even during descent and asking for direct routing wherever possible, she managed to get her landing time down to 10 minutes before the time given to her. The big bird made it safely on to the runway and she made the passenger announcement only during the final phase of landing to ensure the passengers remained calm.

These are not fictional stories or anecdotes from books; these are real accounts of the women who have made it to the cockpit and have been flying commercial airlines in India since 1966. It was easier to break the glass ceiling to reach the cockpit than to change the mindset of people resistant to accepting women as pilots. The idea behind this book came to me when I was medically grounded in 2015. I had put in more than twenty-seven years in Indian Airlines (Air India since 2008) as a pilot, flying different aircraft, from those during my flying school days to commercial airlines ranging from the Pushpak, Cessna 152/152-A, 172 to the Boeing 737s and the Airbuses (319/320/321). I would often come across people who still found it difficult to acknowledge that women were becoming pilots and had been flying for airlines since the 1960s. Even today, eyebrows are raised with an astonished expression as the oft-repeated question, 'Really! Is it true?', rears its head.

This book has been written to help modern India discover the history of these women pilots who worked silently, with utmost dedication, to achieve their aspirations, without asking for any favours or reservations. There were no women empowerment programmes to encourage them, yet they strove to reach their goals, defying all odds and proving their worth as successful commercial airline pilots. No challenge was big enough to come in the way of their desire to excel, and they flew shoulder-to-shoulder with their male colleagues as commanders on different fleets of aircraft. No crisis could defeat them, whether it was a single engine or hydraulic failure, bomb alert, weather navigation or emergency landing – they did it all and sailed through.

The passion with which my career took flight is the same passion that has driven me to put together this book about 'flying women', the women who broke barriers to enter a male-dominated profession at a time when they were generally dissuaded from taking up any profession at all. It is a matter of pride to be a part of this group of women. We are proud of our country, which is perhaps one of the first in the world to have women in commercial airlines flying jet aircraft. We are also proud of Indian Airlines, the first airline in Asia and probably the world to operate with an all-women set of crew, commander, co-pilot and cabin crew on a commercial airline in 1985.

These yesteryear women worked towards their ambitions and goals relentlessly, rendering the seemingly impossible possible. The untold stories of these amazing women who made it to the cockpit of a commercial airline would not have been possible had they not been given the opportunity. It was thanks to the farsightedness of those who took on the challenge of opening up the airline for employing women; it was Indian Airlines that gave them the wings to fly. The focus of this book is on the commercial women pilots of India. Because of the challenges and stress that come with flying passenger planes, the responsibility and alertness required for jet flying cannot be compared to hobby flying. My story would be incomplete, though, if I did not mention some of the early women who had no opportunity to fly passenger planes for lack of access, but they would not be any less inspiring for future generations.

Capt. Sarla Sharma Thukral, the first woman to fly in India as early as 1935; Capt. Prem Mathur, the first woman to get a commercial pilot licence in India in 1955; Capt. Durba Banerjee, the first woman to join Indian Airlines, the only domestic commercial airline in India in 1966; Capt. Saudamini Deshmukh, the first woman commander in India and Asia who operated the all-women commercial airline flight in 1985; Capt. Nivedita Jain Bhasin, the youngest woman to get command on the B-737 in 1989 at the age of twenty-six while raising a two-year-old son; Capt. Anila Bhatia, the first woman instructor of a flying school in India in 1982 and also a proud mother whose only child, her daughter, is a captain on the B-777, making them the first mother-daughter pilot duo in India... the list goes on. This book is my genuine effort to bring out hidden history and record it on paper. May you enjoy every word you read here and take comfort in the knowledge of having safe skies helmed by flying women!

From Sarees To Stripes

True Stories of Commercial Women Pilots of India

The start of my journey – First Officer, Indian Airlines, 1989

Nothing matches the thrill of the first flight – ready to fly the Pushpak, Bhopal Flying Club, 1986

Standing next to the Cessna-152-A at the flying school in Fort Worth, Meacham Airport, USA

Always delighted to be up in the air – flying the Airbus 320

Journey into the Blue Skies

one

Flight to Freedom

Manisha Mohan Puri

The expression 'flight to freedom' perfectly describes how I felt when I sat in the small Pushpak at the Bhopal Flying Club. It was the winter of 1986. I had just received a scholarship for 60 hours of free flying at the club. I still remember that yellow aircraft with its registration 'VT-DLP'. Being up in the sky certainly turned out to be the most amazing experience of my life. I can still feel the sense of exhilaration from that first time; it is very difficult to express the sheer joy of it in mere words.

The journey did not stop there. My big dreams became boundless and there was no turning back. The upheavals in my path did not deter me in any way; I stayed focused and pursued my passion. I did not rest till I reached the cockpit of a jet when I joined Indian Airlines (now Air India) in 1988. I think it merits mention here that this was the only airline in India at the time that hired and trained women as pilots.

Taking a trip down memory lane, I can recall how it all started. In January 1984, I lost my father, Dr Vishwa Mitra Mohan, and I was asked to return home to Bhopal from Chandigarh where I was studying for my master's degree. My mother, Krishna Mohan, was alone and the unbearable loss had shaken us all. Being the third-born in the family, I did not have much say at that time among my siblings. Experiencing this excruciating void in my home, I grew rather quiet as I could not imagine where the future would take us all. Fathers were the driving force in families in those days, and our dad was no different. He was the backbone of our family. Being an educator, he guided us through all the odds life threw at us. Having lost him in a matter of a few seconds while he was at his office was a rude shock that was very difficult to digest. Barely twenty, I was not ready for such a tragedy.

Having moved to Bhopal, I started thinking about what I could and would be able to do there, as it was a small town that did not offer much exposure and opportunities at the time. The Union Public Service Commission (UPSC) exam was the first thing I set my mind on, though my mum and brother thought teaching was good enough before I could be married off. But that was not my plan. Even as a child, I had always wanted to do something adventurous that would keep me going places in life. I started preparing for these exams, aiming to be an IPS officer. After all, Kiran Bedi was one name in the country we all looked up to!

These exams were no easy task, so I started taking tuitions from a neighbour, an ex-IAS officer. As part of our coaching, we were told to read the newspaper like the Bible, front to back, line by line. It was during one such paper-reading session that I spotted the advertisement for a flying scholarship of

60 hours at the Bhopal Flying Club being sponsored by the Godrej group. I cut out the ad and sent in my application even as I continued with my studies. In a few days' time, I got an acknowledgement of acceptance from them, asking me to reach the airport flying club for an interview. I was delighted and resolved not to miss the day of the interview at any cost, even though I was not sure whether I should share this information with my mother at that stage, as I did not know if she would allow me to try this out. It was just my mother and me at home now. My elder brother and sister were in the US. Even my younger brother had left for Delhi to take up a job. So I decided to keep it to myself for the time being, go for the interview and then take a call based on the outcome. In Bhopal, people generally knew one another well, and since we had been living there for years, I was sure that sooner or later, I would have to tell my mother, lest she found out from someone else.

On the day of the interview, I pretended to be heading out for my coaching class as usual but instead requested one of my friends to drop me to the airport. I had no access to conveyance to reach the airport which was a good 12–15 km away from my house. My friends were quite gung-ho that I was venturing into such a daring sport and wholeheartedly supported me. At the airport, I saw many who had applied for this scholarship and, to my surprise, there was one other girl besides me! There was a panel conducting the interview, including persons from the flying club and one from the sponsors' side. We learnt that there were two scholarships for the taking – one for a girl and one for a boy. The interview went well. They only asked a few questions on the basics and checked our aptitude and response to situational awareness. I assumed that they would later hold another round to check if we could cope with the pressures of flying. Interview done, I resumed my studies for the upcoming exam scheduled to be held in a few months' time.

But a few days later, destiny intervened. I received a letter from the club stating that I had been granted the scholarship for 60 hours of flying. You can imagine how surprised I was! Excited, my focus changed. This new venture seemed more inviting and my UPSC studies took a backseat. Instead of going for my tuitions, I would reach Bairagarh Airport in Bhopal (as it was called then) and take to the skies!

Each day would turn out better than the last, each moment more thrilling. Very shortly, I knew I had to appear for my exams, but my interest had shifted, for now the profession I wanted to pursue itself had changed. I did not want to be an IPS officer anymore but a pilot, a captain flying aeroplanes.

Flying gave me a sense of freedom I felt I could not find elsewhere. It was a feeling of pure power and responsibility, of being in control. I was in charge of not only myself but the situation and all decisions that came with it. There was the weather to tackle, as I navigated my way to the destination using the least possible flying aids (this was during the '80s), and even though we were only just learning to fly in a small plane, we were beginning to understand many more issues we would have to face once we were airborne. It was all so new and challenging that I thought this could be a great job. What a 'Wow!' feeling it was to watch the big Boeing from Delhi land in Bhopal every day! As student pilots, we could visit the cockpit before the passengers boarded, and I would be mesmerized seeing those panels, lights and numerous switches. The entire cockpit looked awe-inspiring compared to our humble Pushpak. It would be such a huge dream come true to sit in that cockpit and fly that machine!

I decided it was time to tell my mother about it. Naturally, when I did, she was thoroughly shocked; it did not go down too well with her. She wondered how my studying for the UPSC could possibly lead to this kind of thinking. Immediately, she spoke to my elder brother in the US, who thought I had 'lost it' and he pronounced that it was certainly time for me to get married. I told my mother I had earned a scholarship and that was how and why I was going to the flying club, and I pleaded with her to allow me to continue. I was flying for free; she need not pay for anything. Why should she be worried or concerned? There was turmoil in my house after this announcement. *How could you do this*, she implored. I was supposed to be studying, not gallivanting. I was expected to acquire a good job, rather than hanging out and flying. That would only be a waste of time. I could understand her reasons for saying this. After all, who had heard of a woman holding a pilot's job in those days? However, I had a passion, a larger-than-life dream now that was driving me to simply keep at it, at least till the duration of the scholarship. I must also admit I wasn't sure at the time about getting a job in this field, especially being a girl. I did not know where it would take me, but letting it go was not an option, so I resolved to find some way to continue and, most importantly, to be able to convince my mother and make her understand that I would not be happy in any random office job.

Flying gave me strength, freedom, and independence, things that captivated me. It gave me satisfaction and I just could not think of any job as good as being a pilot. It wasn't easy to get my family to see it as a great profession, or that, even as a woman, I could certainly rise to the challenge. Lines from my favourite author, Richard Bach, kept me going: 'You are never given a wish without also being given the power to make it true. You may have to work for it, however.'

When they saw that I was indeed determined and would not let go of this dream, they threw the first challenge at me:

they would consider my request to fly if I could tell them about any woman in this profession. They were convinced there was no one and I would have to give up this crazy dream. The starting point on the road to success was a tough one. In 1985–86, there was no Internet, no Google search, no mobile phone. Even making an STD call was difficult. Yet, I did not give up. I checked with people in the flying club and with the ATC officers as they would be in touch with Indian Airlines, who operated their B-737 flight daily. Then there was Avro of Vayudoot. With the help of Indian Airlines captains, whom I was allowed to meet, I found out that there were four female pilots in Indian Airlines.

This gave me the impetus I needed and then there was no looking back. I gathered information and wrote a letter to Capt. Saudamini in Calcutta (now Kolkata). She was kind enough to give me some time, and my mother and I went to Calcutta where my maternal uncle lived. It was at their house that Capt. Saudamini met me and my family in May 1987. This not only encouraged me but gave my family something to think about and, ultimately, allowed me to fulfil my dreams! My maternal uncle, Prithvi mamaji, was happy meeting Capt. Saudamini and was convinced thereafter that this could well be a profession for girls. Being my godfather, he spoke to my mother, telling her that he would take responsibility for me and that she should allow me to continue. This enabled me to take the first step towards my ultimate dream.

Next up was the question of the flying school. Back then, girls were the last priority for any instructor as they seemed to think that we were there just to pass time; this was seen as hobby flying for us while more attention was given to male classmates who were considered to be serious about this profession. Being the only girl, classmates did not want to help, and there were only dissuasion and remarks such as, 'She is here to take our slot and waste our time. She will never be able to handle emergencies or the weather.' They would often also add, 'Soon, she will get married and then what, she will not be coming here, but managing her home and husband.' All in all, progress in gaining flying hours was very slow; sometimes, in a month, I would get only 10 minutes of flying time. I did not get discouraged, but became further intent on reaching my goal. I started acquiring as much information as possible and learnt that some of the boys had moved school to finish their flying course faster. A lot of them also opted to go abroad as it was not only quicker, but the flying schools there also offered more modern methods where one could train on better aircraft and acquaint themselves with more advanced systems. I forced my family to let me take this route. I had to finish and get myself a job to prove to them how serious I was. Working hard for this was my topmost priority; I felt most of the boys were younger, being either straight out of school or still pursuing graduation. I was already doing my master's, so I somehow wanted to finish my flying faster. With this in mind, I started checking out schools in the US. As I was yet to complete 60 hours of free flying and there was no further scholarship, I thought the money I would have to spend to fly further in India could be used to go abroad to achieve results faster and get my Commercial Pilot Licence (CPL). I would then be ready to fulfil my aim of applying for a job. I spoke to my maternal uncle and with his support, shortlisted a school in Dallas, Texas. It was a dream moment when I sat in the British Airways flight to New York to go meet my sister, en route to the flying school in Dallas. This was in September 1987.

I felt on top of the world as I landed. This was my first trip to the US, and arriving there from small-town Bhopal was like setting foot on a different planet. There was so much to see. Fast-moving cars, big malls, museums, drive-in movie theatres, highways the likes of which we had never seen anywhere in India, grand bridges over rivers... the list is endless. One could easily get swayed to leisurely enjoy all these wonderful things we could not even imagine back home in the India of those days. Like any enthusiastic twenty-something youngster, I too was ready to explore everything around me, but I remained steadfast about only flying. The dream of operating big aircraft and joining Indian Airlines was the only thing I could think of. Nothing, not even the great American city of New York, could alter my aspiration. It was as if that one aim was all I ate, thought, breathed. All I wanted to do was reach school and start flying.

Finally I got to my destination: Skywings Flight Training School in Meacham Field, Dallas. I was excited and could not wait for my lessons to start. Dallas was a totally new environment, but I told myself that I had chosen to be there and I would have to manage everything. To start with, being a vegetarian was tough anywhere in the western world, and, it was even more difficult in my flying school complex. It had a cafeteria where it was impossible to get vegetarian food. There were times I had to live on French fries or food packets from vending machines. The next big shock came when I started attending lessons. I thought I had chosen to come to the most liberal and advanced country. I never realised that, being a woman, I would be discouraged from flying here! I was taken aback when one of my American classmates would put me down every day, saying that women could hobby fly but making it a career and thinking about airline jobs was not their cup of tea. His reasoning seemed quite illogical to me when, one day, he told me that women would never be able to handle emergencies which were part and parcel of flying big jets in any commercial airline. Even as I made progress, he would tell me this every single day. Initially, it annoyed me, but it also helped me become stronger as I was determined to persist in my efforts.

Moreover, my family had collected money to help me fly. I did not want to do anything where money would go to waste. I knew my mother could not bear the entire cost, left with just her pension and savings. I certainly didn't want to pressurize her with the high cost of flying. Despite my best attempts, I could not manage to get aid from the government and other sponsors for free flying for my CPL. So, the maternal side of my family supported me financially. On my part, I worked for a year as a school teacher, alongside making some paintings that I managed to sell in Bhopal. All this to make as much money as I could in order to continue flying, and get my CPL, without which I could not apply for jobs in the airline.

I decided to teach this American classmate a lesson by showing him how women were up for any challenge. By now, I had flown solo and had been flying regularly. I was able to pile in a lot of hours; I was confident and prepared for anything up in the air. My instructor was good. He would give me a lot of information and flying tips. He was preparing me to take this up as a career and taught me to handle all kinds of emergencies, including negative thoughts. One day, I decided to openly accept this American classmate's challenge. I suggested we put his apprehension about women handling aircraft emergencies to test and invited him to come up in the aircraft with me that evening.

The sun was setting as we took off in the Cessna 152-A and climbed up to 8,000 ft (a comfortable height to manoeuvre the aircraft for any exercise). As we reached that level, we had also flown the distance that indicated that if the engine failed, we may not be able to glide to make it to the runway. There was no other airfield in the vicinity where one could land in case of an emergency. It was already getting dark by now and I noticed he was waiting to see what situation I would create for an emergency. Normally, on a single engine aircraft, people didn't mess around with their engine as there was a possibility that it would not re-start, but I was ready for the worst. I moved my hand and in a split second, shut the engine, the only engine on the aircraft. The aircraft started to glide. I had come prepared for the distance I could glide down to, 2,000 ft, before re-starting the engine). I also knew the best glide speed of the aircraft. As we started to drift down, I turned and saw a strange look on his face as he was not anticipating an 'engine off' situation as an emergency measure. I knew he hadn't, in his wildest imagination, anticipated the step I had taken. There were more situations one could attempt to simulate, other than turning the engine off, especially at night, and moreover with such great distance left to cover for the runway. He sat unspeaking, anxiously wondering what lay in store, though his hands were moving to try and start the engine. However, as I was flying and this was my sortie, I told him to relax, that we would glide and maintain the best glide all the way to the ground, but I knew I would follow the checklist to start the engine around 2,000 ft, as there was no engine fire or engine out for any emergency. He looked extremely uncomfortable. Maintaining the drift down speed, we were slowly losing height and nearing the ground. Finally, as we got close to 2,000 ft, I made the attempt to start the engine, and by 1,000 ft, we had the power on and landed safely. But this incident shut him up. After that day, he hardly spoke to me and would avoid coming to the club when I was there. Hopefully, my actions had clearly conveyed that women could handle anything, even something as tough as an aircraft. It is not about being a woman or a man when it comes to emergencies. It is about your personality and adeptness in handling any situation. Pilots have no gender; a machine does not know whether a man or a woman is handling it. It all comes down to whether one has the skills for the profession or not. Many men I knew were so petrified as passengers, I wondered how they would be if forced into this profession!

Having completed my flying and getting my CPL from the US, I returned to India in July 1988. I had cleared the exams for reconverting an American licence (CPL) to an Indian CPL, before leaving from the US. So on arrival, I only had to send in my papers to the DGCA (Director General Civil Aviation, the licence issuing government agency) for conversion of the Federal Aviation Administration CPL to the Indian CPL. As luck would have it, shortly thereafter, there was an advertisement for induction of trainee pilots in Indian Airlines. I was ready with all the requirements and immediately applied for the job and started to study for the entrance exam. I took all the help available, from friends and colleagues from the industry to the best coaching classes, the most popular being Mr Duggal for technical coaching and Mr Manchanda for aptitude and entrance exam preparation. There was no time to waste or think about anything. My days were spent only studying. On the day of the exam, there were about 150 candidates in all, of which seven were girls. I still remember that 80 students cleared the written test, and of those 80, three were girls. We were informed that there would only be one girl if any were selected for the batch. The next step was a group discussion followed by the final countdown, the interview.

I did my best, then eagerly awaited the outcome. As I did not know anyone in the airline or, for that matter, in aviation, I had no way of finding out when the results would be out. Many of the boys who sat for the exam with me had connections in the industry. I learnt that their fathers were captains and they were overconfident about getting selected. I remember how one such classmate, who had also flown with me in Dallas, would often boast that his father was a senior captain in Air India and would tell me he had the upper hand. He would always ask me,

'Who do you know? How will you get the job?' I would smile and think, 'Let my work talk.' I was confident about my abilities and would respond with, 'Let's see what happens when we get back.' Somehow, I was self-assured and positive that having reached this far, I would make it. Believing in yourself was all you could do those days. Rarely did you get any encouragement from your classmates or others along the way. I remember my excitement when I got the telegram informing me of my selection with instructions to proceed to the Central Training Establishment (CTE), Hyderabad, for the course commencing on 10 October 1988. It felt like the culmination of a big journey and I jumped with joy. I couldn't have ever imagined that my life would take such a beautiful turn. An airline pilot! How many could walk that path in the 1980s?

I was going to Hyderabad for the first time in my life, that too as a trainee pilot with Indian Airlines, one among the few women in the country who were in the airline. There were very few women in those days – eight or nine girls out of about 800–900 pilots in the airline. One girl was selected in each batch. I was from Batch #40 with 24 trainees, of which 23 were boys. We were all going to be trained to become first officers on the B-737, the aircraft I would dream about in my flying school days.

It was only when we reached the training centre that I met my batchmates. Some of them were known to me as we had met or seen each other at flying school and some others when I was studying for the entrance exam. All of us were so happy and excited to be at the Indian Airlines' training centre in Hyderabad. We completed all reporting formalities and got our schedule for classes. We were informed about our classroom and the instructor who would teach us. The first message we got was that classes began at 8 a.m. sharp, and coming late to class would not be acceptable.

On Monday (19 October) morning, everyone was on time. This wasn't an easy profession, yet everyone seemed excitedly geared up for this new life. We waited a while for the instructor to arrive. We greeted him, all pumped up about studying the electrical system of the B-737, one of the first technical chapters that was programmed. Prof. M.M. Rao, our instructor, didn't even greet us as he had just received some sad news before coming to the class. In fact, we were to learn soon that he was never late to class as a rule, but that day, he had been delayed by a good 15 minutes. We realised why when he started talking. He said, 'We are to start with the electrical system of the B-737, but before that I want to inform you all about why I am late for class today. It is with great sadness that I share that one of our Boeings has just gone down in Ahmedabad.'

There was pin-drop silence in the class. All of us were just beginning our careers, our brand-new lives, and what a start to the day – hearing that the aircraft we were going to learn about had just met with an accident! That was an eye-opener. I knew then that this new journey I was setting out on was no bed of roses. It would be tough and one would have to be ready for any eventuality. Such was our first day and first class of training. Slowly, we all got into the rhythm of our aircraft manuals. The Boeing manuals were many and huge. I remember we had a big bag, the size of a cricket kit, filled with our manuals which we had to carry to class every day. With each passing day, we grew more and more familiar with the books. Each of us were here for the final countdown – to be released as first officers!

My acceptance among the batch of 23 boys was also no cakewalk. I was watched every moment. I changed completely, from a carefree person full of life to a quiet, docile one, drawing the line between work and hanging out. Not everyone understood that being in a male-dominated profession, one had to watch what they said, even jokingly, as it could be misunderstood. I did not have much choice but to be very careful in everything I said and did. I realised that the reputation I created then would stay with me when I left the training centre. Some would accept me, but others would not be very happy seeing where I had reached. One of my batch mates would often tell me, 'Why don't you go join as cabin crew? Why have you come here?' Mostly, I would smile to avoid confrontation. Then one day, I politely replied, 'You seem to be very interested in a cabin job, why don't you become cabin crew? You will make a good flight purser.' He was quiet after that. Sometimes, it is important to convey that enough is enough; you are where you want to be and people cannot decide what is good for you. I learnt that people could say what they wanted, but we must continue on our own chosen path.

On another occasion, just to scare me, one of my batch mates put a live frog in my pencil pouch when I had stepped out on an errand. A little later, one of my batch mates asked me to give him a pencil. As I opened my pouch and put my hand inside, I felt something moving and, in a reflex action, I withdrew my hand in a hurry and the frog jumped out. They were all waiting to hear me scream or run out frightened, but to their surprise, I let the frog jump out and opened the door of the classroom for it to make a safe exit instead. The guys were surely surprised at my reaction and how I had handled the situation. There was some silence, nobody wanted to admit who had played this prank. I remained calm and did not bother to ask or scream at those who I believed were behind such a childish prank. A few days later, one of them came up to me and told me he was responsible, as some of them wanted to see me react in fear. I politely told him, 'We are in a profession where the word "fear" is not in our dictionary and "Never Say Die" is what we have learnt and how we got here, so these things are just a waste of time. It's better we get along and work towards learning about the magnificent aircraft we have all worked hard for.' I think my words did change their mindset towards me and women per se from then on.

Soon, the training was over and we were released as First Officers (F/Os). Becoming a F/O was an altogether different feeling, one of achievement. You felt you had worked to earn your wings to fly – the beautiful stripes (even though, at this stage, they were just two stripes), the peak cap, the uniform. It all made you feel great. It wasn't some fancy costume like someone once asked me: 'Are you a real pilot or a pretend one?' It was true that when a woman (even a F/O) in uniform walked around the airport or towards the aircraft, people looked at her in awe. It was the uniform that spoke. For she had made it into a profession that many could not even attempt!

This new life really took off once I was posted to my base in Delhi, in November 1989. We had to start our Line Operating Flight Training (LOFT) before we could fly with any captains as F/Os. Capt. I.D. David, one of the senior commanders and instructors, was to do my LOFT. He had the reputation of being a strict instructor. That did not bother me until I learnt he was a chain smoker. I did not know what effect that would have on me since no one in my family had ever smoked. We started our LOFT normally, with briefings, as with any other trainee captain. There was a pre-flight briefing and I proceeded to the aircraft to perform the co-pilot duties of the external walk walkaround, keeping the aircraft ready with weather and other data. The sector was Delhi–Allahabad–Gorakhpur–Allahabad–Delhi. As instructor/examiner, he could let me handle the controls of the aircraft, which he did.

The first sector went smoothly; although he smoked (smoking was allowed in cabin and cockpit those days), I did not feel anything. But after some time, with his nonstop smoking in the close confines of the cockpit of the Boeing, my head started to feel heavy. By the time we were on the last sector, I had to request him to take over. He didn't like this and, looking at me angrily, he said, 'You girls come and then can't cope with strenuous flying across multiple sectors.'

Before he could speak further or raise his voice, I picked up courage and said, 'Sir, if you can please not smoke till we are out of the cockpit in Delhi, I would be able to cope much more and much better.'

No one could dare talk to Capt. David in this manner; that was the kind of image he had. However, since I wanted to learn and perform well, I had no choice but to speak up. I am sure he was surprised but he did take note of my request and didn't smoke much for the remainder of the flight. The next day, I heard that the entire airline was talking about this 'new girl' who had the guts to stand up to Capt. David.

That was the kind of environment we started our airline careers in. Given how few in number we were, every word we said went around. Today, Capt. David is no more, but I thank him for understanding my difficulty and being ready to accept me and teach me all that was needed to be a good and efficient captain on any aircraft I would have to fly. It was this bold beginning that empowered me to keep going with ease, unfazed by any hurdle that came my way.

The most challenging experience I encountered as F/O was the time I was involved in a Boeing 737 accident. Even today, twenty-five years later, the exact sequence of events replays in my mind. I can never forget that fateful day, 26 April 1993. The time was 1.06 p.m. In fact, that was my last flight on a Boeing as I had cleared the Airbus 320 technical papers and was to proceed to Hyderabad for simulator training after the completion of this flight pattern. The sector was Delhi–Jaipur–Udaipur–Aurangabad–Mumbai and we were on the last leg. We got ready for take-off from Aurangabad Airport, on the 6,000-ft runway, on a hot summer afternoon. The aircraft was filled up to maximum permissible take-off weight. We took permission for line-up on runway 09 and got permission for take-off. The runway (09-27) at Aurangabad Airport had a slope of +2% towards runway 09 and –2% towards runway 27. Therefore, from runway 09 take-off due to an uphill slope, the end of the runway is not visible till you reach your lift-off point. We entered the runway, the captain opened power (throttle), and as the aircraft speed increased and reached the speed of lift-off (Vr), a truck on the highway, at the end of the runway, just outside the vicinity of the airport, came into view. This highway (Beed Road) was declared as part of our clearway in the charts given by the Airport Authority of India (AAI), which was the authority to manage airports in India during those days. This vehicle was overloaded with solid cotton bales on wooden planks. It was an obstacle on our take-off path, in our clearway, as indicated on our airport charts. The cotton bales got sucked into the engine and the No. 1 engine flamed out, as per the cockpit indication, but the actual impact was seen in the wheel being sheared off, (left main landing gear and left engine bottom cowling) which we learnt from the preliminary enquiry later conducted by the DGCA. The aircraft, having been damaged in the wheel that had hit the left stabilizer, was drifting to the left without being able to climb. There was no choice but to bring it down on the best possible open land available. Which, when attempted by the commander, led to a crash landing. All this panned out in about a few minutes after take-off.

My senses heightened at this point. As the co-pilot on this flight, I performed the necessary task of trying to minimize damage and avoid any loss of life within a matter of seconds. Within 120 seconds, we tried to evacuate as many passengers as possible through the only functioning door as all other doors were jammed due to the crash landing. In another 180 seconds, we saw the powerful machine with eight tonnes of fuel burst into flames right before our eyes.

What came next was the enquiry by the fact-finding committee, which lasted nearly two years. This was the first crew that had survived such an accident and was able to state the sequence of events that unfolded, along with the cockpit voice recorder and flight data recorder which carried the exact sequence of events that led to this unfortunate accident. Every dot of the Standard Operating Procedure (SOP) was followed till the last moment of the crash landing. In fact, this was the first CVR till that day where I gave a clear 'Mayday' call in the capacity of an F/O on duty. It was a long and exhausting enquiry with having to hear the CVR every day for nearly a year, along with all the witnesses, to ascertain the causes of such an accident. Finally, the verdict was announced and I was exonerated both by the DGCA and the fact-finding body in Bombay High Court. It was more of a relief for my family, especially my mother who was completely shaken. When the case was closed, she wanted me to quit this profession, but I was not ready to do that yet. I knew we had done our best under the circumstances and I certainly did not want to quit; in fact, to learn more flying and to get my command became my next passion, and amassing greater knowledge my target. A steely attitude and a positive mindset are what I have gained most in this profession, where every moment is different and can be daunting even when one is prepared!

It was also during this phase that I was to get married to a man whom I had met a year and a half ago, though the entire situation and my frame of mind at the time did not permit me to think about marriage. The support he provided by understanding my situation and standing by my side like a pillar of strength gave me the grit and resolve to fight for the truth. After the verdict, we got married and he encouraged me to return to the passion I loved most. No doubt tongues wagged, but I remained firm about going back to the cockpit, for that is where I belonged, back with my seniority, where I successfully flew the Airbus 319/320/321 in command for years.

I wanted to learn more and more so I could get my command. I moved on to the A-320 after re-joining the airline in 1995–96, and subsequently got my command on the A-320. As with all my colleagues, command had its own charm but came with tremendous responsibilities and challenges. My command training started when I resumed work with the airline on completion of maternity leave for the birth of my second daughter. The training was even tougher with having to raise two small children, a situation none of my male colleagues ever faced. It was only with the support of my husband and mother-in-law that I managed to move ahead. By then I had lost my mother, so it was my husband's family, especially my mother-in-law, who gave time to my daughters while I was in Hyderabad for the command training. Her help gave me peace and allowed me to work hard through the most strenuous training to become commander on the A-320. After successfully completing the training and the checks, I was released as a commander in 2002. It was my greatest achievement so far; this was the exhilarating moment I had waited for since my first take-off. After all, we persist in this line of work only to get command!

In this book, most of my colleagues have narrated different experiences as commanders. I agree with them that as a commander, you are responsible not just for your flying but for the entire aircraft. From the passengers to the crew, you are the only person who needs to take prompt and correct decisions. Be it a passenger problem or aircraft issue or the weather, you are liable. As commander, the buck stops with you. You flew less but managed more, which included amicably resolving all issues to ensure a safe flight. Each of us had our own share of experiences. Though we learnt from one another, it was only through handling it hands-on that we acquired a real understanding of every situation.

There are numerous incidents I have encountered in the capacity of a commander, but it seems relevant to mention that, sometimes, passengers would try to create chaos rather than let the commander fly. On this particular flight, I had taken off from Delhi for Bombay (now Mumbai). The flight was full, with not a single vacant seat. We were airborne by then and must have climbed to about 5,000 ft, when one of the cabin crew members called me on the intercom and said, 'One passenger is constantly calling us and complaining that the window is breaking, tell the captain to land the aircraft immediately.' We were still in the climb phase and had not reached cruising level, so I told my co-pilot to inform cabin crew to remain seated as we were encountering bad weather and I would get back to her. As soon as we stabilised, I called her into the cockpit to take information about the cabin situation. The cockpit had no warning, no indication of any door being opened, nor any pressurisation problem for me to divert or return. She told me that the passenger was sitting near the window and the inner frame of that window was loose, and it moved when he touched it, so he thought the window was damaged. I asked her to inform the passenger that there was no problem, the captain had been informed and the matter would be looked into after landing in Mumbai. I also suggested that since the flight was full, she should request any other passenger to change seats with him. But this did not pacify him. He kept creating a scene and would not allow cabin crew to serve. He even sent his visiting card with the crew to be given to me.

We were in cruise mode by then and since there was no issue with the aircraft, I continued the flight. His card said he was a professor at a prestigious university, so in order to dispel his doubts, I invited him inside the cockpit and told him there was no problem in the aircraft. But the minute he came in, I could sense he was not happy seeing a lady commander. He said to me, 'You are going on when you should land as the aircraft has a broken window.'

Calmly, I told him, 'Sir, there is no pressurisation problem in the aircraft, so the window is not broken. It's the inner frame of the window that is loose because of a missing nut, which will be attended to after landing in Bombay.'

By now, we were crossing Jaipur. To my surprise, he was not willing to understand and instead said to me, 'You don't know your job. I am a professor. How can you question my knowledge?' I knew he was making no sense, so I politely replied, 'You can change your seat and we will do our bit.' I asked the cabin crew to take him back.

Back in the cabin, he started making noise again. He had convinced a young man travelling alone to take pictures of the window and went to the extent of telling the cabin crew that he was a reporter and would have this telecast in the news after landing in Mumbai. The crew told this man that taking pictures on an aeroplane was prohibited and they could report the offence, but he would not listen. I sent the co-pilot to give them a warning not to cause any disturbance in the cabin or strict action could be taken against them on landing, but it fell on deaf ears. We had weather issues to handle and I did not want to waste energy on such an implausible matter as this sector could be really bad during monsoons. I then told the cabin crew to ignore them and continue their service. Since the passenger continued to disturb them, we decided to ask for security on arrival.

By this time, we were crossing Ahmedabad and about to commence descent into Mumbai. Once in contact with Mumbai, we informed our company about a passenger creating a ruckus and requested for security on arrival. When the aircraft door was opened after a safe landing, the security personnel came in and asked me for the seat number of the problem-causing passengers, which was provided by the senior-most cabin crew member. They were taken aback when the security asked them to follow them outside the aircraft to be questioned. The cabin crew had prepared the entire sequence of events which I countersigned and handed over to the airline security. Such incidents may be a one-off but they come in the way of a safe flight. It is unfortunate to see people in other professions interfering in things they are ignorant about. It is important to let a professional handle their job, whatever it may be.

These are some of the real-life lessons that each one of us learns, besides the variety of challenges we run into on numerous airfields that we fly. One such airfield I can never forget is Leh, which is at an elevation of 10,682 ft, and is one of the highest-altitude airfields operated in the world. Due to its location between the Himalayas, the approach is precarious, with high terrain all around and a unidirectional runway (that is, whatever the direction of the wind, you have to land on one side and take off from the other). It is difficult if the winds are tailwinds for landing or take-off. The proximity of mountains keeps you on your toes till you have the valley and runway in sight during descent for landing. There is no scope for the slightest of deviation from your SOPs. In fact, it is a common fact that every flight in and out of Leh makes you grow by a few years at a time in your life and profession! On my first route familiarization flight, I still remember looking out to see if the Boeing wing was touching the mountain during the turn from base-leg to final leg; such is the close proximity to the mountains that you must avoid to make a safe landing. The learning graph never dips in this field, where every situation is so inspiring that it is better to keep moving ahead and expanding your horizons by not letting anything affect you.

This is one profession where you have to come to a decision, no matter what. Here, there are no maybes, nothing is left pending or to chance. When you park your aircraft at the end of the flight, you know your work is complete. Flying can get you anywhere you want. As someone rightly said, 'A mile of road can only take you a mile but a mile of runway can take you anywhere.' We are blessed to be pilots, to be able to go anywhere, equipped with wings to fly!

This work is my contribution to all women pilots around the world as it is through the skies that we connect. It is my tribute to those women who have touched the sky and dispelled the myth that the cockpit or the pilot's uniform is the preserve of men alone. My flying career may never have reached its pinnacle had it not been for the wonderful women before me who not only broke the glass ceiling to enter the cockpit as pilots, but also paved a smooth road for us to follow. I am confident that people's mindsets regarding women donning a pilot's uniform will change once they read these pages filled with real stories of women making their mark as pilots as early as the 1930s. It is through their sheer grit and the colleagues in the airlines who accepted them much earlier that, today, India stands ahead of the world in the percentage of women flying as captains in commercial airlines.

Having put in more than twenty-seven years of flying, today I enjoy sharing my experiences as an active member of Indian Women Pilots' Association and as Secretary of International Women Pilots organisation, 'The Ninety-Nines Inc', India Chapter.

Having gained an honour at Amelia Earhart's birthplace, where a plaque bearing my name is engraved in the forest, inducted into the International Forest of Friendship, at Atchison, Kansas, USA; along with some of other Indian aviators. I love to share some of life's real challenges as a motivator and mentor in an NGO, where I mingle with children who give meaning to my life and help them move forward to reach their goals and dreams!

Being honoured for my achievements in flying by an international organisation in Atchison, Kansas, USA

Proud to be donning the captain's uniform. Proud to be a pilot.

The care and share moment at Nai Disha, the NGO I work with

Sarla P. Datt, as a young child, always curious to learn more

The woman in the saree, Sarla P. Datt, ready for her flight on the Tiger Moth

The Legends (The 1930s and '40s)

Two

Flying the Unimaginable Dream

Sarla Thukral

Sarla (Sharma) Thukral is a pioneering figure in women's aviation in India, the first woman to take to the skies as early as 1935. In those times, when many women could not even imagine stepping out of their homes unescorted, venturing out to fly aeroplanes was unimaginable, but Sarla was indeed no ordinary woman. She was a confident, daring and adventurous young girl, twenty-one years old, married, with a four-year-old daughter, dressed in a saree, driving her small car all by herself, her daughter Manjul by her side, making heads turn as she would reach the flying club in Lahore. Manjul still remembers how she would sit on a chair, close to the airstrip, watching her mother's aeroplane lift into the skies and disappear sometimes into the cottony clouds. She would be as excited as she was scared, especially when the aeroplane dipped then vroomed up and down. This would make her want her mother to come down right away!

Born on 8 August 1914 in Jodhpur and brought up in Ajmer, Sarla was the first child of Pt Brij Lal Sharma and Sushila Devi, and the eldest among eight siblings. Even in those early years, her father had the vision to understand the importance of education, and he educated all his children, including his five daughters. Even though at the tender age of sixteen, Sarla was married to Capt. Prabhu Datt Sharma, the first Indian to get an airman pilot's licence and recognised as the best Indian pilot of the time, she considered herself lucky being married into a liberal family as she was permitted to continue her education to the highest level she wanted. The thought of flying had never occurred to her, though. Much later in life, in a conversation with her, she told me that her journey as a pilot was just like a dream!

It all began when her father-in-law, Pt Mool Chand, retired civil engineer, inspired by his elder son, Prabhu Datt, one of the most brilliant pilots in the country, started Himalayan Airways in Haridwar, where his younger son, Brahm Datt, took charge. Pt Mool Chand wanted his daughter-in-law Sarla, too, to become a pilot. However, her husband was more particular. He insisted that she first learn how to ride a bicycle and then to drive a car before she could fly. Taking these remarks in the right spirit, she learnt to ride a bicycle first, then learnt to drive a car. An eager learner, she quickly became proficient in these two skills. Pleased by her effort, her father-in-law took her to the Northern India Flying Club in Lahore in 1935. It was a remarkable and unusual feat for the time, to be a woman getting ready for flying lessons, that too supported by a male member of the family!

The two-seater aircraft in which Sarla started to learn to fly and soared through the skies was a biplane, the Gypsy Moth, with dual control. She still remembers her first instructor,

Capt. Timur Dastur. Flying a biplane was not easy, and doing so in a saree was another challenge, but so inspired was she that nothing could thwart her passion. An anecdote she shared from those initial days reflects her daring and fearless nature which rendered her a good learner and capable of tackling difficult situations right from the beginning. In her words, 'In those days, the pilots had to rotate the propeller by hand to start the engine. The plane was low enough for a pilot to stand on the ground and rotate. However, this could become dangerous if you did not follow the proper technique and could even injure a pilot if they did not move away at the correct time. I had seen one such incident where the learner was injured and finally succumbed to his injuries. But this didn't affect me. In fact, I remained focused by learning the correct technique and would start my plane without any help by rotating the propeller myself.'

The second big challenge with a biplane was that there was no roof above the pilot's head, so they had to wear helmets and goggles. The earphones were attached to the helmet so they could communicate with each other. The strong gusts of wind they encountered sometimes would pose a threat, but all would be forgotten for the sheer love of being in the air. She was dedicated, learning well, and flying with confidence, so while it took other students about 40–50 hours of flying before they could pass the test to fly solo, Sarla managed to get her solo with barely 10 hours of flying! Remembering that moment, her face lit up as she said, 'As my Gypsy Moth took off from the runway in Lahore, all eyes were on my aircraft. This was a particularly remarkable flight as it was piloted by a woman.' Twenty-one-year-old Sarla was making history as India's first woman pilot on her maiden flight. She continued to climb higher as she completed her flying training, ready to get her 'A-licence'.

It must be remembered that the women of that era were mainly expected to perform household duties and they frequently lived in 'purdah'. Getting an education was a task, so flying an aeroplane must have been an unimaginable dream. But Sarla Datt Sharma stood steadfast by her Indian tradition, intrepid in a saree and battling all odds, making history as the first Indian woman to successfully fly and receive her A-licence in March 1936!

She was elated with her achievement but credited it to her father-in-law and husband as she always felt that it was their unstinting encouragement and support that had given her the wings to fly. Licence in hand, she was keen to continue and emulate her husband, with her eye on flying bigger aeroplanes. In November 1937, she gave birth to their second daughter, Anjali. However, even after becoming a mother of two, from time to time, she went to the Northern India Flying Club and flew the Gypsy Moth, either solo or dual with her instructor, not wanting to quit chasing her passion.

Things progressed smoothly till 1939, when tragedy struck. She shivered as she narrated the incident.

'It was dark. My brother-in-law, Brahm Datt, took off in his plane *Vega Gull* from the airport in Karachi to fly to Lahore. A few minutes later, my husband, Prabhu, took off in his twin-engine plane *Beechcraft* from Karachi airport towards Delhi. It was night flying for the brothers. Brahm Datt was taking the senior Cambridge results to Lahore while Prabhu was taking airmail and a passenger from Karachi to Delhi. The passenger was an American, a senior executive of an oil company. About 40 miles north of Karachi, villagers reported that the wreckage of an aeroplane was scattered for 10 miles around. The headquarters of Indian National Airways in Lahore was informed within a few hours. Those in charge of the airways first informed our uncle, Dev Datt (my father-in-law's brother). They told Dev uncle that Prabhu Datt's plane had gone missing. On receiving this news, he called me to his house and told me that Prabhu's plane was missing. I didn't break down but immediately enquired about Brahm's whereabouts. It came as a shock when we got the news that both Prabhu and Brahm had died in their respective plane accidents. I still believe that both my husband and brother-in-law's planes were sabotaged and the target was the American executive. Since both the planes took off in a matter of seconds, they did not know in which plane the American was, so both aircraft were sabotaged.'

Capt. Prabhu Datt's aircraft blew up in mid-air while flying from Karachi to Delhi and Sarla became a widow at the age of twenty-four. The elders of his family invited her to live with them in Delhi, but Sarla declined the offer and decided to live in Lahore with her two daughters. The family did not oppose her decision.

Much had changed for Sarla within those few hours, by a plane tragedy that took away her husband and brother-in-law in a matter of minutes, but she did not let fear overpower her and her desire to continue flying remained unchanged! She resolved to start training for her 'B-licence', equivalent to the Commercial Pilot Licence (CPL) today. For this, she had to move to Jodhpur. Her mother stayed back in Lahore to look after her two daughters. Unfortunately, though, World War II broke out and she could not complete her training, so she returned to Lahore and joined Mayo School of Art. She stayed in Lahore till 1947. In the turmoil of Partition, she got her elder daughter married at the age of fifteen and left for Delhi with her younger daughter.

Having been unable to complete her training for the B-Licence, she still did not give up on her dream to continue flying. In Delhi, she read an advertisement about a vacancy for a lady pilot for Her Highness, the Maharani of Alwar. Losing no time, she applied for it and was thrilled when she received a letter stating that she had been hired! When she reached Alwar to report for the job, she was amused at what she heard. Here's what happened, in her own words:

'Alwar was a small town and there was not much awareness. When I got the job, the city was full of news that a lady pilot had arrived, but no one knew what a lady pilot was! When my cousin brother-in-law walked through the bazaar with me, people yelled, pointing at him: "Look, look at the lady pilot!"'

She was happy to be flying again, but remained in this job only for a few months, dissatisfied with the manner in which the Maharaja was maintaining the planes. She quit the job and returned to Delhi where she stayed with Dev Datt Sharma, her father-in-law's younger brother. There, she kept herself busy with the art education she had acquired, and even stitched clothes for her neighbours. It was during this period that she met R.P. Thukral. He was four years younger, but he proposed marriage to Sarla and they were married in April 1948. Unfortunately, at the age of fifty-three, R.P. Thukral had a heart attack and passed away. This was a great shock for Sarla, but, to overcome her loss, she devoted herself to her art and painting, made costume jewellery and hand-printed sarees for which she had a large clientele, and also supplied to the cottage industries in Delhi.

I had the privilege of meeting Sarlaji at her Delhi residence in January 2008. She was ninety-three years old then and told me that she still painted and designed at leisure; she hadn't retired even then and never would! True to her words, I noticed how, even at that age, she was active, doing her own chores. She confessed that she never took an afternoon nap, did not need help with cooking, cleaning, and other chores, and lived that way till she breathed her last. Capt. Sarla was a great-grandmother and lived in Delhi as the head of three generations where she passed away at the age of ninety-three on 15 March 2008.

Regarding her flying, she once wrote in her diary: 'People have since asked me if I learned anything from my flying experience. Certainly, I have learnt many lessons. First, I found that even under the worst conditions, making a firm decision and sticking to it can bring you to safety. Second, never place yourself in a position where a safe glide cannot be converted into a landing. Third and the most important, regardless of how careful everyone thinks he or she is, there is always that small possibility of an emergency which a pilot should always be prepared for. In other words, expect the unexpected.'

Such is the legendary story and legacy of one of the first women to chart Indian aviation history!

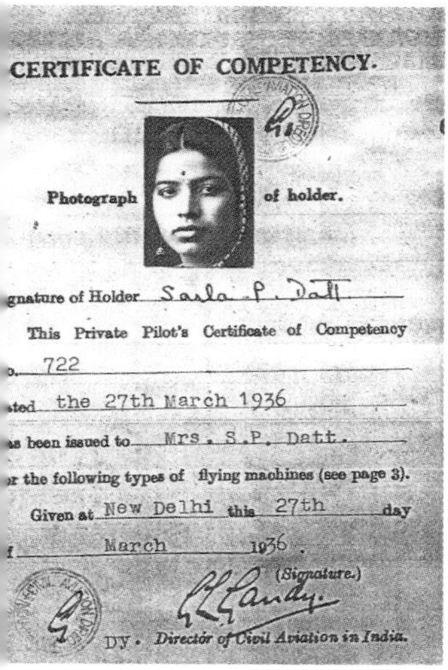

CERTIFICATE OF COMPETENCY.

Photograph of holder.

gnature of Holder Sarla P. Datt

This Private Pilot's Certificate of Competency

o. 722

ated the 27th March 1936

as been issued to Mrs. S.P. Datt.

r the following types of flying machines (see page 3).

Given at New Delhi this 27th day

f March 1936.

(Signature.)

Dy. Director of Civil Aviation in India.

Fédération Aéronautique Internationale

British Empire.

We the undersigned: recognised by the F.A.I. as the sporting authority in the British Empire certify that	Nous soussignés, pouvoir sportif reconnu par la F.A.I. pour l'Empire Britannique certifions que

Mrs S.P. Datt.

Born at India on the 8th Aug: 1914.

having fulfilled all the conditions stipulated by the F.A.I. has been granted an AVIATOR'S CERTIFICATE.	ayant rempli toutes les conditions imposées par la F.A.I. a été breveté PILOTE-AVIATEUR.

On behalf of

THE ROYAL AERO CLUB

THE AERO CLUB OF INDIA & BURMA.

ASSOCIATED ROYAL AERO CLUB OF GREAT BRITAIN.

Chairman

for Secretary.

Date 19th Feby: 1936. No 552.

Sarla P. Datt

(Signature of Holder)

A copy of the private pilot licence of Capt. Sarla P. Datt

In the cockpit, enjoying being up in the air

Capt. Prem Mathur after winning the National Air Race trophies in 1950

Capt. Prem standing amongst the mighty veteran pilots, before the National Air Race in 1950

A confident, independent Capt. Prem with her colleagues.

When she flew the VIPs – with Prime Minister Jawaharlal Nehru and other notable personalities

Three

Standing Apart with Vision and Perseverance

Prem Mathur

While Capt. Sarla P. Datt could not make it as a commercial pilot, ten years later, on 25 August 1924, a girl born in Aligarh, Uttar Pradesh, and raised in Allahabad (now Prayagraj), overcame all struggles to become the first woman commercial pilot in India to fly the Dakota aircraft in 1951. She was Capt. Prem Mathur. The youngest of five siblings, her father Suraj Narain Mathur was the principal of a school in Allahabad. Having lost his wife when Prem was born, her father had a soft corner for her. While the elder daughter was brought up in a very conservative manner and married off at the age of nineteen, he completely changed his stand where Prem was concerned.

Her first association with flying was as an eight-year-old, when she would often accompany her elder brother Anand (who was flying those days) for a joyride. But the journey that shaped her life began while she was pursuing a bachelor's degree from Allahabad University. The dream of flying took root when Capt. Sunder Lal Atal, a pilot friend of her brother, came to stay with them. One morning, he asked her if she would like to come with him for a spin in his aircraft. An invitation she readily accepted.

Once they were airborne, he casually asked her if she wanted to have a feel of the aircraft and guided her to put her feet on the rudders to keep the plane steadily on its course. She felt a thrill as she had never had such an opportunity earlier. Immediately, she did as instructed and managed to keep the aircraft straight. Amazed, the pilot asked her to take the control stick too. She did so without hesitation and didn't let the plane veer off course! Atal was naturally surprised at this performance and thought he would test her nerve and see how long she could sit there with a calm face. Without any warning, he began executing acrobatics with the controls, hoping that she would get frightened, but he found her enjoying herself instead. Truly impressed, he told her she should take up flying as a profession. Her heart leaped at that comment. Anand, a pilot instructor by now, had always fascinated and inspired her, but she had never imagined she too could take up flying. Wondering whether that would be possible, she spoke to her father. He listened to her patiently and did not say no, but told her to complete her graduation first.

Having graduated and enrolled herself in a master's degree programme, in October 1947, she approached her father again. That is when he realised that she had not forgotten her passion, that she was more determined than before, and would remain persistent. After much thinking and consulting with other members of the family, he gave her permission to pursue her dreams, though he still kept telling her that he did not know of any girl exercising such choices in those years. Refusing to be disheartened, she exulted in the fact that she could finally join a flying school. Luck favoured her as well. A flying school had just opened in Allahabad. Overjoyed at this turn of events, she signed up at the club, becoming the first woman from Uttar Pradesh to take to flying and the first to be admitted for flight training in the first batch selected at the Allahabad Flying Club.

Having joined the club, she took another bold step. Not wanting the family car to drop her at the club every day, she persuaded her father to buy her a Harley Davidson motorcycle and would ride it to the flying club dressed in trousers, her hair cut short. That did cause quite a stir in conservative Allahabad where girls were normally chaperoned. Her independence and individuality made her stand apart, letting her colleagues, mostly male, know that she was no ordinary woman. She kept contact with all her friends in the aviation industry, including her male colleagues, until her last days. She had a distinctive personality of her own; she enjoyed music and ballroom dancing, and she never shied away from who she was, in spite of living in such conservative times.

Flying had always excited her and she was on top of the world at being allowed to follow her heart. Her excitement took another turn when, with barely 13 hours in her kitty, she was sent for her first solo flight. As recorded in her diary: 'I could not believe I was all by myself up in the air, what a feeling! I did a good take-off and landed safely.' This flight gave her the boost she needed, and there was no looking back after that. She was now prepared to opt for it as a career, not knowing how many hurdles and challenges she would face going forward.

To pursue further flying and to get a commercial licence, she had to move schools. She chose the Hind Provincial Flying Club Limited in Lucknow, where flying was good. Her brother, an instructor, was a known figure there. Right from the start, she sensed she was in unwelcome territory. No woman had taken up this career so far in India, so there was much reluctance and resistance from all quarters. She stayed strong as she took up this challenge, not letting anyone or anything demotivate her. She worked hard and proved herself by clearing the oral and written tests and was assigned an instructor, Capt. Patwardhan, who was ready to start her flying lessons.

Things brightened up for her in 1950, when she received a letter from the organiser of the National Air Race, Sri Biren Roy, inviting her to join the race. They even offered her extra prize money worth ₹1,000 for being the only woman competitor. At that moment, she was not sure what participating in the competition would help her achieve, or whether it was simply aimed at making her accept that being a woman, she could be a misfit in this profession. But egged on by her instructor, she took this invitation as her first real test to let her colleagues and others know that a woman could navigate the skies and fly just like any male pilot.

She knew she had only 90 hours of flying experience, whereas she needed 100 hours to take part in the National Air Race to be held in Calcutta. Her experience of cross-country flying was limited, but she knew there were ten days left for the race and felt she could easily complete those hours. Without any more delay, she started to pile on the hours, focussing on getting more cross-country experience. Her instructor played an important role, guiding her well to give her complete confidence before the race. He told her that if she could do Jhansi as a cross-country solo flight, she would manage any other airfield. She prepared for the flight, marked her map, and started off for Jhansi. Her experience of this flight perhaps prepared her for the bigger challenge she was to face soon.

She made a note in her diary about this: 'I was over the city of Jhansi and could not see the airfield. I noticed my fuel tank needle; it had begun to inch towards zero. So I started thinking ahead and started to look for an open space to force-land, if necessary. Meanwhile, I decided to go back to the location from where I had flown into the town, to give myself one more chance. To my good luck, I managed to see the windsock this time, though I still could not locate the airstrip. I started to fly low and spotted one place which looked safe enough, circled around and landed safely. At touchdown, I realised I was landing at Jhansi airfield!'

Happy with this achievement, she couldn't wait to reach Lucknow and share her experience with her instructor. He was glad but also surprised as most students who could not locate the airstrip would get lost, confused, and would divert to known airfields so that they didn't go low on fuel, to force-land. To his astonishment, Prem had stayed calm and had thought of the right solution of going back to the starting point to give herself another chance; never did she get confused or panicky and think of diverting course to a known airfield, and therefore, she successfully found the landing field. It was obvious that she would certainly go a long way in this field.

Her 100 hours of flying time to qualify for the race was now completed. The next day, she was to leave for Barrackpore Airport where the race was scheduled to begin. It was no simple contest. There were twelve veteran pilots taking part in this triangular cross-country race covering approximately 350 nautical miles, going from Barrackpore to Jamshedpur and Asansol, then back to Barrackpore Airport. Young Prem Mathur was up for the challenge, though, the only woman pit against the might of experienced male pilots and, indeed, she surprised everyone by winning it! She spoke to her nephew regarding the race later. He recalls her experience:

'She was nervous about the race but did not want to lose

this opportunity to let everyone know that women are not behind men in any field. So she took off in her aircraft, the *Luscombe Silvaire*, from Lucknow and first went to Allahabad to meet her father. Then she flew to Banaras, refuelled her aircraft, and flew to Patna where she spent the night. Next morning, she took off for Calcutta, halting briefly at Gaya and Asansol. She reached Calcutta, where the authorities had made arrangements for all the pilots to stay. Here, she met up with the other competitors, some of whom she knew, having flown for some time now. It was a tense evening for all of them, but she began to feel at home with the other fliers and started to think about the race.'

The next morning, on the day of the race, there was much hullaballoo and everyone reached the airport with a single thought on their minds – of winning the great race. She narrates: 'The time had come; each one of us was settled in our aircraft. It had been determined who would take off first, in accordance with the performance of the machine. My brother Anand took off first, then came another competitor; I was third. It was a clear and sunny day, the take-off went well, and I gained height and went along steadily. I hadn't gone far when I spotted the second plane. I could not believe it and thought I must have drifted off the track. As I flew a little ahead, I spotted my brother's plane. This made me even more uneasy as he had taken off first. I thought I must have gone off-track by miles, so I took out my map and marked a location point which I could see within ten minutes. When I spotted that, I felt very relieved. Soon, I zoomed over Jamshedpur Airport, the first landing in the race. I noticed there was no other plane, and I thought the others must have come and gone. When I landed, there was a huge crowd around, and as I jumped out of my plane and walked towards the crowd, there was a tremendous ovation and much cheering and excitement. I learned that I had landed first. I could not believe myself! A little later, other planes began to land, and I noticed they were not very happy to see me here.'

She felt more confident now as they all moved on to the next leg of the race. When she zoomed over the final destination, Barrackpore Airport, she spotted other aeroplanes coming in too. She continued her finish with the same perfection and zeal, and as she landed, there was a great cheer from the crowd.

While everyone was eagerly waiting for the winner to be announced soon, an experienced instructor pilot, Capt. Maj. Gen. Misri Chand assumed he would definitely be the winner and started to celebrate his success. While this celebration was on, around mid-afternoon, the results were declared. To her amazement, Prem saw her friends running towards her from all directions. They shook her hands almost violently, congratulating her. Composing herself, she asked, 'What are you all congratulating me for?' They shouted in utter glee, 'Don't you know you have won the race?'

She recounts: 'I could not believe what I heard and exclaimed, "What!" I confess it was the most exciting moment of my life. So unbelievable yet so true! I won three trophies that day – one as the winner of the National Air Race, the second for economic cruising, and the third for being the only woman competitor. I also received ₹3,000 in cash. It was the happiest day, and I decided this was what I was made for!'

Then onwards, she continued flying more seriously and regularly. Although her crusade to become a commercial pilot was not taken seriously initially, she completed her required hours and received her commercial licence (B-Licence) on 24 April 1951, becoming the first Indian woman to achieve this glory. With this licence, she could apply for a job in any airline, but she needed some experience of flying a Dakota. There were six or seven airlines at that time, but no one was ready to offer a job to a woman. She remained undeterred in her aim. To her luck, her colleague from the Allahabad Flying Club, Capt. Nam Joshi, managed to persuade Deccan Airways to let her fly on their scheduled service as an apprentice pilot to gain experience. They agreed and put her on for training, after which she was allowed to fly as a co-pilot on their service but without any salary or overstay expenses. She still accepted the offer, happy to be able to fly to gain experience on the Dakota aircraft.

Airlines would permit her to fly, but without paying a salary or any other expenses. Her persistence would only result in excuses. They would tell her there were no women pilots flying any scheduled airline in the world and, therefore, they could not offer her the job. They were also worried that passengers may lose confidence in their airline on seeing a woman as a pilot. This would cause them financial losses and give them a bad reputation. Even though there were six or seven airlines at that time and she applied to all of them, the response was a standard 'Being a woman, we cannot offer you the job of a pilot.' She did not give up, and instead, wrote to the Ministry of Communication and the heads of all the airlines that she was willing to take any test to prove that she was capable.

The ministry restated its point via a letter dated 6 May 1952, saying: 'Airlines are unable to offer you a pilot's job as women are not used as pilots by any airline in the world.' She countered this by suggesting that the airlines subject her to the stress test mandated by the job. In fact, she volunteered to take the test herself. The test proved that her reflexes were far better than those of many of the male pilots. If not for her gender, she would be selected immediately, having outdone more than half the male pilots. This further toughened her resolve to fight to make sure women were inducted to the cockpit and not just the cabin, as was suggested to her by many airlines.

Telegrams :—
"COMMUNICATIONS".

D.O. No. 132-5/52

Ministry of Communications.
New Delhi,
6th May 1952

Dear Miss Prem Mathur,

Please refer to your letter dated March 12, addressed to Air-India Ltd. Hon'ble Minister forwarded it to the Air India Ltd. But I am sorry to say that I have just heard from them saying that they are unable to offer you employment as a pilot pointing out that women are not used as pilots by any airline in the world. H.M. regrets that she is unable to persuade the Air Company to accept you as a pilot in a scheduled passenger service. I would repeat, if I may, as advised by the D.G.C.A. you may try first to obtain employment in a Freighter service to begin with.

Yours sincerely,
A.V.Pai
(A.V. Pai)

Miss Prem Mathur,
12, Windsor Place,
New Delhi.

The letter from the Ministry of Communication

When the airlines were nationalised in 1953, once again she tried to get a job. Finally with her persistence and persuasion, Deccan Airways did hire her. She got her endorsement on the Douglas DC-3 and flew as co-pilot on the airline's scheduled routes.

As a pilot myself, I want to emphasise that co-pilots do not merely sit in the cockpit; they have an important role to play there. The co-pilot is second-in-command, and in the eventuality of the commander being incapacitated, the co-pilot takes over as commander. There are specific duties and responsibilities that each pilot performs, be it a commander or a co-pilot. Flying a commercial airline is in itself a tough call, and she did it!

However, the job did not last long. She had to give it up because she felt she was kept off flying and given excuses that were attributed to her gender and not her skills. She wrote about this discrimination to politician and diplomat Vijaya Lakshmi Pandit, who was also the sister of then Prime Minister Jawaharlal Nehru. Mrs Pandit hailed from Allahabad, and having grown up there herself, Prem felt the former would understand her agenda of trying to make airlines realise that gender did not matter in a pilot's job; it was the capability, temperament and skill that counted – all qualities that she possessed.

It was after this that she applied to one of the leading industrialists of the country, G.D. Birla, and subsequently got employed by them to fly their planes. Since there was no offer coming through yet with any commercial airline, she grabbed this opportunity. Starting in 1955, she worked with them for six years, flying DC-3 aircraft (Dakotas) as a co-pilot. During her stint there, she had the privilege of flying VVIPs – Lady Mountbatten, Pandit Nehru, Mrs Indira Gandhi and many more dignitaries. In fact, Pandit Nehru was very proud of the fact that a girl from Allahabad had become the first female commercial pilot in India, and expressed his joy whenever he flew the Birlas' plane with Capt. Prem as part of the cockpit crew.

EMBASSY OF INDIA
MOSCOW

20. 7. 48.

My dear Prem,

Indian news reaches our part of the world rather late & it was only yesterday that we saw a picture of you in one of the papers & learnt that you [illegible] have secured your 'B' licence for [illegible] I cannot tell you how very happy this news made me. Please accept my warm congratulations.

It is so important for our girls to look beyond the very restricted field in which they have so far functioned & I am specially glad that a girl from Allahabad should have been a pioneer. I hope others will come forward to follow your lead.

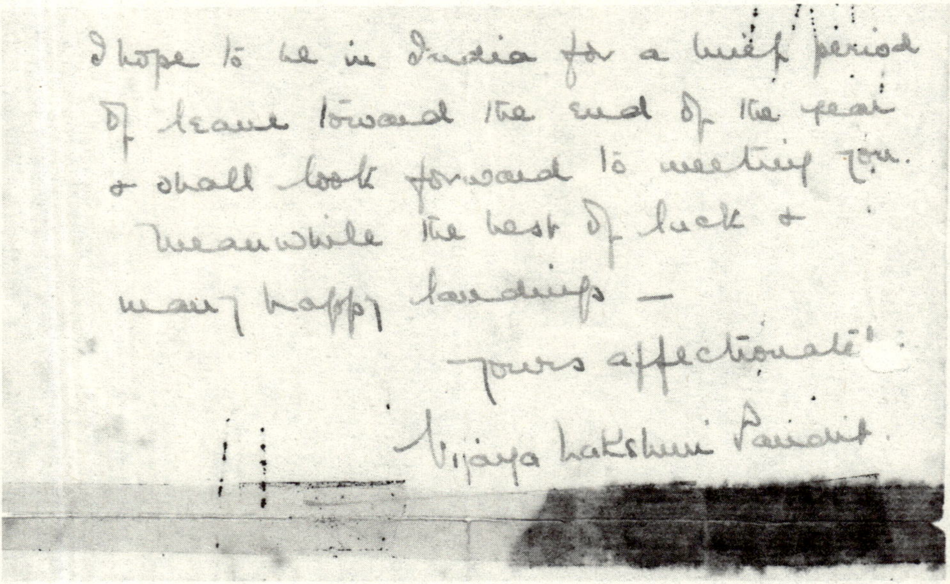

I hope to be in India for a brief period of leave toward the end of the year & shall look forward to meeting you. Meanwhile the best of luck & many happy landings —

Yours affectionately

Vijaya Lakshmi Pandit.

A letter of encouragement from politician and diplomat, Vijay Lakshmi Pandit

He would introduce her to his entire team with great pride. On one occasion, he told her that he had travelled to the UK and the US, and even though these counties were advanced, they did not have any women pilots flying passengers. It was an honour to hear this from the prime minister of the country.

She flew with the Birlas for a long time. When it was time to retire, she was not ready to sit idle. Having dedicated her life to aviation, she wished to give more time to the profession. Her dream remained 'to see women flying commercial airlines on par with men'. Even though she did not get the opportunity to fly as a pilot, she applied to Indian Airlines in 1965 and was inducted as assistant manager, Flight Safety. This was again a job she enjoyed as she would be involved in investigating aircraft accidents both in the air and on the ground. She would be questioning the pilots, engineers and ground staff involved, making statements and preparing preliminary reports indicating the probable cause of the accident.

Being a pilot, safety was naturally her top priority. Her elder brother Anand, a pilot instructor and her early inspiration, had died in an air accident in Lucknow, in 1952, while trying to do a reverse loop in an air show before a crowd which included both friends and family. She was not present during the show and never learnt the exact cause of the accident, but she didn't let it demoralise her and kept flying. Nevertheless, her mind was made up that, given an opportunity, she would work to promote safety in flying. She was very systematic and orderly in conducting safety investigations because she felt that unless one was disciplined and systematic, it always affected flight safety.

During her tenure in Flight Safety, she worked on another major issue: pilots' drinking problems. She would not spare anyone and would be openly critical if any pilot was reported for this offence. The image of the airline and the profession must be above personal choices. Besides, a profession such as this required full focus, concentration and alertness, which is not possible to sustain with a drinking habit. Her focus and dedication towards Flight Safety was rewarded and she was promoted to Deputy Flight Safety Manager where she served selflessly for more than nineteen years, retiring on 30 August 1984.

In her later years, she lived with her younger brother at Jor Bagh in Delhi. It brought her contentment to be close to the Delhi Flying Club at Safdarjung Airport which she would often visit to keep her interest alive. When her brother passed away, she moved to Green Park where she bought her own apartment.

She would visit her niece and nephew often and talk to them about how she was happy to see women flying commercial airlines shoulder to shoulder with men now.

She spoke about her only disappointment in life – that being a woman, she was never made a commander in spite of having the requisite experience and qualification. She had the skill and capability needed, and could handle stress better than most men she flew with during her time. She was brave enough to have undergone a voluntary stress test, which most pilots would avoid. Then with barely 100 hours of flying time in her kitty, she had taken part in the National Air Race with veteran pilots, overcoming every challenge to beat all the men and take home the trophy as winner of this prestigious race. The fact that even Prime Minister Jawaharlal Nehru always wished to fly on the aircraft that she co-piloted stands testimony to her greatness. She was a commander in every sense, only inhibited by discrimination on the basis of her gender!

She passed away in 1992 in Delhi. Her dream of seeing women flying commercial airlines came true when Capt. Durba was inducted into Indian Airlines and flew for more than twenty years, getting her command. The moment of crowning glory for women in Indian aviation came with Capt. Saudamini and Capt. Nivedita leading the first all-women crew in India – making news around the world as the first all-women crew on any aircraft, among airlines that are members of the International Air Transport Association (IATA) – to fly passengers, in 1985.

Capt. Prem once told her nephew: 'I am a woman, and for me, a sense of freedom is very important. When I look up into the sky and see these birds fly... I always wonder and think they have a wonderful sense of freedom; they have a vision to see things that one can't see from the ground! I often think how great it would be to be able to do something like that and since we have the opportunity to fly, it would be a great tragedy if I would not be able to emulate the joy of flying.'

Her dream is now a reality.

Being honoured as the Flight Safety Deputy Manager at Indian Airlines. Also seen on the dais are other dignitaries, including Prime Minister Rajiv Gandhi.

With President Giani Zail Singh in New Delhi

First ever woman pilot retires

eadquarters : Miss Prem Mathur, Dy Manager Flight Safety receiving a resent from Capt. B.K. Bhasin, Director Flight Safety on her retirement.

NDIA'S first ever woman pilot, Iiss Prem Mathur retired from idian Airlines after over 19 years rvice.

Having qualified for a Private lot's Licence in 1949 and the ommercial Pilot's 'B' Licence in 951, she joined Deccan Airways as n apprentice pilot. She earned an ndorsement on the DC-3 and ew as a co-pilot on the airline's heduled routes.

She has had the distinction of ying VVIPs including Lady Mountatten, Anurein Bavan and our resent Prime Minister Mrs Indira andhi besides several Cabinet linisters.

In March 1965, Miss Mathur oined the Flight Safety department as Assistant Manager and etired last month as Dy. Manager ight Safety.

IA image

Editor
Ajit S. Gopal
Associate Editor
K.G. Rajpoot
Sr. Editorial Assistant
Ashok Sharma
Representatives
Bombay: R.N. Pathak Dy P.R.M.
Calcutta: P. Subramanyam, Dy. P.R.M.
Delhi: R.K. Khanna, Sr P.R.O.
Madras: B.P.N. Kavlekar, Sr. P.R.O.
Published by Ajit S. Gopal, Public Relations Manager, Indian Airlines, 113 Gurdwara Rakabganj Road, New Delhi 110001.
Printed at Veerendra Printers, New Delhi 110005.
For internal circulation only.

September 1984

Media coverage of Capt. Prem's retirement

Durba Banerjee – the first woman First Officer in Indian Airlines, 1966

Dedicated to her work with Airways Limited

In the cockpit of a Boeing 737

Breaking the Glass Ceiling (The 1950s)

Four

Destiny Calling

Durba Banerjee

Living the dream of Capt. Prem Mathur, Capt. Durba Banerjee, born on 1 December 1930 in Patna, became the first woman pilot in the country to join a commercial airline in 1966.

Third among seven siblings, from early on, Durba wanted to do something extraordinary. Nearing completion of graduation studies, one day, she saw an advertisement by the Bihar government offering flying scholarships. Girls were encouraged to apply and there was a separate scholarship set aside for one girl. The year was 1953. Flying sounded exciting and Durba thought it would be challenging and different, although it wasn't something girls talked about or signed up for at the time. But ever-ready to venture into new territories, she welcomed this opportunity as godsend and sent in her application. To her surprise, she got the scholarship, and so did her brother, Shibesh. When their parents were informed, they were delighted and happy with this turn of events. It didn't bother them that aviation was not a field girls were conventionally exposed to. Those days, parents hardly allowed their children to follow their dreams. But Durba's parents, Suresh C. Banerjee and Malina Banerjee, even though they had not heard of any girl learning how to fly an aeroplane, were broad-minded and educated, not only believing in higher education for their children but also giving them the freedom to dream big and all the support and encouragement needed to pursue those dreams!

Her mother came from a family of doctors and had cultivated attributes of courage, calmness, fortitude and the capability to face every situation with aplomb. Her father was benevolent and generous, loved reading, and was of the opinion that every child must be bold, brave, adventurous and ambitious. Her parents' qualities and beliefs indeed inspired her to tread a very difficult path, gathering her strength to surmount all obstacles and enter the domain of flying, an exclusive male preserve at the time.

The scholarship she won was an impetus to explore this uncharted field although, at that point, she never thought this would be a viable career option in the 1950s. Moreover, women becoming professional pilots in any airline was unheard of. Durba and her brother started flying in Patna Flying Club on scholarships simply to learn and enjoy something new. She knew that, despite winning the scholarship, there were chances that she might not be viewed as an equal in this male-dominated space. And being the only woman, all eyes would be on her and she had to perform to prove herself. Complete focus and dedication would be required in order to master this skill.

Soon, her flying lessons started. She made every effort to stay calm and collected as she sat in an aircraft for the first time. 'Tiger Moth', the training aircraft, was something novel.

This is how she described it: 'It was so much fun, the feeling of the lift-off, leaving the ground beneath, up in the open sky, it felt like a bird. I could not imagine this was real! Tiger Moth being a biplane, had an open cockpit, so as one got airborne, one could feel the wind hitting the face; it was more for the joy of being up in the air and being able to fly the aircraft. I realised the open cockpit helped me to keep a look on the runway and where one was flying. It was a good training aircraft, though difficult to fly well; moreover, the tail-wheel did make it difficult for landing, which one had to master to perform well.' As training progressed, the amount of skill required increased. It was an aircraft that would not fly out of trouble, so one had to be mindful to not let it stall or spin. She never gave up in her quest to learn, and thus flew to perfection, empowering herself to successfully earn her Private Pilot Licence (PPL) in 1954.

Even as this opportunity gave her a taste of flying, she realised it had now become a passion. Her journey to become a commercial pilot had begun. PPL in hand, she decided to talk to her parents about her aspiration to enter the profession.

To her surprise, they did not object to her ambition, even though they did not know how this could become a career. 'Who would hire a lady pilot?' they wondered aloud. Nevertheless, her mother motivated her daughter to go ahead. On the other hand, she discouraged her son and asked him to choose some other profession as they would not be able to afford financing two children's flying ambitions. To help ease some of the costs involved, Durba decided to take up a job as a teacher in Patna. With zero knowledge about the prospects of a flying job, but self-belief and family support firmly in place, she set out to fulfil the uphill task of getting her Commercial Pilot Licence (CPL).

Once again, she joined the Patna Flying Club to complete the required flying to obtain a CPL. She was surprised to note that training now took place in two types of aircraft – Tiger Moth and a new arrival 'Chipmunk', a two-seater with one seat in the front and another at the back, both having dual controls and instrument panels. It certainly appeared to be a better version of the Tiger Moth. In fact, she learned that the Chipmunk was a successor to the immortal Tiger Moth, and flying schools around the world were opting for it. She was enthusiastic to get started on the phase ahead.

Flying the Chipmunk was another thing altogether, but she gained confidence. She had a wonderful instructor who taught her the correct handling technique, keeping it simple and effective. She grew adept at handling the throttle and rudders together and keeping the aircraft more or less straight, which helped her understand the superb characteristics of this beautiful aircraft. She began enjoying flying even more now. It became a routine, and she was mostly flying solo, logging hours to get her CPL. In 1956, she had to complete 200 hours of solo flying, including cross-country. With little or no aid, she struggled to go to places such as Gorakhpur, Darbhanga, Bagdogra, Benares, Allahabad, Bhopal, Agra, and Delhi, among others. Everywhere she flew, she sensed that people were wondering why she was doing what she was doing – flying high!

Not letting anything come in her way, holding her head high and eyes trained on the future, she went on to do something more challenging by asking for special permission to carry passengers with her on the two-seater aircraft. According to her, 'When I got clearance to carry passengers, I flew my elder sister as my passenger to Delhi and visited the first industrial exhibition of India there. I think this event became a record, as in the year 1956, where would one find a female pilot carrying a female passenger in a two-seater aircraft from Patna to Delhi, a distance of approximately 800 miles. We surely made heads turn and I became a known figure in aviation!'

Her excitement knew no bounds when, in the same year (1956), she secured her CPL from the Bihar Flying Club. She sees it as one of the greatest achievements of her life. Even in the face of opposition from people in the club and outside, she continued to add feathers to her cap and secured a second-class navigator's licence in 1957 from the Bamrauli Flying Training Centre in Allahabad as also the 'Dakota' Aircraft Endorsement (specialised training a pilot undergoes to be able to fly that particular aircraft) in 1958. It wasn't easy; not many pilots were able to do this and there was no scholarship for these training/ratings. Society was clearly not yet ready to accept a woman in this field, so no one wanted to help or support a woman. She was lucky to have parents who believed in her and stood by her wholeheartedly.

With the Dakota endorsement advantage, Durba considered joining an airline as a pilot, but met with only hindrance from everywhere except her family members and a few friends who staunchly urged her to keep up her efforts. She said, 'People tried to dissuade me from selecting a flying career. According to them, I would be entering an exclusively male domain and that was not acceptable.' This was proven when, during one of her medical reviews, an eye specialist gave her a report that would have proven to be detrimental to her pursuing flying as a profession, but she took up the challenge and refused to accept that report. She appealed to all higher authorities and got permission to be examined by Dr Geeta Chanda (Ghosh) at the Air Force Central Medical Board, New Delhi, and sure enough, she got a genuine and correct report that enabled her to continue flying. However, this was just the beginning of the many battles to be fought.

Quite early on in her search for a regular pilot's job with

airlines operating in India, she understood that being a woman in this line of work was almost a disadvantage. In her own words, 'My applications to the airlines for a pilot's job were not answered, again and again. I knew I had the advantage of an endorsement but I kept getting no response, till one day, I decided to omit "Miss" and wrote my name as D. Banerjee. I wasn't surprised when I was promptly called for an interview. But before the day of the interview, it was cancelled. Somehow, they found out that I was a woman. Disheartened but not giving up, I approached the Civil Aviation Authority, even forced myself to get an appointment to meet the then civil aviation minister, but nobody helped me on the pretext of the existing convention across the world of not allowing a woman to fly scheduled passenger airlines.'

She was offered every other kind of work possible. In fact, the authorities tried to dissuade her from becoming a regular airline pilot. They went to the extent of promising her four increments at one time if she accepted any other job in the aviation sector, but she remained unfazed. She wanted to be an airline pilot and no temptation whatsoever could change her mind. She refused all such offers and resolved to keep trying till she achieved success!

During these hard times, her family – parents, brothers, sisters – stood by her side constantly, reminding her how great her achievements were. Their support kept her going. She once said: 'People have many great personalities as their inspiration to move ahead in life during their struggles. I thank God I have my family, my inspiration to keep going to reach my goal.'

With no work and weighed down with the worry of keeping her licence valid, she knew she had to find a flying job somehow, so she started to opt for flying jobs even without pay. Finally, with the help of family, friends and well-wishers, she managed to get a pilot's job with Air Survey of India in 1959. Although this was not what she was aiming for, she accepted the offer. The work was very strenuous and monotonous, but she did not complain as she wanted to fly and thought all experience gained would take her closer to the goal of flying passenger planes. In 1960, an opportunity came her way with an offer to work as a pilot with Airways India, a private charter company. Seeing this as a chance to prove herself, she accepted the offer even though her male colleagues were paid higher salaries and given other allowances. She didn't object or protest; she had only one objective at that time. As she had said, 'My aim was to break the world's rigid convention of not allowing women to fly any scheduled airline as a regular line pilot and pave the way for other girls to take up flying as a career.' Joining Airways India, she thought she would be able to get into a commercial airline, sooner or later. Being in the private sector, Airways India mandated nearly 13 hours of work time for their staff. Not only that, they flew in the most difficult environs of Assam. However, Durba was happy that she was flying Dakotas (DC-3) and getting the opportunity to fly many VIPs, including Vijaya Lakshmi Pandit, V.K. Krishna Menon, Kailash Nath Katju and Indira Gandhi, to name a few.

It was during these years while flying for Airways India that lady luck finally acknowledged her struggle and determination. She succeeded in opening the doors of the commercial airline, Indian Airlines, for herself and for many more women who followed suit in this profession. It was not only her individual dream that came true but those of many women ever since. In her own words, 'I piloted the West Bengal government's plane during the Durgapur Congress Session. It was an important event in my life. I was flying the national leaders, all VIPs. Sure, I had flown many VIPs earlier, but here was Mrs Indira Gandhi, Minister of Information and Broadcasting. I was introduced to her and she was proud to learn that women in her country were pilots. In fact, one of the leading news reporters quoted: “A Lady brought a Lady to meet a Lady” since the president of AICC was also a lady. This coverage made my presence known, and I was suddenly being talked about as a “lady pilot”! On the return leg of the flight, Mrs Gandhi learnt about my struggle and rejection from airlines for not offering me the job of a pilot only because I was a woman. She spoke to me about this and asked me to inform her office when I applied for this job in any airline next. It wasn’t long before Indian Airlines advertised for the vacancy of pilots. I took no time to apply and also sent a copy of my application to Mrs Gandhi. I truly believe that it was at the insistence of Mrs Gandhi that I was called for the interview and finally got selected as a pilot with Indian Airlines on provision. I could not believe myself, first for being called for the interview being a woman when on many occasions I was not called because of my gender and, second, that I qualified and was selected! Till date, I thank the goodwill of Mrs Gandhi. Her intervention gave me the privilege to break the world convention that women should not fly scheduled airlines and, thus, I became the first professional line female pilot on a scheduled airline in India and probably the world. I finally managed to break the glass ceiling. The year was 1966… it changed my life and created openings for many women who dared to dream!’

She was now ready for the new venture ahead. Her ambition of flying for a scheduled airline had been achieved. She had to quit Airways India where she had worked from 1960 to 1966, not regretting a single moment there. In fact, she feels that by giving her a chance, Airways India provided her the stepping stone to reach her ultimate destination: the cockpit of a commercial airline! On joining Indian Airlines in 1966, she learnt that it was not a very friendly environment. She had shattered the glass ceiling, but mindsets in a male-dominated profession could not be changed easily. She was the only female pilot in the airline and in the country, but she had to survive all difficult situations thrown at her to prove her mettle in this field.

Her training started with the Avro Aircraft. Her experience with flying Dakotas helped her tremendously in coping with the Avro training. She surprised her colleagues and batchmates when she completed her endorsement and emerged with flying colours. Meeting challenges head-on had become second nature by now.

She flew the Avro for a while, and then her batch was moved for their second endorsement, the turboprop Fokker Friendship F-27. Here, too, she overcame all hurdles and not only got her endorsement as a co-pilot but also went on to get command on the Fokker Friendship in 1972, breaking all barriers as a woman to be in charge as commander in the schedule airline aircraft. But this came with its own difficulties. Though she qualified, there were some issues to be dealt with. As she described it: 'I got my command; I didn't even want to celebrate even though it was the most thrilling moment for me and my family. I was a commander but I had to wait for nearly two months to actually fly as a commander, as the authorities felt that no one would fly with a lady as a commander in the cockpit. I was the only lady pilot; I could understand their apprehension. But how could the authorities make their decision without trying? My persistence and good record finally had the authorities change their mind, and with much reluctance, they finally rostered me for a flight as a commander.'

However, no problem ever arose with Capt. Durba as the commander. She flew thousands of passengers in the F-27 before moving on to the Boeing 737 and, later, the Airbus 300. In fact, her stories as a woman captain reached other parts of the world. She felt happy that her success paved the way for women in

India and other countries and inspired them to take up a career in flying. She recalled with pride: 'In Bangladesh, two women cited my case in Bangladesh Parliament and were, subsequently, allowed to join as pilots in their scheduled airline. Moreover, one Japanese general whom I had flown as a commander in the F-27 to Imphal was so impressed that he sent Japanese television reporters to do a feature on me as the "Indian Woman Pilot" for showing all over Japan, to inspire ladies there to take up professions like these and the scheduled airlines to create an opening like this for women.'

Her journey as a pilot too took her places. She represented India in the World Lady Pilots Convention held in Philadelphia in 1976 as the only regular lady pilot in the world among scheduled airlines controlled by the government. She got featured in UNESCO-sponsored programmes as one of the ten prominent ladies in action in the '70s. She was also featured in the BBC and Japanese television as 'Lady Flying Commander'. She carried herself with dignity and pride, and never let her profession take a backseat for anything. Yet, she felt she was constantly looked upon differently for being a woman by the public, probably more so because for fourteen years, she was the only woman pilot flying passenger planes in India.

She recounted: 'I joined Indian Airlines in 1966 and I was all alone for fourteen long years. I was overjoyed when the second lady joined IA in 1980. She was Capt. Saudamini. Around the same time, I heard that there were one or two women joining different airlines in the world.' The world may not have been ready but the ambitions and aspirations of women made them reach the skies. She always felt that young women should come forward in large numbers to avail of any opportunity given to them, enabling them to achieve their goals. Flying remained her passion even after a full tenure with Indian Airlines. She retired in 1988 and, on the eve of retirement, she was happy to see the number of female pilots joining the national carrier going up to nearly ten. This was surely the start of a new chapter for women in this male bastion. She said, 'I believe that women would make better pilots than men. They are calm, more disciplined and able to handle emergencies better, being composed and quiet.'

After retirement, she lived in Kolkata with her brothers and sisters. She was a known figure among Kolkata's elite and received many honours and awards there. These include the Jawaharlal Nehru Centenary Award in 1989, the Lokshree Award in 1989 by the Indian Institute of Economic Studies, and the Abhinandan Patra (memoirs) from the renowned old Swadhinata Sangramis, the freedom fighters of Bengal, to name a few. She was also felicitated by the Limca Book of Records in 1990. She led an active social life, mingling with her colleagues from aviation, especially the women, and people from different walks of life. She passed away in 2011 in Kolkata.

Her life was an inspiration not only for younger generations but for everyone. The story of her life can never be forgotten – the strong woman who took on every challenge and overcame every obstacle to make a success story of her life. Her words still echo to hundreds of women flying commercial airlines as pilots in India and elsewhere in the world: 'I was considered stubborn, but I kept on persisting, to fly, fly commercial airlines, passenger planes, so that I could pass on the torch of airline piloting to other women in my country and see them becoming line pilots in great numbers, removing the myth that line piloting was exclusively a male domain.'

Capt. Durba's life and achievements were given due honour and recognition in 2011, during the 100 years of Aviation celebration organised by the Civil Aviation Ministry in Delhi. True to Capt. Durba's words, she handed over the torch of airline piloting to Capt. Saudamini in 1980, as the second woman in the country. Since then, there has been no looking back. That torch is kept alive to this day, shining ever so bright with the number of women pilots growing every year!

During the First World Congress in Delhi in 1986, with Prime Minister Rajiv Gandhi

Ready for their flight – the first two women pilots of India, Capt. Durba Banerjee with Capt. Saudamini Deshmukh.

Flying school days – at the Bombay Flying Club in 1977. Saudamini with Margaret Callaway (centre) and Mohini Shroff (extreme right).

Felicitation of women airline pilots of the world in 1988, at Oklahoma City, USA. Capt. Saudamini (front row, second from left) represented India as captain with Indian Airlines.

The first all-women flight in Asia, under Capt. Saudamini Deshmukh's (second from right) command, along with First Officer Capt. Nivedita Jain Bhasin.

Professionalism and Dedication (Early 1980s)

Five

Creating Her Own 'Firsts'

Saudamini Deshmukh

Capt. Saudamini Deshmukh became the second woman in the country to join Indian Airlines in 1980, after a long gap of fourteen years. Little did that stop her from creating her own history with her many achievements!

Recalling her childhood days and her first experience of a flight, she smiles at the memories and says, 'My family told me this story. I was a child when, once, a small aeroplane spraying pesticide to protect crops came to our little town, Akola (where we lived for two years). The pilot was nice and he was giving joyrides for a price. I was the only one from my family who rushed ahead and went for one. Even though I was a child, not for a moment did I feel uneasy or worried. In fact, I enjoyed every moment of that ride. I was full of excitement and ready to tell everyone about the fun I had. I could do anything to go back for this joyride! My family was surprised that being a girl, I was so daring.' Saudamini would look up at the aircraft zooming past her house with curiosity. She did not know at the time where destiny would take her, but her fascination with aircraft was already established. Her family had shifted to Poona (now Pune) by then. In her own words: 'I was probably eight years old when I pointed to an aeroplane passing over my house in Poona and told my family that I was going to be a pilot when I grew up.' At that tender age, she did not know much about flying and certainly would not know how that dream would take shape, but it was a dream she saw through to the end. She could not have imagined then that it would become a reality one day.

Born on 9 March 1952 in Poona, Saudamini was the second child of Madhav N. Deshmukh and Suneeti M. Deshmukh. Flanked by an elder sister and a younger brother, she was the middle child in a large joint family, where it was very common for girls and married women to engage in sporting activities, such as cycling, swimming, and a game of cricket with the boys. She never felt as if she lacked anything. She was barely twelve years old when they moved from Poona to Bombay. Her childhood fascination with aircraft carried forth into adolescence and, in Bombay, she felt there would be more opportunities available to make her dream of becoming a pilot come true. She located and visited The Bombay Flying Club and found out that the cost of obtaining the Private Pilot Licence (PPL) had been subsidised by the government. However, further training was exorbitantly priced. When she mentioned this to her parents, her father said, 'We can afford your training up to the PPL. Don't just talk about becoming a pilot, show that you can do it.' Her mother too motivated her to pursue her dreams. With their backing, she joined the Bombay Flying Club at the age of seventeen.

But she had to wait patiently for two years before starting her training as there was a long waiting list at the flying club. At this stage, she didn't have much idea where it would take her or how she would manage to continue. The support at home was enough and she felt reassured that she would reach her desired destination somehow or the other. Along this journey, her persistence, hard work and dedication helped her to fulfil her goal.

The flying club was very popular, and the elite in society were known to be members there during the 1970s, around the time she joined it. None of this mattered to her of course; all she wanted was to fly, and what could be better than receiving professional training to learn how to fly! Recalling her flying club days brings forth wonderful feelings, memories of unforgettable moments and pleasant experiences. Her eyes shining, she narrates her most memorable experience of that time.

'Some memories still bring smiles, this was my first solo way back in March 1972. I was on my routine flying sortie with my instructor. We did a few take-offs and landings, then he suddenly stopped the aeroplane on the runway. I was wondering what the reason was when, unexpectedly, he opened the door of the aeroplane (Piper Super Cub PA18) with the engine running, got off the plane and told me, 'Go, go alone'! I looked at him stunned, spoke to the ATC, took permission for solo flight, pushed the power and, before I realised, I was up in the sky! I did one take-off and landing and returned to the parking area. That was an exhilarating, joyful and unforgettable experience for me. During that flight, I was smiling happily and laughing and singing to myself. The world was below me and I was on top of the world!'

That solo was the beginning of a career path born of passion and grit, one not easily heard of and talked about in those days. She successfully finished her PPL in 1973 from the Bombay Flying Club. A number of women came there for hobby flying, but few showed interest in staying the course to obtain the Commercial Pilot Licence (CPL), because the future for women in this field seemed bleak. Saudamini, however, was very keen to take her flying forward from a PPL to a CPL. With monetary constraints in the family, she did not have any choice but to look for other ways and means to work and earn money. Being a graduate (BSc), she scouted around for a bank job and was happy to get selected to join Bank of India's Poona branch as an officer. This was in November 1973. Even though she felt she had a very good job for those times, her mind was still on flying. Somehow, she needed to put together the necessary finances to fuel her ambition. Her heart was set on the ultimate goal—to fly as a pilot with a commercial airline.

While working in the bank, she learnt about an organisation of women pilots called Indian Women Pilots' Association (IWPA). She thought this would keep her connected to her passion for flying and, more importantly, allow her to meet and interact with like-minded women who were interested in flying. Making friends associated with aviation would likely help her on her chosen path, so she decided to join the organisation.

The IWPA was established in 1967 by Chanda Budhabhatti, Rabia Futehally and Mohini Shroff along with four other women. Chanda, Rabia and Mohini had met each other at the Bombay Flying Club in the early 1960s, where they were pursuing their passion for flying. Here's the interesting story behind how the IWPA was conceived.

There is an international organisation of women pilots called 'The Ninety-Nines Inc.' based in the USA. It was established in 1929 by 99 women pilots with world-famous aviatrix Amelia Earhart as Founder President. Individual members were called

99s. This organisation has many sections all over the world and many chapters within a section.

In 1964, Isabelle McCrae Hale, a 99 from the El Cajon Valley chapter in California, USA, came to Bombay on tour. Isabelle had served as a pilot in World War II as part of the WASP (Women's Auxiliary Service Pilots). She was employed as a nurse on a passenger ship sailing around the world. The ship had docked at Bombay Port. When she learnt that there was a flying club in Bombay, she decided to pay a visit. She was taken by surprise to see the number of women flying in the Bombay Flying Club. She observed from a distance a woman (Rabia) dressed in a saree, walking to the aircraft and, soon after, taking off. It amused Isabelle that these women were so actively involved in flying and thoroughly enjoying it! Although she could not meet Rabia or any other women during the visit, she began corresponding with them on returning to the USA. She was instrumental in suggesting that they join the International Organisation for Women Pilots called The Ninety-Nines Inc. Since it was not possible in those days to make a payment in dollars for membership fees, Isabelle, along with her El Cajon Valley chapter, decided to give membership to five ladies from India by making payments through their chapter till the women in question were able to make their own remittances. Such was the generosity and closeness of women around the world having a common passion for flying. Chanda, Rabia and Mohini were among the five women who became 99s. They then discovered the existence of the British Women Pilots' Association, the Australian Women Pilots' Association and the French Women Pilots' Association. And that's how Chanda conceptualised the Indian Women Pilots' Association (IWPA). It was established in 1967, with seven women as founder members and Chanda Budhabhatti as founder president. Besides Chanda, there were other ladies, including Rabia Futehally,

Mohini Shroff, Dr Sunila Bhajekar, Fulmala Maniar, Kumadini Rawal and Mangala Joshi.

The organisation was formed mainly to keep records and information regarding women belonging to different flying clubs around the country. Its other purpose was to reach out to them whenever they needed help and support to pursue flying. The IWPA still exists and has grown over the years. It keeps alive women's interest in aviation. In 1976, Lois Feigenbaum, the then international president of The Ninety-Nines Inc., travelled to Bombay and created the India chapter of The Ninety-Nines Inc.

After joining the IWPA, Saudamini learned more about the international women pilots' body. She felt that by joining the international organisation, she would be able to connect with women around the world who shared a passion for flying. Even today, she feels happy and proud as she remembers: 'I was one of the founder members of the India Chapter of The Ninety-Nines, an international organisation of women pilots. It was in 1977 that I got an opportunity to go to Los Angeles in the USA, as some individual 99s came to Bombay in March 1977, and offered me help and sponsorship for flying training with them. These were life-changing moments for me. My dream to continue flying and acquire my commercial licence seemed to have come closer to reality when I hopped on to the aircraft to leave for Los Angeles.'

She continues: 'It was my first trip outside India. I did not know what to expect when I reached LA. It was mind-blowing to see America, its people and their lifestyle. I thought I had arrived on another planet! I cannot even compare anything with the India of that time; even big cities like Bombay were nowhere close to what I experienced. I was to stay in LA for six months. All the Ninety-Nines members there were so friendly and helpful and extended their full support for my stay and for my flying training. I started my flying with full enthusiasm, wanting to get my commercial licence as soon as I could. I still owe a lot to my chief mentors, Wally Funk, Margaret Callaway and Norma Futterman, who lived in LA. Wally Funk was one of the famous Mercury 13 women who were in a race to become America's first female astronauts. As part of a privately funded programme, they successfully underwent the same physiological screening tests as had been undergone by the male astronauts selected by NASA in 1959 for Project Mercury; they never flew in space, though.

'My flying kick-started with the help and support of these three 99s and many other 99s from California and other states. I flew day in and day out, flying a Cessna 150 which belonged to Norma Futterman. She was generous enough to give me her Cessna for my training during my stay, free of charge. I also flew the single-engine V Tail Piper PA24, which belonged to Margaret Callaway who also generously offered her home and hospitality for my stay. Both Margaret and Wally Funk were my flying instructors. Wally was, however, in charge of my training. She arranged for me to take all the written tests and flying checks for my licence. Not a single day did I feel I was among strange people; I lived in the friendliest atmosphere and, before I realised it, I was completing 300 hours in 6 months, getting my much-awaited CPL, Instrument Rating and Instrument Ground Instructor Rating. It is a moment that I do not want to ever forget. I owe a huge debt of gratitude to the IWPA and The Ninety-Nines Inc. It was through their support that I could see my dream turn into reality!'

There was no turning back after that. Saudamini returned to India in 1978 with the CPL. Once back, she converted the licence to an Indian commercial licence, clearing the required written tests and flying checks. Then she eagerly awaited any opening for a pilot's job in a commercial airline. It wasn't long before she saw an advertisement put out by Indian Airlines for a pilot's post, and applied for it. Till then, Indian Airlines had only one woman pilot, Capt. Durba Capt. Saudamini became the second woman pilot to join Indian Airlines when she was selected as a trainee pilot based entirely on her merit and qualifications. In her own words, 'I was thrilled when I came to know that I had got the job and that I was to fly the Fokker Friendship (F-27) aircraft. Indian Airlines was the national carrier and the only domestic airline in India at the time. It was a proud moment for me. I resigned from my bank job and joined Indian Airlines in January 1980.'

It was a new beginning and a new adventure. She described her career as 'very interesting, fascinating and challenging'. Flying the Fokker was a thrill in itself. It was a twin-engine Turbo-Prop aircraft with 44 passenger seats and 2 seats for the flight attendants. She still remembers her experiences of flying during that time. She relates that the F-27 did not have a voice recorder and no simulator either for the aircraft training. Their six-monthly training and checks for licence renewal had to be conducted on the aircraft itself. Their instructor cum inspector would take 3 to 4 pilots in an empty F-27 for a check ride. They would do a series of take-offs and landings, and practice emergency procedures like engine failure in the actual aircraft. This training made them confident and perfect with all emergency procedures. Additionally, this made them fly completely by the book, following all standard operating procedures (SOPs).

Her first posting in the airline was to Calcutta. Flying from Calcutta was also a tough task. The flights were mainly to the North-East sector which provided her with new experiences. Though every field that she flew from taught her something different, her early years of flying from Calcutta always remind her of the special challenges that each pilot encountered there.

She remarks: 'From my base in Calcutta as a young first officer, I got accustomed to the airfields in the North-East region. We used to fly to all small airstrips. Many runways were just about 5,000 ft in length (considered short-field runways) having no Instrument Landing System (ILS). Flying into those airfields was the learning that helped each one of us realise how we have to navigate, keep the flight safe and perform a safe landing. Navigating and flying was done on flying aids like VOR (Very high frequency Omni-directional Range), ADF (Automatic Direction Finders) and NDB (Non-Directional Beacons). Though these aids were considered old in the western world, here, for us, it was a done thing. It was something that was accepted as part of our flying training and therefore, every day taught me something new. I still remember there was one airfield called Tezu, which was available only for the daytime. We were told elephants roam on the runway at night! But we did operate there during daytime and were lucky to have faced no problems. Not only that, but the North East sector being on the foothills of the Himalayan range resulted in the weather conditions becoming tough and challenging.'

Nothing seems to be too tough to handle when one takes up a profession like flying. The fact is that one is prepared for the worst at any moment and always ready for action. Pilots are trained to think positively so that they can handle any situation, anytime. Capt. Saudamini's focus, dedication and hard work brought results when she successfully completed her training and qualified to become a commander on the F-27, in September 1985. Adding another feather to her cap, on 29 November 1985, Capt. Saudamini commanded the first all-women crew flight. Although women were not even heard of in this profession, Indian Airlines, the only domestic airline in India, decided to showcase their women captains and proceeded with the first all-women flight. So Capt. Saudamini, along with First Officer Capt. Nivedita (who joined IA in 1984, becoming the third woman pilot in the country), and two female flight attendants formed the first all-women crew in an aircraft when they operated an F-27 aircraft from Calcutta to Guwahati, onwards to Tezpur, Jorhat, Lilabari and Chabua. They created history among airlines which were members of the IATA (International Air Transport Association) as the first all-women crew flight in the world, where the Captain, First Officer and cabin attendants were all women.

India may not have been ready for many things in the 1980s, but women had proven that they could scale the sky! The world was to see many more successful all-women crew flights. This was just the beginning. It was also an eye-opener for women in India who dreamt of becoming pilots. Thanks to the professionalism and dedication of Capt. Saudamini and Capt. Nivedita, women would go on to garner both recognition in this field and the confidence of the airline and passengers. Women were now not only flying but also joining airlines as pilots. The number kept rising slowly but steadily. Capt. Saudamini created further history when, in 1987, she successfully completed her training to become a check pilot on the F-27, the first woman in Asia to become one in a commercial airline.

Having flown on Fokkers for a few years, she was moved to the jet engine aircraft Boeing 737. When she started her training on this new jet engine aircraft after a turboprop (F-27), it felt like a big change, but she lost no time in adapting to this and successfully completed her training. Having a yearning to fly any aircraft, she took this as an opportunity to forge ahead in her career and to fly the advanced aircraft of those times. Adapting to the jet technology was arduous, but she quickly grasped the concept and started enjoying handling the new machine. She moved on to the B-737 and was posted from Calcutta to her own city, Bombay.

For any ambitious flyer, it is a desire to move on to bigger and more advanced aircraft. It always takes a certain number of flying hours to get the hang of a new machine. Capt. Saudamini smoothly mastered the new aircraft, which was faster, better equipped and took more passengers on board (compared to the Fokker). She concedes that the stress and responsibility also increased. Moreover, what motivated her to excel was that even though they changed to a better aircraft, a jet aircraft, their ground facilities did not change much. She remembers the details. 'We were operating the Boeing but flew to airfields having no advance aids like the Instrument Landing System (ILS). Many of these airfields had very short-length runways of little more than 5,000 ft, and under 6,000 ft. We had to land at the correct touch-down zone. Also, making an approach in bad weather conditions using landing aids like ADF/NDB was not easy, as these aids do not bring you on the runway centre line; you have to keep your runway in sight and align yourself to the centre line of the runway and land safely in the correct touchdown zone.' This was the actual situation, but she felt the training allowed her to handle each flight with ease. Furthermore, each day's experience taught her to become a better flier. Performing well in such difficult conditions gave her a great sense of job satisfaction and happiness.

She became commander on the B-737 in 1988, the first Indian woman to be a commander on a jet engine aircraft. Here, too, she got the opportunity to operate the first all-women crew flight on 16 September 1989, with Capt. Nivedita as her co-pilot and only female flight attendants. They flew from Bombay to Goa and back. This was the first all-women crew flight on a jet aircraft in Asia.

By now, the first captain of the Indian Airlines, Capt. Durba, had retired and Capt. Saudamini became the senior-most female captain. During her tenure, she witnessed many changes in this industry: the modernisation of airports with new Air Traffic Control (ATC) systems. The ATC built new and modern control towers, acquiring new and improved radars, with a larger range of detection to help the flow of traffic that increases over the years. Aircraft equipped with modern radars TCAS (Traffic Alert and Collision Avoidance System) and other instruments helped perform an auto-landing even in zero visibility during fog conditions. Most runways were now equipped with ILS and runway lengths increased. Also, the number of new domestic airlines and new passenger terminal buildings with aerobridges rose. Most importantly, she witnessed the upward change in the number of women pilots joining different airlines.

This was also the time that the world saw the latest fly-by-wire technology aircraft, the Airbus 320 (A-320). Indian Airlines was one of the first airlines to have acquired this aircraft. By the early 90s, Capt. Saudamini started her training on this machine. Moving to better aircraft and technology always excited her. She successfully completed her training and got her command in 1994, thus becoming the first woman in Asia to be a captain on the A-320, a computerised, fly-by-wire technology aircraft, totally different from the conventional type of jet aircraft. In 1995, she commanded the all-women crew on the A-320 along with First Officer Capt. Sangita K. Bangar from Mumbai to Madras (now Chennai) and back. This flight again is marked as the first on the Airbus 320 in Asia and probably the world.

Capt. Saudamini's career boasts of many firsts and her name is well-known in aviation circles. Yet, for her, nothing matches the respect, love and affection she received from her colleagues from all departments of the airline and the ATC and the thousands of passengers she flew in her long career. Having joined Indian Airlines in 1980, she had a smooth and fulfilling flying career until her retirement from Air India in 2010 (Indian Airlines was merged with Air India in 2007–08). She retired as general manager of Western Region, Air India (Narrow Body).

Remembering her grand last flight, she narrated: 'It was a great morning on 31 March 2010. The flight was from Mumbai to Bangalore (now Bengaluru) and back to Mumbai. Capt. Sangita was my co-pilot for this flight. I knew my time to retire had come; I had enjoyed and cherished every moment in this fantastic profession from the time I joined in January 1980, and I wanted to do my last flight the same way. I reached the airport, was greeted warmly by the entire ground staff, did my pre-flight medical, took the Meteorological Terminal Aviation Routine Weather Report (METAR) and flight plan briefing, went through security and proceeded to the aircraft. The entire crew was waiting to greet me with a smile. I sat in my seat in the aircraft, scanned the cockpit, went for my external walk around, did my preliminary cockpit checks and saw the passengers boarding. Little did they know this was my last flight, but I wanted to give them the most comfortable and smooth experience that day. These thoughts were running through my mind as I saw the passengers boarding. Finally, we did our push-back and taxied to the runway. We took permission to line up on the runway and take off, I pushed the throttles for take-off, and it seemed like the first day I had started my career, full of excitement and a great feeling. During the flight to Bangalore and back, the ATC officers congratulated me on my long and outstanding career as a pilot. We reached our destination and the passengers deplaned. We waited for the return sector, and it was time for the return leg, the final countdown, back to Mumbai. As we approached

Mumbai, the ATC officers welcomed me back and cleared us to land. And I made my landing, the aircraft smoothly touching the runway. We vacated the runway, entered the taxi track and two fire brigade trucks showered water on our aircraft from both sides. *What a last flight*, I thought to myself. Surely one could not ask for more. My eyes grew moist as Capt. Sangita patted me gently on the back.

Capt. Saudamini formally retired on 31 March 2010 but was inducted as a contract pilot with Air India, where she flew for another two years before finally bidding goodbye to flying in July 2012. Capt. Saudamini lives in Mumbai, keeping herself active by interacting with her colleagues from aviation and the Ninety-Nines Inc. She is a yoga enthusiast and a student of spirituality. She describes the goal as a balanced state of mind. Over the course of her life, she has had many honours and awards bestowed on her. As early as 1977, when she was given the achievement award by the International Women Pilots Organisation at their annual convention in San Francisco, USA. In 1988, she received a Certificate of Appreciation from The Ninety-Nines Inc. on an occasion where all those airlines in the world who had employed women pilots were honoured and felicitated. She was invited to represent Indian Airlines. The function was held in Oklahoma, USA. In 1991, she received the F.I.E. Foundation award at Ichalkaranji, Maharashtra, from the then prime minister of India, Mr Chandrashekhar. The foundation was established in 1973 to promote outstanding achievements in the fields of science, technology, arts and humanities.

The torch that Capt. Saudamini held aloft has been carried forward by a number of women pilots who joined and continue to join the airlines as pilots. Capt. Saudamini will be remembered as an avant-garde woman aviator, opening up this profession for hundreds of women who dreamt of becoming pilots. Her vision and perseverance lent wings to many other women who were inspired to become achievers like her.

The first all-women flight in Asia on Airbus 320, under Capt. Saudamini Deshmukh's (extreme right) command, along with First Officer Capt. Sangita K. Bangar (extreme left)

(L–R) Capt. Saudamini Deshmukh, Capt. Durba Banerjee, Prime Minister Rajiv Gandhi, Capt. Nivedita Jain Bhasin and Capt. Anila Bhatia at the First World Congress in New Delhi in 1986

Beaming with satisfaction and contentment born out of a rewarding journey – her last flight on Airbus 320, before her retirement

On the Boeing 737, Nivedita Bhasin (R) as First Officer with Capt. Saudamini Deshmukh

Proud mother, Capt. Nivedita, with daughter, Niharika, captain with Indigo Airlines

(L–R) Capt. Nivedita Bhasin (co-pilot), Ms Korobi Pathak (air hostess), Capt. Saudamini Deshmukh (Commander) and S. Roy Choudhary (air hostess), after completing the first all-women flight in 1985

Young Achiever

Six

All in the Family

Nivedita Jain Bhasin

She had just finished her Class 10 exams. Still in her school uniform, she decided to go to the Delhi Flying Club at Safdarjung Airport, unmindful that she would appear as a little school girl. The way she saw it, she would soon be in Class 11, and surely that was a big deal. That visit to the club for young, enthusiastic Nivedita was the most natural extension of her rapture at the sight of small aircraft flying overhead every day, which she would watch from her classroom window. 'My school was in Delhi's Chanakyapuri area which was behind the Delhi Flying Club. Every day, I would see the reflection of small planes take off and land, on my classroom window, and I would be mesmerised by the sight. I particularly remember when one day, my algebra teacher asked me a question and she caught me daydreaming as usual. "You'll get nothing but a big zero," she thundered, pulling me out of my reverie.' And there was a round of suppressed giggles all around.

Born on 6 July 1963, Nivedita, the younger daughter of Bijendra and Amita Jain, had always dreamt of doing something different from the rest of the crowd. She was determined to be unique. She wanted to excel in a field not many women had set foot in. She was not keen on pure academics, and was very sure she did not want a desk job that would keep her in an office from 9 to 5.

The fact that her sister was very good in studies and that she was always compared to her did not seem to bother her; it only strengthened her resolve to steadfastly follow her dreams.

But as soon as she reached the flying club, the clerk who saw her said with a smirk, '*Abhi aap wapas* school *jaaiyye aur padhaai khatam keejiye*.' Roughly translated to mean: 'Go back to school now and complete your education.' Ignoring his condescending attitude, she replied, 'No, I want to become a pilot. I have come to find out about how to learn flying.' To this, he laughed and said, 'You go and study in your school. This is no place for you.' But seeing that she would not budge, he relented and pointed to the way to the gliding club and said she could start by learning to fly gliders, as she was too young to learn flying.

His cavalier dismissal made her sad. But not willing to give up so easily, she walked towards the Delhi Gliding Club. There, she was lucky to meet the gliding instructor, Capt. Wason. She recalls the incident: 'Capt. Wason was a very kind gentleman and responded pleasantly when I asked him very plainly that, as I was too young to start flying, could I learn gliding? I wanted to be an airline pilot, I told him. He listened patiently and said, "We would love to have you here for gliding, but you have to be sixteen years old."' And he asked her how old she was. Despondently, she told him she was fifteen. To her surprise, he did not dismiss her. Instead, he advised that she could start with aeromodelling, which could give her an understanding of the science of flying, and when she turned sixteen, she could come back.

Within a few days, Nivedita found herself at the India Hobby Centre in Connaught Place. She was surprised to see that there were only boys there, making aero models. However, she didn't mind being the only girl, and in fact, the store manager, a very kind gentleman named John D'cruz, encouraged her and taught her the first lessons in aerodynamics.

Retaining focus, she started making small balsa-wood Chuck gliders and was encouraged by one and all. Soon, she took part in an aeromodelling competition, and was awarded the first prize in the 'Chuck Glider' category. This only piqued her curiosity and a month before she turned sixteen, she went back to the kind instructor who had counselled her and requested him to start teaching her gliding. She was happy that he kept his word, and soon enough, she enrolled for gliding classes.

This was a different experience altogether from aeromodelling. Here she was, inside the glider, feeling like a bird up in the sky, soaking up the serenity of silence and filled with unimaginable joy! She was learning and experiencing how the glider flies without an engine. The glider was connected by a cable to a motorised winch on the airfield, which lifted the glider into the sky up to a specified height and, when released, the glider would glide down. Each circuit lasted all of three minutes. It was a wonderful feeling! She enjoyed every launch in the wooden gliders with the instructor training her. Not before long, he started preparing her for her first solo. She grasped the different techniques and started replicating the glider flights as per her instructor's guidance. Complete focus and dedication resulted in her sorties turning out perfect every day. Her instructor was convinced that she was now ready to fly the glider on her own and it was time to send her for her solo. She narrates with pride what an experience that was: 'I was on top of the world. This was what I had been dreaming of all my life – to be able to fly like a bird. It was pure ecstasy. Freedom. This was in 1979, and when I look back today, I feel sixteen is too young, but there I was, gliding away in the sky, enjoying every moment of that experience. An interesting fact is that I first learnt how to glide, then to fly, and only then did I learn how to drive a car!'

In a few months, Nivedita was giving joyrides to passengers in the twin-seater gliders and no longer needed to pay for her launches. She gave demonstration flights at the Annual Gliding Club Day and also became adept at soaring, a technique in which one takes the help of thermals or hot air currents and can fly higher and longer. Her longest flight was 2 hours and 47 minutes long.

The year was 1980, and women were not flying or known to show much interest in aviation. Nivedita had been gliding for over a year and was now ready to start flying. It was a totally male-dominated field and no one considered it a suitable profession for women. Nevertheless, she felt increasingly ebullient about flying, and told her parents all about her dreams, aspirations and determination. They were encouraging and understanding, even though she did not know where this desire would lead her. Moreover, it was expensive to learn flying. Her father had just left his job with DCM and started his own work, so they couldn't easily afford such an expensive vocation (at that time, nobody could imagine that this could be a profession for girls). But they never said no. While her father encouraged her to continue her training, he always laid emphasis on the fact that whatever she started, she must complete it well. That is to say, in today's lingo, 'It should reach a logical conclusion.' On the other hand, her mother gave her the assurance that she would save money whichever way she could and help out with the finances. Nivedita's mother did most of the household chores herself in order to save money on domestic help. She gave tuitions to children at home, travelled by bus instead of taking a taxi, stitched the children's clothes at home, and all of this without letting the children know what hardships she was facing. She was a housewife with no professional work experience, yet her children learnt to be resilient and conscientious. They understood that they would have to make the best of any opportunity that came their way.

Capt. Nivedita ponders: 'Today, I realise how many sacrifices she must have made to allow me to fly, not knowing where it would take me, what kind of job I would get, or whether I would ever even get a job as a pilot. It was my own passion, my dream, and I am extremely proud that my parents supported me and helped me pursue it.' She feels that having the support of her parents helped her take her ambitions forward with determination and courage, and gave her the confidence that she could definitely achieve her aspirations of becoming a pilot. And so, she continued to learn how to fly, a dream that must have been really difficult to fructify for many women in the 1980s!

She finally joined the Delhi Flying Club and began flying those small yellow aircraft she had so often seen from her classroom. Here she was now, inside one of them, learning to fly them on her own! It all seemed like a big wish come true as she found herself right in the middle of it. The next step was to work hard towards her goal of becoming a commercial pilot, and finally join Indian Airlines as an airline pilot. The real thrill came when she got her solo. In her words: 'This was in April 1981. I had just finished with my Class 12 board exams and was giving joyrides, when Capt. Karmendra Singh, adviser of Civil Aviation, visited the gliding club. He saw me and enquired if I had gone solo in the plane. When I responded in the negative, he immediately asked me to accompany him to the flying club so that he could test my gliding skills. He was the senior-most flying instructor at the time. After flying with me for 15 minutes, in the evening, he asked me to return the next morning. And I flew solo the next morning. The rest is history.'

Nivedita then went to Patiala to log some solo hours and also enrolled for the Aircraft Maintenance Engineer's course alongside. While flying in Patiala, Nivedita met Anila Bhatia. Anila was doing her instructor's training and they spent many a happy evening together. They took walks, exchanging notes and sharing experiences. They have been friends for over forty years now.

Nivedita was still unsure of how her parents would arrange the finances required. While she was in Patiala, unknown to her, her mother (on her behalf) applied for a flying scholarship at the Bihar Flying Institute (BFI), Patna. The Bihar government was providing scholarships for obtaining a Commercial Pilot Licence (CPL). Her parents belonged to Bihar and had domicile there, and as such, she could apply for this scholarship. Her maternal uncle had conveyed this to her parents.

This was a golden opportunity for her. She was not very pleased at the thought of living in Patna, but this was the only way to complete her CPL. She sat for the qualifying test held by the BFI and was elated when she learnt that she had won the scholarship. It felt like a big burden off her shoulders. She knew she could now fully concentrate on flying and not worry her parents about the finances.

As a young convent school girl, given the cultural differences and the way girls were treated in Bihar, it was with a lot of trepidation that Nivedita reached the BFI. Her fears were not unfounded. She met with a lot of resistance. Born and brought up in Delhi, the difference in the kind of exposure she had got was vastly different from what she saw in Patna of the 1980s. It was a culture shock for her, even though she had been there many times. Most of the boys in the flying club did not like her. First, she was a girl and, second, they felt she had usurped their scholarship. They would have bets that she would lose her way on a cross-country flight. They even tried to sabotage her flying by putting paper in the fuel tank. She found herself trapped in a very hostile atmosphere. The only saving grace was that she was staying with her maternal family, which included her grandmother, and their love and support comforted her while she was away from home. Her peers at the club thought she had come to pass time as they all wondered what she would do after getting a CPL. To overcome this first hurdle, she decided that she should study and clear her papers. So, within three months of getting there, she worked hard, appeared for her CPL papers, and cleared all of them in one shot, a feat hardly anyone could accomplish. This made a lot of difference. Now the instructor had to allow her to fly and her other colleagues, who could not clear the same papers, had to keep mum. The message she wanted to convey to her colleagues was that she was serious and was there to perform, and it had hit home.

It was while flying in Patna that she first met Capt. Saudamini, a co-pilot with Indian Airlines, who had joined the national carrier in 1980 and was posted in Calcutta. She was India's second airline pilot. One day, Nivedita found out that Capt. Saudamini was landing in Patna from Calcutta. She waited patiently near the tarmac. When Capt. Saudamini walked towards the terminal, everyone stared at her. The uniform made all the difference. 'It put every one of us, including the boys, in awe of her,' she says. This made young Nivedita even more focused on what she was doing and she resolved to work extra hard to be able to join the airline as soon as possible and fly for the country.

By February 1983, she successfully completed her hours and got her CPL. She became the seventh woman CPL holder in the country. She recalls proudly: 'It was one of the happiest moments of my life. I had no idea where life would take me from there, but certainly the first step – the first hurdle – I had overcome. It was a proud moment for my parents, my sister, my brother and myself. I did not rest after that. I knew I still had a long way to go. I now had to work on getting into the airline.'

On completion of her CPL, as a gift, her sister presented her with a one-year membership of The Ninety-Nines Inc., the International Organisation of Women Pilots. As a member of The Ninety-Nines, Nivedita was introduced to women pilots from around the world. Over the course of her airline career, she has made hundreds of friends across the globe. As governor of The Ninety-Nines, she feels that aviation education is her ultimate calling and she leaves no stone unturned in sharing her experience with budding pilots and school children.

She returned to Delhi and started making enquiries about jobs, but there were no vacancies. It was a bit disappointing as she was so eager to join the airline. The image of Capt. Saudamini was so clearly etched in her mind. Nevertheless, she did not lose heart and decided that instead of doing nothing, she should work to get her instructor rating, and went about finding out how that could be done. In Patiala, she successfully got her instructor rating in January 1984, and also managed to get a job as an instructor with the Ludhiana Flying Club. As she was about to take up the new job, she heard about pilot vacancies in Indian Airlines, which had been announced after four long years. She knew there would be many people sitting for this exam, so she put her heart and soul into preparing for the entrance tests.

She wanted to do her best, and for that she realised she needed guidance, perhaps some expert advice on the method of the examination being conducted. She learnt about coaching centres others were attending to study for the exam and she approached some of these, but found they charged a lot. This was indeed a deterrent. Not intending to give up, she took a chance, went to one of the most popular coaching centres run by Mr Duggal, and told him that her parents could not afford the tuition fees, thereby requesting him to take her in with minimum tuition fees. She remembers this incident very well. 'He saw me and probably understood my need and was kind enough to allow me to sit in the classes and not take any money from me. I still remember this gesture; he is no more today, but I will never forget him. I owe my job to him, his compassion and his kindness.'

She cleared the written test and the next thing she knew, she was excitedly holding a letter in her hand which informed her of her selection in Indian Airlines. This was July 1984. The batch comprised fourteen pilots including her; she was not only the youngest but also the only girl. She was the third girl in the country to join the national airline as a pilot, to have forayed into a predominantly male-dominated field of work. She was ready for this new journey that destiny had shaped for her, for the big dreams, the passion that had finally paid off, for the reality of being a part of the airline as a pilot.

Where life would take her from there was another story, but it was the start of a different struggle. This was clearly the world of the rich and famous. There were a handful of boys whose fathers were airline pilots, some colleagues who had prior experience in the airline in other departments, and some were even working as flight instructors. For them to see a girl as one amongst them was not so easy, to say the least. Having just turned twenty-one, Nivedita was naive and gullible. The boys would gang up and she felt lonely at times, but this was expected and nothing new. Perhaps men were not yet ready to have women share their space and classroom, partaking of the same knowledge, having the same passion and being readied for the same challenges as they were; so there were mixed reactions. Some of her batchmates were friendly while some others were not, and there were certainly quite a few hiccups initially. It was a lonely, tough and arduous path, where she had to bravely deal with everything that was thrown her way, be it academics or the hostile attitude of her colleagues. Even though she worked very hard, she was average in class. She realised that boys had the added advantage of hanging out together with instructors and they visited the simulators secretly. Thus, they were always one step ahead. During that time, she was the only girl in the Indian Airlines Central Training Establishment (CTE) in Hyderabad. Capt. Durba and Capt. Saudamini were flying as co-pilots from their base in Calcutta.

This was the time that Nivedita met Rohit Bhasin. He joined the CTE, Hyderabad, for training on the Fokker Friendship, though he was not her batchmate. He had joined India's third-level airline, Vayudoot. Vayudoot also operated the Fokker Friendship aircraft and the pilots were trained in the Indian Airlines Training Centre in Hyderabad. She said, 'It seems strange now that I met Rohit during our training, and we got married within a few months. I think the fact that I had heard that both the first two lady pilots, Capt. Durba and Capt. Saudamini, never got married, stayed in my head. Very early in my career, I had made up my mind that I would get married and have children. Marriage did me good. After my training was over, I was posted in Calcutta. My father-in-law was a senior pilot in Indian Airlines, which was a big blessing for me. The whole base started treating me like their own daughter-in-law. He was a very loving person and, as such, was liked by all his colleagues. I was accepted without much of a problem, even though women pilots were few; I would think I was lucky!'

The rough patches encountered during her flying club days were different. As a girl, people had wondered why she had chosen to do this. Once in the airline, it seemed like another challenge altogether. Everybody would notice what she was doing. Simple things such as how she talked and dressed were commented on. It was because girls were so few in number. Of this fact she says: 'I felt this changed my personality. At home, I was fun-loving, open and carefree but at work, I became very reserved. This was also because one could not show their fun-loving side as the profession was such. You had to look mature and serious. Being a woman, we could not take things easy or lightly; we were being watched and judged constantly. Of course, being professional was part of it. It's funny, though, but interesting to share that whenever Capt. Saudamini and I would fly, everyone (despatchers, pre-flight medical doctors, engineers and ground staff) seemed to be concerned and would give us strange looks. We would wonder why this kind of attitude was directed towards us when we were just as trained and qualified as our male colleagues. We had gone through the same training as our male colleagues but we always seemed to be under scrutiny, especially when we flew into rough weather. It was like they wanted to know if we would be able to cope! Capt. Saudamini was very professional and, I think, kind of strict. Being a woman in a male-dominated field, we always had to be extra careful, to be disciplined and dedicated.

'We both were Calcutta-based and also became the first to operate the all-women crew flight, the first in the world to do so. It was a proud moment for us, our airline and the country.'

Capt. Nivedita became the second woman in the country to get command on the B-737 jet aircraft. At twenty-six, she was also the youngest woman to get command on the B-737 in the world at that time (1989). She says: 'I feel grateful and thankful to Indian Airlines for having given me this opportunity. Working hard was my responsibility!' She talks about how a lot of change came over her as a commander. People started looking at her differently. She had to prove herself at every step, coping with professional challenges on one hand while, on the other, her personal challenges were not trivial. She had a two-year-old son when she flew her first flight in command. It was with the help and support of her husband, and his and her parents, that she was able to continue working as a pilot. She managed both, being young and having family support. She had her second child, a daughter, but never thought of quitting the profession, although the mindset of people assumed that once women had a family, they would quit their jobs.

In fact, it was only when Capt. Nivedita became pregnant, that Indian Airlines formulated a maternity policy for pilots. There had been no need till this time. The minimum period to report for flying after childbirth is 6 weeks, or 42 days. And after each of her children were born, Capt. Nivedita did just that. She did not take any extra leave. She did not want pregnancy/childbirth to be the reasons for airlines to be biased against recruiting women. She proved that women could come back to work after giving birth and attain the desired level of competency.

Of course, now she shudders at the thought of how she had the courage and strength to leave her infants at home when they were just forty-two days old!

She continued even though it was really tough, with the struggle to keep herself fit, look after her family and commandeer the flights, all at the same time. It was also during this phase that she was moved from one aircraft to another for her command. The flights also became more frequent and long sectors were quite tiring too. It was challenging to handle the emotional turmoil, physical exhaustion, the ups and downs of flights and the work conditions, among other things. She was grateful to her in-laws for helping look after the children which enabled her to keep going.

While in school, Nivedita had got limited opportunities to play sports, but her husband was a tennis champion and an expert swimmer. She was petrified of being in the water, but once her children were old enough to swim, she found the courage to learn swimming. She was in her thirties then. She started swimming five days a week. For more than two decades, this was her regular fitness regime. Today, she can swim non-stop for hours and is also a certified open water diver, certified by the Professional Association of Diving Instructors (PADI).

Her husband was in Air India by then, so they were both posted in Bombay, where bringing up kids was quite an ordeal. She remembers one such time, when her kids were small and her husband was off on a long international flight, with both her parents and in-laws living in Delhi. 'One such time, I remember, I was pulled out for a night-stop flight, and leaving the kids alone was not an option, so I had no choice but to take my kids on the flight with me. I think my children also took it as a way of life. There were times they would open their eyes and find themselves in the aircraft. It became part of their life as they were growing up.' No wonder both her son and daughter are pilots today.

Capt. Nivedita's son and daughter followed in the footsteps of their parents and both took to flying after school. While her son joined Air India and is a Boeing B-777 Commander, her daughter didn't want to join Air India, as three of them were already there. She wanted to show that what her parents achieved, she could too, without being in their shadow.

Capt. Nivedita reflects: 'As women of the 80s, we faced many different challenges in getting where we wanted to be. Though some women may not agree, each one of us did have to go through more for being a woman. Whether it was in simulator checks or actual aircraft checks, there were fewer women, and some men were not ready for women to fly with the same ease and handle the big jet without any difficulties. Yes, women were very conscientious in their work. They were serious, dedicated and thoroughly professional, leaving no chance for any error, as all of us wanted to be the most ideal women captains.'

During her long tenure as captain, she has flown all aircraft from Fokker to Boeing 737 to A-300 to A-330, and is currently flying the Dreamliner B-787. In the long span of her career, Capt. Nivedita has handled many demanding situations, like engine failure, smoke in the cockpit, and hydraulic failure. Recently, though, she faced a very different experience, which she felt was more important than her handling emergencies in the cockpit. 'Flying the B-787 from Delhi to Birmingham, we were two hours into the flight when cabin crew informed that one of the passengers complained of breathlessness and, as a routine procedure, they had made an announcement for a doctor. They also told me that three doctors who were on board had volunteered to look into the passenger's problem. In the cockpit, my co-pilot and I geared up, keeping all the closest airports en route on our list, in case we were required to divert. In the meantime, we were informed that the doctors on board were looking after the patient and he was stable. So after some time, I went into the cabin and saw that the passenger had been well taken care of. They had laid him down on three empty seats. I met with the three doctors and took their names and their contact details. I then made an in-flight announcement informing all the passengers about this incident and called out the names of the three doctors who had attended to the ill passenger. We also made handwritten notes thanking them. After landing, I informed Air India about this whole incident. The airline took note of this and sent its appreciation to the doctors and cabin crew of the flight. I felt satisfied that the doctors who had volunteered were acknowledged by the airline. Gestures like these will always help make airlines a happy place for everyone.'

On another note, she narrated an incident that took place when she was commander on the B-737 during the early days.

She still remembers that time and the attitude of the people in the airline. 'It was a flight from Mumbai to Jodhpur. The aircraft had a snag and due to rectification of the same, we got delayed in Jodhpur. At that time, the Jodhpur runway did not have lights and so we had night flying restrictions. My operations manager from Mumbai wanted me to bring the flight back. He said, "Take off with gooseneck flares on the runway." A gooseneck flare is a type of wick-in-kerosene runway lighting arrangement provided where permanent airfield lighting systems are not installed. I could take off, but what if I had to return in case of an emergency and the gooseneck flares had extinguished by then? It didn't seem the right thing to do. I told him that I would not operate at night with gooseneck flares. The flight got grounded overnight in Jodhpur. We returned to Bombay the next day and I was asked to explain my decision. Following procedure is the correct thing, and I would still suggest this to all the juniors. In a profession like ours, it is also important to make the right decisions with a lot of thinking so that you don't take hasty action for anything.' Safety is the prime concern.

Growing up through adversity, Capt. Nivedita's siblings, an elder sister and younger brother, excelled in their respective fields. Her sister pursued physics and computer engineering and has had a long and successful career in software, secrecy laws and HR. She's married to a professor of physics. Her younger brother and his wife are both architects. Their father taught them to be 'honest, sincere and truthful' and from their mother they learned to be resilient.

Capt. Nivedita's aviation journey taught her many things. The biggest lesson was to accept every challenge. In her career, she has accomplished many feats, some of which are unthinkable for most. She has done sky-diving, deep-sea diving, run half marathons, climbed mountains, Mt Fuji being one of them, and has even done wing walking. She has learned and practised

Iyengar yoga for three years. She has played golf for many years. She has also learned photography from a professional photographer. These are the hobbies that she made time for during her hectic life as an airline pilot and she hopes to be able to spend time after retirement keeping busy with these. She realises that being truthful and honest is sometimes detrimental to a career, yet this is what she derives her strength from. As a captain, she has embraced these life lessons. 'Whatever one does, wherever one lives, one must enjoy, appreciate whatever one has, be thankful each day and never take things for granted,' she concludes.

As an international pilot, Capt. Nivedita has flown to every continent except South America. She makes it a point to meet women pilots across the globe and over the years, has made some very good friends. She has won many national and international awards for her contribution to aviation, including the Rajiv Gandhi Rashtriya Ekta Award. She was inducted into the International Forest of Friendship, at Atchison, Kansas, where a plaque bearing her name is engraved in the forest. She was also inducted in the Captain's Club of the International Society of Women Airline Pilots.

As 'Wide Body' training captain, Capt. Nivedita says that one learns a lot when one teaches. She first became a training captain in 1999 on the A-300 and continued on the A-330 and Boeing B-787. In 2012, Capt. Nivedita became the first woman airline pilot to fly the state-of-the-art Dreamliner. She was privileged to take delivery of the second Dreamliner of Air India and flew it to Delhi, from the Boeing factory in Charleston, South Carolina, in September 2012.

Today, Capt. Nivedita feels she is not as reserved and serious, whether it stems from years of experience, hers and other women pilots' gradual acceptance over the years, or even the fact that with a jump in the number of women pilots, people's attitudes have changed. The fact that, as women pilots, they went against the prevalent trend and proved themselves cannot be ignored. After more than thirty-six years of being with the airlines, she feels she has been there, done it all, and would like to share her experiences like an open book from which different leaves can be taken out and shared for the benefit of others. She wishes to encourage the younger generation and guide them in the best possible way. It is her way of paying it forward.

She makes an observation: 'I feel the new generation of women are not like us. They don't take any nonsense or criticism if they know they are right; they do not flinch at anything. My daughter is a captain, flying in command with Indigo. I see how she addresses her junior or senior captains. Our times were certainly different, but in spite of all odds, it has been the most satisfying, adventurous and exciting profession that I cherish and enjoy each day. I do not think I would have been happy in any other job. If I had to live my life again, I would replicate it. My wings are the most precious things in my life and I have a lot to be thankful for every day.'

Capt. Nivedita kept herself busy when the COVID-19 pandemic struck. Air India, like all other airlines, had to shut shop and pilots became redundant. During this time, Capt. Nivedita enrolled for several courses in Flight Safety, Human Factors, Flight Safety of Remotely Piloted Aircraft, as well as Accident Investigation and Auditing, at the University of Southern California and IATA and soon completed the Certificate Program in Aviation Safety & Security.

Along with flying the Dreamliner Boeing B-787, she became a qualified Aircraft Accident Investigator, IOSA Airline Auditor, Quality, Safety and CORSIA Internal Auditor, as well as Safety Management Trainer. With these and several other accolades in her kitty, she was soon promoted to the position of General Manager, Flight Safety.

In 2020, Capt. Nivedita was appointed the Executive Director and Chief of Flight Safety at Air India and created history by becoming the first woman airline pilot in India to hold this coveted post.

It was in June 2021 that, as a challenge, she along with three other crew members flew the Dreamliner along the best route from Washington DC to New Delhi and, in the process, set a world record for the fastest commercial flight in a B-787.

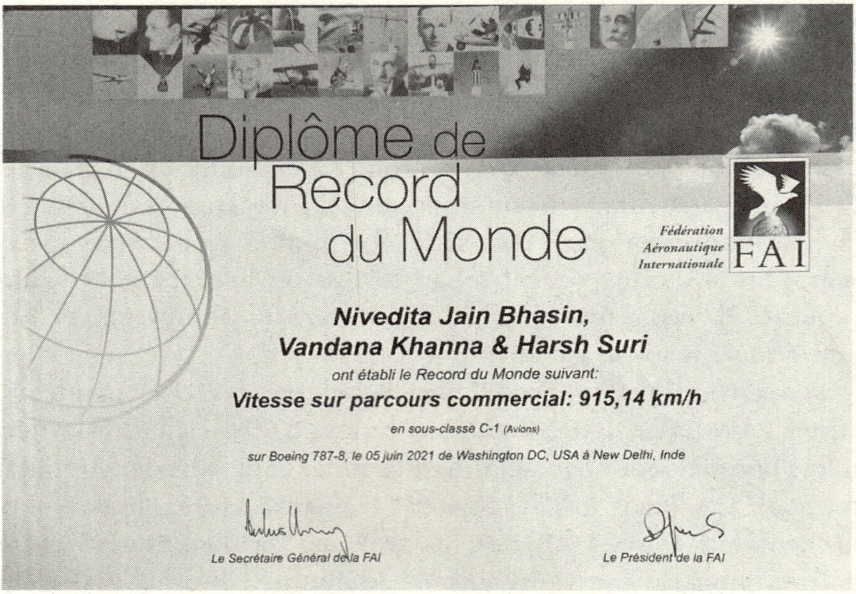
Diplôme de Record du Monde

Fédération Aéronautique Internationale FAI

Nivedita Jain Bhasin,
Vandana Khanna & Harsh Suri

ont établi le Record du Monde suivant:

Vitesse sur parcours commercial: 915,14 km/h

en sous-classe C-1 (Avions)

sur Boeing 787-8, le 05 juin 2021 de Washington DC, USA à New Delhi, Inde

Le Secrétaire Général de la FAI — *Le Président de la FAI*

The certificate Capt. Nivedita received for achieving the feat of flying the Dreamliner from Washington DC to New Delhi in record time

Capt. Nivedita's last flight at Air India was in July 2021 from Heathrow to Delhi. She got a warm send-off at Heathrow Airport.

Today, Capt. Nivedita beams with pride as she shows us her report card that reads: Superannuated in July 2021 after thirty-seven years as an Airline Pilot in Air India with 22,000 hours of flying.

She leaves behind a legacy of pilots – her daughter and son-in-law, both Airbus A-320 captains and her son, a Boeing B-777 captain. And who knows? Perhaps her grandson, a handsome two-and-a-half-year old, might just follow in his grandmother's footsteps!

Nothing can compare to the joy of flying – Capt. Nivedita in the cockpit of Boeing 787, the Dreamliner

The passion for flying runs in the family. Capt. Nivedita with daughter Niharika, son Rohan and husband Rohit.

On the occasion of International Women's Day, the all-women flight crew of Boeing 787, with Capt. Nivedita (sixth from right) before their departure from Delhi

Capt. Anila Bhatia, First Officer with Indian Airlines, 1986

A happy moment with daughter Miriya after a flight

Little Miriya, growing up among aircraft

First Mother-Daughter Fliers

Seven

Self-motivation to Success

Anila Bhatia

The year 1981 saw another young girl in her teens join this elite group of women fliers, writing her own history by overcoming all odds and becoming a pilot. With complete belief in herself and her dreams, she was successful in getting her CPL. Come 1982, she also got her instructor rating. Since the only domestic airline at that time had no vacancy and she wanted to capitalise on her flying start, she worked towards bagging the job of assistant flying instructor at the Karnal Flying Club, the place where she had acquired her training. She broke all gender barriers by becoming the first female instructor of a flying club in the country in 1982. This is none other than Capt. Anila Bhatia, a lady who firmly espouses that however much people may want to quell one's ambition, one can always make it to the finish line, just as she did!

Self-motivated about becoming a pilot one day, she joined the existing league of women pilots in the country in December 1984. She was the only girl in her batch and became the fourth girl to join a commercial airline as a pilot in India. Born on 19 September in Nurmahal, Jalandhar district, Punjab, to Maj. Krishan Kumar Bhatia and Santosh Bhatia, she was a quiet child who would dream and imagine the things she would do when she grew up. She describes an incident from the time she was barely four or five years old.

'We used to stay in the Sarojini Nagar area in Delhi, very close to the Delhi Flying Club. Those days in summer, we slept on the rooftop and while we were sleeping, early every morning, I would hear the sound of aircraft. There were small yellow-coloured aircraft flying over our house and I used to wonder what they were, who flew them, and why they flew so early every morning. Though today I understand what they were doing and why they were flying early in the morning, as a child, I found this very mysterious and wondered how one could do something like this, that it must be God who flew them. I think this generated a fascination in me for flying. Even though I was barely four or five years old, they seemed to be inviting me to come and try and feel for myself what it would be like to be in the sky! Even today when I see these small aircraft, especially the yellow ones, they bring a smile to my face.'

Entirely self-driven, it is this sturdy sense of motivation that eventually fuelled her yearning and made her a successful pilot.

Her dream took further shape in 1971, when war broke out between India and Pakistan. During that time, there was a period of blackouts when they had to switch off the lights and remain indoors. The only thing they heard in the dark was the loud noise of aircraft flying over their heads. Still a child, she had no idea that these were fighter planes. Though there was no possibility of seeing anything outside, this experience ignited a curiosity in her about how fast these machines moved. In just about ten seconds, one could hear them and then they were out, gone, leaving behind only a faint sound.

Her brother, who is two-and-a-half years older than her, would also be thrilled to hear these aircraft. He would often make paper planes and fly them, imitating the same sounds. She would join him, making her own small paper plane. They would often target each other in their game, talking animatedly about aircraft and how fast they moved. That's when she began pondering how great it would be to be a pilot. Her brother also felt the same way. In fact, he wanted to operate these very machines they would hear, and he pursued his dream by joining the Indian Air Force as a fighter pilot, eventually flying his dream machines. What started as an innocent sibling pastime grew into a serious life purpose, and they became India's first brother-sister professional flying duo.

Their parents played an important role in encouraging them to follow their passion. Anila says her father was more excited than her when she said she wanted to enrol at the Delhi Flying Club. An army officer himself, he was happy that his daughter had ventured into a challenging field. He would share with them the many life lessons he learnt as an army officer. She still remembers his words: 'War is never won with weapons or by aircraft fighting; war is won by the courage that people have.' That lesson also taught her to be courageous, to fight all odds and try her level best to never give up in life. She feels that her father's message has stayed with her and helped her forge ahead in her profession.

While her family was supportive, people around her were difficult and discouraging. Even at the flying club, she felt boys were given priority in flying. When her brother found out, he decided to take her to the Karnal Flying Club. At Karnal, much to their surprise, everyone asked her brother where he had brought his sister as this was no place for girls. They also told him that many of them had their CPLs in hand but no job, and his sister would never get a job after her training there. Her memory of this time is crystal-clear.

'I was standing next to my brother, listening to every word of what was being said and even though I was just a teenager at the time, I wondered that if they were not successful, why should they think nobody else could be? I felt that if they had performed well, they would have been successful. Never did it come to my mind that if they were not successful, I wouldn't be too. So, I told my brother to let me start flying, that we would think of the job when the time came.'

She admits she felt a bit apprehensive when they kept telling her brother how difficult it was to get a job in spite of having a CPL; they were experienced after all, and she wondered whether she should listen to them. But her brother understood her feelings, and encouraged by their father as he himself was interested in flying, he made the decision to get her to join the flying club. And that's how she got started. Thinking about those times still brings a smile to her face.

'I still remember that day – 20 September 1977. People in the club mocked me and would say, "We will see how far she will go!" Such was the start but my passion and determination persisted; I knew I was in Karnal Flying Club for a mission.'

Around this time, her brother joined the National Defence Academy (NDA) and started his flying. 'In fact, we both started our flying together,' she says, remembering how their close relatives would ask their parents what they were thinking by sending both children into this field, but they were lucky their parents did not bother. For both of them, it was an exciting time. They got their solo around the same time. It was fun; they would write to each other discussing their flying. Her brother always encouraged her and would give her tips on many occasions.

With excitement, she describes the experience of her first solo.

'I can still recall the first solo from my flying school days. It was 6 December 1977. I reached the flying school as I did every day. After doing one or two circuits and landing, my instructor got out of the aircraft and said, "Anila, go, go feel the sky." I looked at him, a little dazed, and then contacted the ATC for permission for another circuit and landing, announcing the pilot in command as Anila Bhatia, solo. The ATC gave permission and clearance for circuit and land.' She smiles as she continues. 'It still seems fresh in my mind. I rolled the little aircraft and soon was up in the air, turning on down-wind. I saw the aircraft empty. It was like something I was dreaming. I started singing '*Panchi banu udti firoon mast gagan mein, aaj mein azaad hoon duniya ke chaman mein...*' with my standard call-outs, making sure I didn't miss out on my circuit pattern. I made my turn to down-wind, then turned base, and finally landed and parked. When I came out of the aircraft, I felt tears rolling down my cheeks on realising that I had lived my dream, the dream of learning how to fly. As a child, I used to think God flew these machines. Today I realised it's us, we can fly and I can do it!'

It was an emotional moment. She wrote a letter to her father, telling him about her solo, that too completed in under 9 hours. Then she wrote a long letter to her brother. She knew he had got his solo a few days ago and realised how he must have felt. The excitement continued when she reached the club the next day for flying. She wanted to go solo again and again and it was as if destiny was listening to her. Today, she can proudly say that she has forty-two years of flying behind her and the solos continue.

Anila completed her flying to get her CPL in 1981, but since there was no vacancy for jobs in the airline, she continued and got her instructor rating in 1982. She worked as an instructor for nearly two years before she got into Indian Airlines as a pilot. Doors opened for her when she got selected to join Indian Airlines in December 1984. There was no going back from then on. She knew there were two or three girls who had made it before her, but it remained a male-dominated territory and she faced her share of challenges just as the girls before her had. Her batchmates were very welcoming when she reached the training centre in Hyderabad. However, at the start of their training, the then director of training came for the orientation class. She recalls his opening statement: '"I can see a lady sitting among you all, so I would like to inform you all, that the aircraft knows no gender. The aircraft only knows who flies and responds to all inputs in the same manner. Training will be at par for each and every one." I realised he had done my work; I did not have to prove anything to anyone. Our training would be the same. I needed to perform, and my batchmates had no choice but to accept me as one of them—a pilot.'

She felt a woman met with more resistance in flying school than in the airline. Early on, women were looked down upon for whether they would cope with this hard and stressful job, both during training and as a line pilot, but seeing their performance, people's reactions changed. In other words, the feeling of 'how dare they come here!' later turned into acceptance and afterwards, it was as if all of them were buddies, colleagues who stood together to discuss all emergencies and remedies.

Their batch started the training on the Avro HS-748, a medium-sized turboprop aircraft, which, Anila remembers, was, 'so different from the small Pushpak aircraft we flew in the flying school. Training was strenuous but one was excited about learning to fly a new aircraft. We all knew that after Pushpak, we have to work hard, learn and understand the cockpit layout to master the skill of flying this aircraft.' It was sheer dedication, discipline and focus that helped her successfully complete the training. She remarks, 'There was a sense of achievement when

I was posted as First Officer on Avro and I enjoyed every flight that I operated.'

After flying the Avro for a few years, the next transition was to the B-737, a narrow-body, jet aeroplane, faster and different from the Avro. 'Here again,' she recounts, 'our training was even more vigorous, but we all put in our effort and, with the guidance of our well-qualified instructors, we were able to master the skill of flying this jet aircraft.' She flew as a co-pilot till 1990, and then came the next major event of her life, when she started her command training – every pilot's big dream! Whether in flying school or the airlines, command is what one waits for. From the Avros to the B-737, the transition was one step and the command was a major jump.

By 1991, she was flying as a commander on the Boeing 737-200 series. Command made her somewhat serious as the responsibilities increased, but it instilled in her a feeling of complete satisfaction. It also changed the way she thought. Now she was taking decisions by herself and these decisions mattered a lot; in no way could one let their decision be affected by anything. She feels that with the responsibility, one grew more confident and started relying on their judgement which became more analytical and self-assured. She also started looking at her co-pilot differently. S/he was second-in-command and her backup; therefore, she made sure she got their full support whenever needed. Command also made her calmer. It relieved a lot of the pressure to do things in a hurry. It was a great feeling to be in command, to be able to take passengers safely from Point A to Point B. She says, 'It is true of this profession that one had to shut oneself out from other worries for, otherwise, it is difficult to perform. For example, if one's child was unwell, one had the option to choose not to come for the flight, but once one was in the cockpit, one had to be detached from the outside world. Preparing for a safe flight is paramount duty.'

Capt. Anila felt it was difficult to juggle work and family as a pilot. They would have to sacrifice many important occasions, which may sound insignificant to some, but she gets emotional as she admits that she missed seeing her daughter grow and couldn't be part of some milestones, one among them being 'her first step to walk'. Another was cutting her first tooth. During flying hours, many times she had to throw away her breast milk in the aircraft toilet so that her uniform wouldn't get wet and show. This was just one stark example of how demanding this profession was. As a pilot and mother, she learnt another important thing – to compartmentalise her life. When in the cockpit, it would be just about the flight and nothing else but when at home with her daughter and husband, it was only them. Prioritising and living a disciplined life became an intrinsic feature of her daily life. She says, 'I think no other profession would have taught me this! In an emergency, one knows what to prioritise and when, even at home, and my husband can also understand all this, even the kind of stress and challenges attached to this profession as he is also a pilot, though retired now.'

Flying threw up numerous challenges off and on, and for Capt. Anila, it was better to learn from them and improve herself. According to her, every incident should be treated like a new experience, even if it happened to somebody else. It is a profession in which one works in a very dynamic environment. Everything changes in seconds. As she puts it, 'I could say that on one hand, it is most exciting as every day is different even if we are going to the same airfield. On the other, every flight throws some challenges and we have to rise above it and control it. That is why after a smooth or safe landing, when we park the aircraft and go home, we are so satisfied and completely relaxed. Sometimes, you even think of patting yourself because nobody else will do that. You know you have come out of a major storm and got your passengers safely on the ground; you know you have done justice to your profession and the flight, and it's a great feeling!'

If one were to compare this profession to other demanding ones such as that of police officers and fire brigade personnel, here, one single-handedly manages the aircraft and all manner of situations accompanying it. At any point of time, be it an emergency or evacuation or a smooth flight, it is always handled by that one person alone. In other words, it is a 'one-person' show. There is a team on duty but they cannot interfere in decision-making when a critical situation arises. Unlike other professions, where there is a team that actively helps in some way, in the air, one is operating on their own while also being responsible for a safe flight. The job satisfaction compared to that elsewhere, therefore, is so different that it cannot be expressed in mere words. Another key difference is that, here, one finds satisfaction every single day. There is no pending task; each day is different yet complete in itself. It is a tough job dealing with machines alongside humans and it does involve emotion; only a pilot knows how each flight is undertaken and what all goes into it.

Capt. Anila says, 'It may sound strange but passengers do not know that captains are constantly observing them when they are boarding the plane, thinking that it is their responsibility to get them to their destination safe and on time, and after the flight, one watches them deplane with a calm and relaxed mind, knowing that they have reached their destination safe.' She narrates an interesting incident from the year 1991. She was a commander on the B-737 and the sector was Delhi–Ahmedabad–Delhi. 'It was from Ahmedabad when passengers were boarding that one passenger saw me in the cockpit. He called the cabin crew and asked who I was and what I was doing in the cockpit. When the cabin crew informed him that I was the captain of the flight, he exclaimed, "What, a woman! Is the airline okay, how can they do this?" All this was spoken in Gujarati. The end result was that he refused to fly in that aircraft. He had rejected me even before knowing how many years I had been flying and how much training had taken place before I sat in this seat. He made a lot of noise and, finally, a member of the commercial department (which handles passengers from the time of boarding till the aircraft doors are closed) came to the cockpit to ask me whether he could be deplaned. It involved delaying the flight. His baggage had to be removed. I thought I could go and convince him but something held me back. Being an elderly person, I left it for him to be comfortable, took the delay and got him offloaded.'

Such is the reaction sometimes; it has indeed taken people very long to accept women as pilots! Capt. Anila emphasises though, 'These incidents never discouraged or demoralised any one of us. We believed in ourselves and worked diligently. Nothing like this could or should affect any one of us.' She recounts another instance. 'While one passenger got offloaded, during the same year, a few months later, while operating a flight from Delhi to Mumbai, there was a wonderful experience with a passenger. An Army Lt General in uniform saw me doing the walk-around of the aircraft. After completing it, I was boarding the plane along with my two-year-old daughter in my arms who was coming with me on my flight. I must admit I was a bit embarrassed thinking about how passengers would react, but to my surprise, the army officer who was boarding the aircraft said to another passenger, "Today's flight will be the safest. The captain has her daughter on board." I was so happy with his remark. It showed confidence and acceptance by the passenger. Where one wanted to get offloaded, another felt differently. This for me is empowerment. There is a lot of talk about women's empowerment. In fact, empowerment is needed to change the perception of the people. It is and should not be for women only; it should be for society at large. Why talk of women's empowerment today? Women were always empowered, even in the 1960s, '70s and '80s. In a profession like flying, being pilots, we are the living examples. Who spoke of empowerment then or gave schemes? Yet, we worked and achieved. We fought till we succeeded.'

Capt. Anila feels women are self-powered. They may need reassurance or a boost at times but negativity around them only makes them stronger and automatically empowers them furthermore. She believes they must work calmly and diligently to move ahead and to show people that they are performers. Letting their work speak for them and their capabilities can silence other people who then see that women are made of a different mettle and no challenge is too big for them.

Flying has been a childhood dream, a passion she fulfilled, battling all sorts of barriers, to be where she is today, having put in more than thirty-six years of flying in the airline. She feels she can go on for another thirty-six years! For her, despite it being a serious profession that one cannot take lightly, the high of lifting off and seeing the horizon, the beautiful sunrise and sunset, lightning dancing in the sky, zero-visibility landings, rain, slush, high-altitude landings, the runway lights on a fog-filled approach... all make for an amazing and wonderful experience. While certainly not an easy task, it is one that is full of satisfaction, the kind that cannot be traded with any other job. Capt. Anila is currently flying the B-737 and her daughter Miriya flies the B-777. Together, they make the first mother-daughter pilot duo not only in India but in all of Asia.

Capt. Miriya belongs to the new generation of pilots. This millennium child has worked with the same passion and dedication as her mother to be where she is today. Her journey may have seen lesser gender bias and more advanced facilities but the profession permits no shortcuts. The next generation has seen much more in terms of technological advancement than their predecessors. Modern technology is the key word for them, where the touch of a button is the need of the hour. And aviation is not far behind. Today, the world has shrunk. Getting from one part of the world to another is quicker, easier and more accessible. Even reaching outer space is possible and crossing time zones is the most normal thing for people to achieve. Aircraft are modernised with better technology for speed, safety and comfort. Time is precious, and so air travel has seen a huge increase as has air traffic. Airway routes are congested, but there are aids available to make it all a smooth operation. In this fast-paced life, the meaning of flying has changed. One is constantly on the move and it's no longer a small, closely packed group of pilots. The numbers have gone up and keep increasing. The year 2000 saw prodigious growth in the number of women pilots in India and probably the world over. Yet, women as pilots flying across the world still pose a 'wow' factor to most!

There are a large number of women pilots on duty today and all airlines showcase their feminine strength every year on 8 March, International Women's Day. It is a fact now that every day, on every flight, there is at least one woman in the cockpit. An all-women crew is now de rigueur and typically a daily routine. It indeed became a challenge for me to shortlist who could be portrayed amongst this generation to represent this history of Indian women pilots. After telling the story of the pioneers who were the backbone of women's aviation in the country, the focus of the narrative moves to three young, dynamic, fearless women pilots (Capt. Miriya Cheema, Capt. Deeksha Sharan and Capt. Aashna Sharan) who grew up in aviation households but went on to write their own stories. They faced more challenges growing up as pilots' daughters, so taking their passion forward with a unique zeal came naturally to them.

Eight

In the Footsteps of Her Mother

Miriya Cheema

On a flight from Delhi to Mumbai, barely ten years old, she was sitting in the cabin when she heard her mother's announcement on the PA system: 'Ladies and gentlemen, this is your captain, Anila Bhatia, from the flight deck...' Like the passengers, she sat glued to the announcement. She still remembers it vividly, so impressed by it at the time that she decided this is what she would do when she grew up. She wanted to be on the flight deck making the same announcement. So confident and clear was the voice that it made everyone feel totally safe on the flight.

Daughter of Capt. Anila and Capt. G.S. Cheema, one cannot imagine that Capt. Miriya Cheema would have chosen any profession other than this one, to be a captain on the B-777 with Air India. Her mother was amongst the first four women pilots of the country. She flew for Indian Airlines and later joined Jet Airways, flying the Boeings. Her father was the Chief Flying Instructor (CFI) of Pinjore Flying Club and, later, Karnal Flying Club where she started flying under his mentorship and guidance. Capt. Miriya belongs to the new generation of fliers and considers herself a born flyer. She remembers how, as a baby, she would wake up in her father's lap, under his jacket, zipped up with her head popping out, thrilled to be in the Yellow Bird with him. Born on 10 August, she practically grew up in the cockpit instead of the backyard of her home. No wonder flying came naturally to her. Even her name 'Miriya' has been taken from the Russian-named largest aircraft, and it means 'dream come true', reinforcing the fact that flying runs in her blood!

She remembers how her father's regular stories of flying got her curious about this profession as a child. Her mother, on the other hand, was her pride, flying as a captain with Indian Airlines. She would often go to the airport to pick her mother up after her flight and would be fascinated with her uniform. She loved her mother's cap and would be enthralled to wear it herself. Being an only child growing up with flying parents, she was absolutely enraptured by this profession.

Even though the thought of flying had been on her mind since childhood, it was when she was in Class 10 that she gave it serious thought. Initially, she felt that dreaming of a profession was different from having the talent to hone such a technical skill. While still at an impressionable age, what helped firm up her mind after Class 10 were the sessions her school counsellors held to suggest different professions to students. She attended them all and realised that everyone wanted to do something that would let them explore the world. She decided it would be best to see the world by becoming a pilot!

After her Class 12 board examinations, when all her friends were shortlisting and making choices among different colleges, she approached her parents with complete clarity and told them of her desire to join a flying club to become a pilot. So confident was she from the start that she took the bold step not to apply to any college as she only wanted to fly and become a pilot. It didn't come as a surprise to her parents; they were probably waiting for this decision to be announced. So after relaxing for a week, she headed to the Karnal Flying Club with her parents in March 2007.

It was a strange feeling for them. She recalls: 'My father was the CFI there and now his daughter was joining as a student. My mother remembered her time at the Karnal Flying Club where she had done all her flying and was also a flying instructor before she joined the airline. She remembered how, during her days there, people would look at her and wonder what she would do with her flying licence. Things may have changed from that perspective, but people still look at you strangely for pursuing a profession like this as a woman. I realised then how my mother must have struggled during her time to make people understand and believe that women can fly.'

She went on to finish her formalities at the flying club and was briefed by her dad. She still remembers his stern words. 'You are not a CFI's daughter here; you are just another student, so don't expect any preferences. You will get your licence if you work towards it.' She had never heard her father say something like that, and knew that she would have to maintain the decorum of the school without letting others know her identity. While she stayed intent on that, other students were already talking about her. She heard everyone discussing that she belonged to a privileged class. She was often asked, 'Your father is a CFI and your mother an airline captain, where would you choose to go, airline or flying club instructor?' It was not a comfortable feeling to be confronted with such remarks. She knew that nothing was easy and one had to work hard and perform well to get anywhere. 'Once you get your licence, you realise there are many others from flying backgrounds. The competition is tough to get into the airline. I kept myself focused and did not let any of these things bother me,' she says.

Her first sortie as a student pilot was with the CFI, her father. It may have seemed advantageous to others that she was fortunate to have a comfortable start, but it was not so, as her father had a lot of expectations from her. And as the flying progressed, each day got tougher. Her performance mattered or she would be taken to task. There is one incident she still remembers.

'It was circuit and landing. Everything was going good when suddenly the winds changed. We were informed by the ATC of that. Now I needed a different heading on my down-wind to maintain the track. I think I was a bit relaxed knowing my father was there to help me and I kept going off-track. Finally, even when my dad pointed that out to me, I was still not keeping the proper heading by applying the wind correction. He waited for the corrective action, but when it was not done, he took over the controls and shouted at me for my performance. I had never been shouted at by him and I was taken aback. I realised I was distracted by my thoughts which affected my performance. After we had parked, I went to him and said, "Papa, I am sorry, I got distracted. This will not happen again." He looked at me and I still remember what he said that day, "Miriya, I am your instructor, not Papa, here in the flying club. You can either call me Sir or Capt. Cheema, like all the other students. And like all other students, when you don't perform, you will repeat your ground lesson and only then be allowed to fly. So now you redraw the circuit, show the headings you will fly with the wind corrections, and only then can you leave for home.'

She was subjected to the same procedure that was followed by all the other student pilots. She followed his instructions, and from that day onwards, would address him as Sir in the flying club and Papa at home. It was the best thing that happened to her; she was no longer relaxed and was subjected to all tasks that each one would go through during flying school days: cleaning, washing the aircraft, filling fuel, carrying big, heavy cans of fuel, cleaning spark plugs, and so on. Sun, rain or dust, she had to do what she was programmed for. Her father made sure she did everything, like the other students. Every bit of the aircraft had to be known to her, and as an aviator, he prepared all his students to master their aircraft in case of an emergency landing eventuality.

As she gained experience and piled on more hours, like everyone else, she too waited eagerly for her solo flight. By now, she was moved to another instructor. This was more so because, as a CFI, her father had to give guidance to other students who were completing the course. She had put in around 9 hours by now, and every morning, she would be ready for the day with the hope that her solo would happen soon. Even though her father was a CFI there, her solo would be based on her performance. So, daily, she reached the venue in the morning and started her sortie as usual. She remembers one such day when she was flying, doing the circuits, when after two circuits, her instructor looked at her and asked, 'Are you ready?' She thought it was for another circuit and promptly replied, 'Yes, Sir!' To this, he stopped the aircraft after landing, opened his door and told her, 'Go, enjoy your solo.' She looked at him blankly as he simply smiled and walked away. She looked around, spoke to the ATC, took permission for her first solo flight, pushed the power, and before she knew it, she was up in the air all by herself!

'There was a mixed feeling of excitement and responsibility,' she recounts. 'I thought to myself that I can make no error. I became more careful, checked my down-wind heading, keeping the runway in sight throughout. The winds were favourable. I joined the base leg with ease and went on to the finals for my landing. This must have been my first sortie where I did not let the runway out of my sight. The strong words of my dad played in my head, getting me a perfect first solo flight! Once I landed and taxied for parking, I could see all my colleagues standing there to welcome me, probably more excited than I was. As I came out of the aircraft, everyone began congratulating me. My dad was waiting. There were tears in his eye, tears of happiness and satisfaction, I gathered. Here was his daughter aged seventeen years, just out of school and she had flown her first solo flight, a head start to her flying career! I went up to him and met him. Today, he was my dad in the flying club, excited and happy for me and I was on top of the world! Then I spoke to my mother. She was already briefed about my solo flight. Her excited words, "Congratulations, Miriya, you did it, we are so proud of you!" are still fresh in my mind. The dream of flying big aircraft, to reach the cockpit of the B-777, started henceforth. There was only one aim left: to finish flying as early as possible and get into the airline.'

Flying school teaches many life lessons. Although she had heard many stories from her parents about their flying days, unless things were experienced first-hand, she could never understand the real situation and its outcome. Textbooks were there to teach, but real learning in a situation could only come with hands-on experience that brought the kind of confidence no learning from books could. She shares an experience that taught her a lasting lesson, one she gains from till date.

'I remember learning old methods of flying was something our generation would argue about in our flying school days. This incident will narrate what I am trying to imply. It was 2007 when I was flying and the GPS had become part of our flying those days. Even our Cessnas were equipped with the GPS, but my father insisted that I should also have the experience of flying without the GPS, using the conventional method of visual clues through the cross-country route. I would argue with him for hours about that. I would ask him that with all modern aids, why must I fly using remote methods? But he would insist and eventually took me on cross-country training with the GPS switched off and made me open my maps for route familiarisation and to mark visual clues through the route. I was not happy and would often show my displeasure, but I did it. I would tell him I must be the only student who was doing such a thing in the era of all modern aids! I did some cross-country flying with him without GPS and, honestly, after a few flights, I did not mind it. In fact, at times, I would see the actual visual clue below, cross-check with my airway map and would be thrilled to see how accurately I was flying. Then came the solo cross-country day. I selected my route: Karnal to Hisar and back. I prepared myself with flight planning and kept my maps with all the clues that I had marked. I was now confident enough to go with or without the GPS. Another colleague of mine was also planning his cross-country and decided on the same route. So we took off with a few minutes' difference so that we could follow each other. I was ahead of him and, after flying for a few miles, he contacted me on guard frequency and told me that his GPS was not working properly and requested me to give him some route clue. I told him I was not flying with the GPS but had my map with bearings and checking my visual clues, so I was on track. I kept giving him headings and told him to check the visual clues. He had not flown like this; he was so dependent on his instruments. I realised what added pressure he was going through just because of no GPS. It was our (first) solo cross-country flight and definitely there was stress to not get lost as it would affect our flying. As we were not very far from each other and going to the same destination, he requested guidance and followed me for the route. I was now more careful with the responsibility of helping my colleague reach his destination. Finally, we both landed in Hisar safely and returned to Karnal as planned.'

Even though this was a small event, she learnt a different kind of responsibility and understood how important it was to learn all methods possible to ably handle any situation. She was responsible for her colleague's correct route and did it thanks to the conventional flying methods that were taught to her. This sense of responsibility has stayed on; it has now evolved to ensuring her passengers reach safely from Point A to Point B.

By 2008, Capt. Miriya was ready with her CPL. Luckily, Air India had advertised for trainee pilots (this was the last batch that Air India hired before the merger of Indian Airlines and Air India). Since this advertisement appeared after a long gap, there were about 7,000-odd candidates who applied and she was among them. It was a close competition, but she decided to put in whatever effort it took and hoped for the best. The exam was held in Mumbai. Those days, her mother was flying for Sahara Airways; she did a flight to Mumbai to be with her. Miriya was staying with her mother in the hotel and after finishing her exam that night, she slept like a log. It was like a huge pressure off her mind. Now she eagerly awaited the result.

The next morning, her mother had an early flight and probably left the room at about 4–4.30 a.m. Capt. Miriya had no idea that her mother would be going towards the Air India building before her flight to check if the results were put up. After some time, she heard a knock on the door. Her mother walked into the room and, shaking her, said, 'Miriya, you have passed the Air India exam, get up, get up!' She was dead to the world and thought she was dreaming. Her mother forcibly shook her and she had to pinch herself to believe what she had heard. She was one step closer to her dream of being in the airlines, flying a big jet, and becoming an airline pilot like her mother. She was so emotional, she started crying. Then she picked up the phone and called her father in Delhi. It was 5.30 a.m., but she wanted to inform him immediately. She was still crying when he picked up the phone. She told him she had cleared Air India's written examination. Since she was crying, he thought she had not cleared it and started consoling her, telling her not to worry, that she could try again. Then in a clearer tone, she told him, 'Papa, I have passed, I have cleared the Air India exam.' His first remark to her was, 'Then why are you crying?' He congratulated her and told her to go for the interview with full confidence.

The interview took place the very next day. A total of 54 students had cleared the written examination. The day of the interview is imprinted in her memory. She entered the room in the presence of all seniors: a judge, an HR official, a psychologist, pilots. All eyes were on her. She calmly told herself that this was her golden chance to do her best to be able to reach her dream airline and the dream aircraft she wanted to fly. *She had to make it*! Everyone there made her feel relaxed. She was asked many questions and was able to answer almost all of them. She was asked about any aircraft she knew. She talked about the B-777, the engines, the make, the type, etc. They seemed impressed and asked her if there was someone in her family who was in aviation. She told them about her mother flying the B-737 and her father who was a CFI. They started asking her about the B-737. She could not reply as confidently. So they asked her how she knew so much about the 777 and not the 737. To this she promptly replied, 'Sir, my dream aircraft is B-777. Since my flying school days, I have been wanting to fly the 777. It's this interest that automatically helped me gain knowledge about the aircraft.' That seemed to satisfy them.

She was thrilled when she received the letter stating that she had been selected as a trainee pilot and was asked to proceed to the medical round, the final leg before the letter of induction was handed to her. Finally, she got confirmation of her selection by speed post and joined Air India on 19 April 2010. The delay was because of the merger. There was a lot of discussion around their induction and she thanks her stars that their induction happened despite the delay. They later learnt that their batch was the last to be employed on permanent basis. Henceforth, because of the merger, all selections would be on contract basis. It all went well for her and she continues to fly the B-777, the aircraft of her dreams!

Her mother, Capt. Anila, had joined Indian Airlines in 1984. Air India would not hire women as pilots then. And now, after more than twenty-five years of flying, her only child, her daughter, was joining Air India as a pilot! They became the first mother-daughter pilot duo flying a commercial airline in India. Her name 'Miriya' proved true to its meaning. Her achievement was a dream that came true for her parents as well as for her! She was in Air India and going to fly her dream aircraft, one of the few women pilots that Air India can boast of till date.

Today, she feels blessed flying the 777, and travelling around at the young age of twenty. Flying as a co-pilot, she has had her share of experiences, be it turbulent weather, go-around or diversions, but she feels that every day is a learning experience. One of her greatest moments was on a flight to the US. She felt proud of her job and her country when she met another lady captain of Air Canada on one of her night-stop flights to San Francisco. This was what she experienced in her own words: 'I was in the elevator going to the room along with another lady captain who was in uniform too. She started a conversation, asking me which airline I was flying for. I told her Air India. She was in awe that I was so young and flying the B-777. While talking, I also mentioned that my mom had been in Indian Airlines and flying B-737s since 1984. She seemed to be in complete admiration and, with an astonished expression, asked me if I had a picture of my mother in uniform to show her. I did and felt so proud as I had always thought the western world was much ahead of us in everything. Surely they found it difficult to believe that women in India had been flying for decades and were commanders in a commercial airline much before them.'

Being a next-generation child who took up a challenging profession at a very young age, she gives credit to her flying and the experience of flying big jets that helped her grow as a person. The profession has taught her a lot; it has given her a sense of freedom with responsibility that has made her confident. She is not worried about going anywhere and can face any challenge with ease. She sees kids her age who are still not ready for most life challenges or fear many situations, but handling and surmounting any situation comes easier to her. In fact, she faces everything with a never-say-die attitude. The grass is greener for her here and she considers it the most rewarding, thrilling and satisfying profession one can be in. She is thankful to her parents for having exposed her to this wonderful life and line of work. Sometimes, she wonders where she would be if she were not flying, because for her, aircraft, runways and blue skies are nothing but a part of everyday life, difficult to live without!

First mother-daughter pilots in India

Proud mother, Capt. Anila

Daughter Miriya Cheema, captain on Boeing 777, Air India

Capt. Indraani Singh's passion for flying...

...is matched by her passion to serve the underprivileged. Empowering children and adults, Capt. Indraani is dedicated to her NGO, Literacy India.

Making Dreams Their Fuel (The Mid-1980s)

Nine

The Airbus Woman

Indraani Singh

In her own words: 'I am referred to as an Airbus Woman. I am still a dreamer; dreams are my fuel. Even when I am flying, I am dreaming ahead, keeping myself ahead of my aircraft. I am also a very stubborn person. The more people throw challenges at me, the more I want to overcome them. If I am told something is not possible, I prove it by doing and showing that it is possible. I personally feel, most women, when given any challenge, will rise above it.'

She is Indraani Singh Grewal, born on 25 September in Delhi to Namita Singh, a homemaker, and Durga Prasad Singh, a businessman. From childhood itself, she was a dreamer. Being the eldest child with two younger brothers, she felt she was treated by her parents as one of the boys. In fact, her father would often tell her she should look after her brothers and mother in case of any untoward eventuality. As destiny took its course, today she is the one looking after them.

As a child, she had always wanted to do something different, something fun and full of thrilling adventure. Growing up, she discovered a love for painting and often thought it could be a good career for her. Being a dreamer, she could transfer anything from her mind onto canvas or paper. Quite naturally then, after schooling in Summer Fields School, Delhi, she applied to the College of Art there. But destiny had different plans for her and she did not get admission. Dejected with life and the shock of not having been selected to the only college she had applied for, she was too demoralised to do anything. With some difficulty, her father managed to get her admission in Kamala Nehru College. This was in 1984.

That's where her journey began. She recalls, 'When I entered college, the first thing I saw were some students in the NCC uniform. I was fascinated by them. The uniform looked stunning, so instead of going to my class, I went and signed up to become an NCC cadet. As I was joining, I was also informed that in the NCC, one would be required to go for camps, outdoor activities, etc. It all seemed like an adventure to me and I got even more excited. My mind started to dream about this new venture.' As a cadet, she attended a couple of camps, which gave her exposure to the Air Wing of the NCC. She saw the blue uniform and the cap which looked even smarter and was thoroughly charmed. She enrolled with them in no time.

However, the real adventure began when they started going to Safdarjung Airport, where she would see small aircraft flying. Her world started to open up. When she was just a junior, she would hear the squadron leader telling seniors to do a sortie, winch pulling in a glider, and other such tasks. She would see the glider being pushed out of the hangar. Her eyes and ears would open wide in wonder. To her, all this spelt fun, adventure and excitement. She was excited to fly the glider herself too. So, one day, she went up to the squadron leader and asked him if she could try it. He smiled at her and said, 'Your time will come. First you have to slog. You have to start with aeromodelling, marching, etc. Also, you have to be on time and regular, and then we will see.'

Indraani took his words seriously, started reporting well on time everyday, and could be found pushing the glider out of the hangar for others, waiting patiently for her turn. The squadron leader would see her every day, and one day, he asked her if she really wanted to fly. He offered her a chance to hop into the glider, saying that he wanted to see how much guts she had. She did not want to lose this opportunity, so she took a seat, and it turned out to be one of the most exciting experiences she had ever had. He gave her a tough start, a tough sortie with loops, barren roll, wings over and whatnot. When they landed and parked, he asked her how it had been. One look at her face and he already knew the answer; her eyes were popping out in sheer excitement. She promptly said, 'It was like being on top of the world. It was an awesome experience, Sir, when can I start?' He was both surprised and happy as he had seen that, generally, students would feel sick and giddy, but she had done just fine. He told her they could start gliding lessons the next day. Hearing this, she jumped with joy. And so, in 1984, she started gliding and enjoyed every moment of it. At that point, she had no idea there could be a career in flying; it had never occurred to her. She wanted to take one thing at a time.

In 1985, she represented Delhi in a gliding competition. She won the championship and was declared the best cadet. She was the only girl till then who had won a gliding contest; mostly, boys would participate and win. Her instructor, Sqdn Ldr Verma, was very happy with her and said that if she wanted to fly, she could get subsidies flying through the NCC. She was thrilled but worried too as she had been missing college classes in order to take part in all these activities and she knew her father would be angry if he found out. Moreover, her exams were due shortly and she knew she had to clear them or her parents would not be happy. But she gathered courage and talked to her father, telling him about the gliding championship and her win and how she could learn flying with subsidised rates through the NCC, an opportunity not many got. He was not very happy as he wanted her to concentrate on her studies. She begged him, assuring him she would work hard and manage both flying and classes. By then, she was in the second year of college. Reluctantly, he agreed. She was overjoyed, and with hard work, managed to get a scholarship for 60 hours of flying. She admits it took a toll on her studies as she barely managed to clear her exams.

She got started at the Delhi Flying Club. It was here that she first saw and later met Capt. Nivedita, a senior who had already completed her flying hours. It was here that she also met her future husband, Kirat, who was flying at that time. One day, she asked him if there was any career for women in flying. He told her about Capt. Saudamini, who had worked in a bank while pursuing her flying. He also told her about Capt. Durba, the first woman to join Indian Airlines. Indraani was worried about what would happen once she completed 60 hours of flying. It was expensive to continue and her parents would not be able to pay for further flying training. But her positive thinking assuaged these worries. Learning about other women pilots who had also been employed in airlines was a big boost and offered consolation; it was something to tell her parents in the hope that they would consider allowing her to continue flying.

Her father had mostly allowed her to do everything she wanted, so she mustered the courage to tell him about her interest in making a career of flying. She could tell that he was not very happy with what she had said. Her mother too was unsure; she said she didn't know what Indraani was thinking, that she seemed to have grown too big for her shoes and was unnecessarily letting her imagination run wild. Indraani wanted her parents to understand and believe in her dream. She repeatedly narrated the stories of other women who had made careers in flying, having learnt about this from a colleague in the flying club, but that too did not satisfy them.

Her father was somewhat comforted once she mentioned the two women pilots flying with Indian Airlines. Moreover, when he could see how determined she was, not ready to take no for an answer, he started telling her about the negative aspects of such a profession. While it all seemed great to dream about, he said, it would be a tough and thorny path in a male-dominated field with just a few women that one had heard about within the aviation circle. Outsiders would continue to disapprove of it. He warned her that she would be in unfriendly surroundings which could make her feel unwanted in the long run. A flying job would also keep her on the move constantly and force her to live out of a suitcase. She listened to every word patiently and said that it was fine with her, that she was prepared and ready for anything. She just wanted to continue being up in the air. Flying and forging ahead in this field was all she could think of!

So, her parents agreed to let her continue. The first hurdle had been overcome, but other challenges soon emerged. Motivation kept her going. Her parents could not afford the high cost of flying. After completing her 60 hours, she could not get any scholarship. Money was not easy to come by, so she took up a part-time job alongside attending college to be able to meet some of the expenses. Even so, it took her a lot of time to finish her flying hours for lack of funds. At one point, she started to question herself on how she was putting her parents through so much trouble for the sake of her dreams without even knowing if she would get into any airline. One day, she told her father that she would stop flying and do whatever he wanted her to do. He smiled and said, 'You go and complete your flying with full dedication, don't give up on it now. I will somehow manage to fund your flying, don't worry about that.' This encouragement let her carry on and she could focus fully not only on completing her flying but also on getting a job and supporting her parents as long as they lived.

Being free from financial worry, a second issue presented itself, one which she felt most women who were out to become pilots during that time must have faced. Women were constantly judged. She clearly remembers one of the boys in the flying school telling her, 'Why are you here? Because of you we are getting delayed. You take up 30–40 minutes of flying and eat into our flying time. Why don't you get married to Kirat? He is flying; you can look after the home.' Such comments made her very angry but she always kept her cool and did not let them thwart her desire to become a pilot.

Another problem was reaching the flying club, as there was hardly any public transport going in that direction. She asked her father to get her a motorcycle, after which commuting became easy and she was able to reach well in time for her sorties. The boys, however, did not take that well. She still remembers how some of them deflated her bike tyre just to trouble her while she was flying. This happened once when she had gone for a night sortie. She had to drag her bike herself and reach some place she could get it repaired, with no help forthcoming from her colleagues. This was a common phenomenon at that time. An absolutely unwelcoming atmosphere, no help, no encouragement. Yet, whether it was out of passion, dedication or the drive to achieve, all of them strove on and successfully managed not to let negative incidents and feelings interfere with their dreams.

To keep her flying progressing at a good pace, she had to move schools from Delhi to Hisar, then to Jaipur and Karnal. The only thing that kept her going was that the instructors imparted fair training. There was no distinction between men and women, both in the flying school and subsequently in the airline when she joined in 1987, becoming one amongst the few women commercial pilots in the country.

She joined as a trainee pilot to be trained to fly the B-737 as First Officer. She was the only woman in her batch, and though her batchmates accepted her, she did have to face challenges from some conservative quarters. She explains, 'Even though I kept myself aloof, I became quite popular, I think, because I had my bike. And a lot of my batchmates became friends with me for that reason.' She completed her training and started flying on the B-737 as First Officer sometime in 1988. By 1989, she was moved to the latest fly-by-wire A-320 aircraft. As part of the initial batch, she was sent along with her colleagues to Toulouse, France, for training in these. Later, after these aircraft were grounded, she got moved to the A-300 as co-pilot and went on to get her command on this aircraft in 1995, becoming the first woman commander on the wide-bodied A-300 in India.

Until then, Indian Airlines was the only domestic airline hiring women as pilots in each batch. Air India was still not ready; they had not inducted any women so far. It was inevitable then that the few women who were flying were constantly scrutinised, with the result that women had to give more than 100 per cent. Every check of theirs was monitored; it was as if their performance, their way of approaching their colleagues, all of it was fodder for conversation.

As a co-pilot, one was being constantly assessed but after getting command, things did change, though women were still watched more than their male colleagues. Command gave people a different approach towards you, as she points out. You were now the sole in-charge of the aircraft from the word go, so people realise that if you were a commander, you were there to stay. They start respecting you in a different way and you realise there is a change in your personality too. Command brought with it a lot of responsibility, not only of the aircraft or flying but of passengers too. It is the entire gamut of situations that arise before, during and after the flight that makes one disciplined, organised and alert at all times. As a commander, one understands that the trust of the passengers and the entire crew rests solely on their shoulders. Capt. Indraani feels, though, that male pilots looked at things differently, maybe because men were mostly perceived as bread earners. She feels that due to this kind of DNA, men walk into any kind of profession appearing cooler than their female counterparts. Even though she was never made to believe that women could only do certain jobs while growing up, in the cockpit, she was made to feel that a favour had been done by allowing her to be there. She ponders, 'This probably leads to most of us taking our work more seriously and with more discipline.'

She continues: 'When I had joined the NCC, it was a turning point in my life. I was driven by the feel of that uniform; it instilled in me the disciple that I think helped me to achieve my goal, my mission of becoming a pilot. I did dream of becoming a fighter pilot but that was not allowed; there was no opportunity, though my male colleague from the NCC could go ahead and do so. Nearly more than twenty-five years later, the first batch of women were inducted as fighter pilots. Surely one wants to ask the government what the women of earlier years had not proven as to be denied that opportunity. Many of us have paid the price for just being a woman, and it is not that we are not capable of doing what we want to do. Most of us have flown in command for many years to let people know that one can do anything if given an opportunity. We were given this opportunity by Indian Airlines and we proved that it doesn't matter whether you are male or female; if you are given the chance, you can be who you want to be.'

Having flown in command for more than two decades, Capt. Indraani recalls the many hardships women encounter. She thinks they face the toughest challenge when they become mothers. Bringing up a baby and managing this profession is very tough; she still remembers that phase of her life. Even though her only child, her son, is a pilot today with Indigo Airlines, when he was a baby, it used to get tough managing him while juggling flight schedules, especially when both her husband (also a pilot with Indian Airlines) and she had flights with the same departure time. She recalls one such time when she could not leave her son alone as he was very small, and had to reach out to a batchmate to babysit her son as there was no one at home to look after him. They had to resort to such measures simply to keep themselves there in the cockpit. She says, 'Although most women around the world have to juggle work and kids, our work involves being up in the air, that's our office. We cannot take our babies there, neither can we keep in touch via phone, etc. And then we know it's a machine; we can be grounded on any outstation and can return only the next day. Many arrangements have to be made before the flight unlike other professions where one can be back early or keep in touch constantly.'

Besides, she reiterates, as women, there are different kinds of issues they have to deal with. Flying can be handled with ease but reforming the mindsets of passengers and their approach towards women commanders has not been easy. During one of her command flights on the A-300 (wide-bodied aircraft), she recalls an episode that occurred during the monsoon season, on a flight from Delhi to Kathmandu. Approaching Kathmandu, they were informed that the current visibility reported 5 km with total cloud cover. The Kathmandu airfield is surrounded by mountains and has a special let-down procedure. There were many aircraft holding over the airfield as the sky was overcast. As visibility reported was within minima, Capt. Indraani continued her approach, decided to go overhead, and requested descent below 10,000 ft to break the cloud layer. Since she was over the airfield, she was given permission to descend. Once she started the descent and reached a height below 10,000 ft, she was victor-mike—which means, she could now clearly see the airfield. She knew if she went outbound for approach, she would again get into the cloud, and may not be able to make the approach, so she decided to ask for a visual approach. Keeping the airfield in sight, she initiated a steep descent to get into profile for a visual approach. By then, it had started to rain. Maintaining composure and staying focused and alert, she went ahead with her approach and landed safely. As commander, she knew she could take this decision within the safety range. She was confident and knew she could manage this situation, and kept herself prepared for a go-around in case it was required. She continued her approach and made a safe landing. This was one situation where she felt the good training received from all the instructors gave them the necessary confidence to handle the aircraft and made them more optimistic as commanders.

She then stood at the cockpit door watching the passengers deplane. To her surprise, a foreign passenger came up to her and said, 'You landed this plane?' She responded with a simple yes, but he kept asking the crew about this again and again. She could make out he was not very comfortable seeing a woman as a pilot and landing this big plane in such bad weather. She surprised him and said, 'You are on ground safe in Kathmandu, Sir, it is too late to think about who landed the plane.' Landing during the monsoons when the weather is playing havoc is a tough call for any pilot, male or female; what matters is how well one understands the situation they are in and whether they can handle it. She adds that the more one encounters weather vagaries, the humbler their attitude towards it is. In fact, one even starts to respect the weather. She also feels that things are more manageable if one takes each day as it comes and does their best. It is one's experience, knowledge, confidence, training and, to some extent, destiny that takes them through tough decisions.

Capt. Indraani's passion for flying is matched in equal measure by her passion for contributing to the social sector: empowering children and adults through literacy. In 1996, she became part of the Literacy India Trust, a non-profit organisation operating out of a construction site in Palam Vihar, Gurgaon. She embarked on a mission to lead the trust to new heights with education and employment as its target. Literacy India has today benefited over 55,000 children and women across three states of India through its education and employability programmes. She says, 'In the school I run, most of the girls want to become a pilot like me. The uniform does attract people. It's very satisfying. I feel I am an achiever if I can motivate another girl to join this profession and help her achieve her dreams. I also feel we have not achieved anything big by taking up the challenge to become a pilot. When I see these underprivileged women and girls around me in my school, I realise they are the ones who have achieved something, as the struggle and challenges they go through are ones we have not faced nor even imagine. They have far more challenging lives than ours. I dedicate my profession and the wings of freedom that it provides to these girls, and want them to rise and fly in life. This is the true Capt. Indraani to you and the world.'

Capt. Indraani Singh (right) after an all-women flight on the occasion of International Women's Day with Capt. Avantika Rastogi on the Airbus 320

Spreading the wings of freedom amongst the children of Literacy India

In Atchison, Kansas, USA, where Capt. Sangita Kabra Bangar was honoured for her flying achievement with a plaque that has her name inscribed on it

The aircraft she loves to fly – the Airbus 320

The all-women crew of the Mumbai–Karachi Indian Airlines flight Airbus 320, led by Capt. Sangita Bangar (R) and Capt. Anupama Kohli (L) at Sahar International Airport. The flight was organised by the airline as a symbolic gesture on the occasion of International Women's Day.

Ten

The First Flying Marwari Girl

Sangita Kabra Bangar

Born into a Marwari family, one would think marriage was the only thing in store for Sangita Kabra Bangar. But things turned out differently for her, as her grandmother was forward-thinking for her times, having taught herself and becoming an ayurvedic medicine expert in the village. She had a clear vision and wanted all her grandchildren, especially the girls, to be educated. Today, amongst all her cousins, the girls are more educated than the boys. Such is her family.

Sangita Kabra Bangar was born on 5 September to Geniram Kabra and Vimal Kabra in Sangli, a small town in Maharashtra, popular for the production of turmeric. She was barely four years old when she was adopted by her uncle and aunt, Nandkishore Kabra and Vijaya Kabra, and moved out of Sangli as her father worked for Union Carbide and was posted in Hyderabad. Her early years were spent in many places, from Hyderabad to Mumbai to Bhopal and then to Kolkata. It was in Kolkata that her father decided to leave the company and start his own work, so they could settle in one place. And there she got the exposure to flying that brought her to her present position, that of a pilot with Air India.

Recalling her younger days, she narrates, 'Coming from a liberal family, I was very tomboyish. I remember I had more boys as friends as I loved playing cricket, football, etc. Dreaming big and doing something different became my goal, though as a child, I did not know that I could or would become a pilot. It was when we were in Kolkata that I had a friend whose father was a pilot with Indian Airlines. I would always ask him about aircraft. It was something that fascinated me, I remember I would always look up to the skies whenever I heard an aircraft pass, but flying them was not on my mind then. It was only after I finished my BSc that one of my college friends, Dharamraj (whose father was with Indian Airlines), came over to tell me that he was going to the US for flying. He suggested that I could also think about this as I was so inquisitive about aircraft. My parents were sitting across and listening to our conversation. They were smiling as if they read my mind and I think my journey in aviation started then.'

To her astonishment, the very next day, she saw Capt. R.R. Rao at their place and her parents were talking to him, gathering information on flying. Capt. Rao's first remark was, 'First things first. We need to check her height as she is not very tall and that is a big concern.' He added that before they started discussing or thinking of flying, they could go to the Behala Flying Club in Kolkata to get her height checked so that there was no issue regarding her medical examination, a mandatory requirement for a flying licence. They did so the following day, and, to her joy, she had the required leg length.

Next thing, she was told by Uncle Rao to proceed to the Class 1 medical to get her fitness requirements for flying before joining any flying club anywhere. She proceeded to Delhi as she had to go to the DGCA-approved medical centre. It was after she got clearance from the Air Force Central Medical Establishment (AFCME) in Delhi and had the medical fitness certificate in hand that she started dreaming of actually flying and becoming a pilot.

She had seen pilots around her home in Kolkata (mostly male), and the uniform had always made her visualise being in this profession. She is sure that, even today, children and adults alike from all walks of life find this uniform, this field fascinating. Once pronounced medically fit, she decided to scout for flying schools in the US, so she could set out to achieve her goal. Her parents were very supportive of the decision, but on the other hand, there were people in her extended family who objected, their concern being what kind of job this was for a girl and that if she did become a pilot, who would marry her? However, her grandfather put an end to all these remarks, bidding her parents to let her continue and not bother about what others said. This was encouraging and propelled her onward.

As luck would have it, she was going to meet her cousins in the US. This was the summer of 1986. She reached Albany, the capital of New York State where her cousins lived, eagerly looking forward to pursuing her ambition to fly.

A few days later, she visited the flying schools in Albany with her uncle, but to their dismay, not much flying was happening there. The weather was not very favourable either. Yet, they decided that she would start there and shift elsewhere later. Her father differed in opinion, however, and on his approval, they shortlisted a school in Long Island. Next thing she knew, she was heading to Long Island to join the American Flying Club at McArthur Airport in August 1986.

She had zero experience of flying at the time. She remembered how her friend Dharamraj would often talk about flying and she could never understand why he was so thrilled about it. Until she got her own first feel of being high above the ground. The feeling of the lift-off, being up in the air, was just mind-blowing and remains fresh in her memory. Off to a great start, each day got better as she learnt and actually handled the aircraft controls. The Cessna didn't seem like a small aircraft in those days. In fact, sometimes, one sensed that they themselves were slower than their aircraft. Today, after flying the Airbus, one can say, 'Oh, that small Cessna!' But one cannot forget that it did take time to understand and acquire the knack of flying those little Cessnas. Sangita was putting in as much effort as needed to learn the skill of flying, enjoying every moment without the fear of anything.

Then came the D-day, as she vividly recalls, when she was on her regular sortie with her instructor, doing circuits. She felt she was on her best performance but wasn't sure what her instructor was thinking, when suddenly he informed the ATC about a full-stop landing. She was a bit disappointed as she wanted to fly more, but as they landed and she stopped, he coolly opened his door, alighted and told her, 'Go! Get going, get the feel of solo flying!' The instruction came out of the blue; she just wasn't expecting her solo then. Before she could even look at him to acknowledge what he said, he was out of the little Cessna. She did the pre-flight preparation, informed the ATC, opened the throttle, and there she was, up in the air again. Till she was airborne, she didn't realise she was all by herself, all alone! She stayed calm, more focused both on Radio Telephony (RT) and keeping the runway in sight, joined down-wind for the circuit turned towards base leg, not letting the runway out of sight. When she finally turned on to the finals, she saw that there was a big aircraft (much bigger than a Cessna) in front of her that she had not noticed while concentrating on her perfect circuit pattern. With whatever experience she had, she continued on the final track behind the big aircraft. Suddenly her aircraft started to shake, she didn't know why. Today, one would understand that with a bigger aircraft in front, one would encounter wake-turbulence. But she wasn't aware of the concept, definitely not on that first solo. Even so, she gauged that she was not stabilised in her approach, and even though she did not have much exposure to all this yet, she knew she could not continue in the same way and must do a go-around. She took a firm decision, informed the ATC and did a go-around.

Then she was up in the air again. This time staying even more careful, keeping an eye on other aircraft too, until she made a final smooth touchdown. So where a student usually did only one circuit on their first solo, by default, she had managed to do two! She admits to having been a bit anxious when she encountered the wake-turbulence but once she did the go-around, she enjoyed that experience on the first solo. Honestly, she did not know then how her instructor felt about the go-around; after she landed and parked, he seemed relieved and chose not to say anything till the next day's briefing class.

After that, she was flying every day for hours, growing increasingly confident, getting more solos and doing cross-country flying. It was now time for her cross-country solo, a requirement that all fliers have to fulfil. Remembering one particular experience, she says it brings on a laugh today, but as a student pilot, it sure was not funny. As it happened, her instructor, Paul, had asked her to shortlist the airfield which she would like to explore for her solo cross-country. He then accompanied her once on the same route to bolster her spirits. He explained all visual clues, making her even more confident of the route. Feeling self-assured, she planned her solo cross-country, choosing a place she had been before so that she would be able to hold on to visual clues as backup.

She had heard of many fliers getting lost during their first solo, but she felt confident as she had done her planning with utmost care. She started fine, presumably doing well until she flew past the river where she knew she had to take a turn. She was navigating using her route map but was also cross-checking with visual clues. Somehow she jumbled up the turn; visualising it wrongfully, and turned right instead of left. As she flew a little ahead, it struck her that while flying with the instructor, after the turn, she was to look out for and fly towards a city, but here she saw hills all around and they seemed to be almost at the same height as her. She also noticed that everything looked different from how it had been on the last round she had made with the instructor. Keeping calm, she took the next step and called the ATC to relay her position. But there was no response on the frequency she was calling (since she was on the opposite route, the frequency would change, but she did not realise that she was calling on the wrong frequency). So, she began thinking about her next step. There was no time to panic; she immediately set the emergency (guard) frequency 121.5 MHz and gave her position, hoping for a response. Luckily for her, there was a response, she gave her bearings, and was lucky she was identified on the radar; she was given her location and guided to the nearest airfield. She got the ATC frequency and was asked to inform them once she had the runway in sight. She spotted the airport beacon first, then a runway on top of a hill. She was asked to make the approach and land on this runway. It was the first time she was landing on a runway atop a hill, a 'table-top' runway. (A tabletop runway is one that is located on top of a plateau or hill with one or both ends adjacent to a steep precipice which drops into a deep gorge. This type of runway creates an optical illusion which requires a very precise approach by the pilot.) She did what was instructed by the ATC and, to her good luck, she managed to land safely. It was only later, she learned more about table-top runways and how critical these airfields can be. She had taken the plunge with little experience and knowledge.

After parking the aircraft, she found out which city she was in, how far it was from her actual destination, and then called her instructor to give him her location. He had figured out by now that she had got lost and reached another city. He spoke to her calmly and showed concern once she told him where and how she had actually landed. He probably knew that table-top runways were not the best option to land for someone on their first solo cross-country, and he told her to wait there until he came to pick her up. However, she knew she must find her way back, so she bravely told him, 'Sir, I will make a flight plan and call you with all the details. Please let me make an attempt to come back.' She took some time, finished everything and called him. She hoped he felt confident about her approach and preparation. He just advised her to take as much extra fuel as she could and return. His go-ahead gave her the reassurance she needed after what had happened. So she took off, keeping more visual cues at hand, being more conscientious all along the route, and landed safely back at her flying school.

Her instructor was waiting. He helped her park the aircraft and told her to go home and come back the next day. She was taken aback as she was expecting a long debriefing and a proper scolding, but he said nothing. The next day, she reached the flying school very early and learnt that her instructor had just got married the day before. So, the previous day, he had been hoping to go back early after her cross-country but had to be there nearly the whole day till she reached. She felt really foolish. When he met her, he said, 'If you had asked me to come pick you up, you would have had it from me. The fact that you realised your mistake, prepared yourself, found your bearings and reached back safely, is how I know you will not get lost again, so go fly and enjoy yourself!'

This was the impetus that gave her the wings she was looking for. She completed her flying with zest to get her Commercial Pilot Licence (CPL), an achievement she felt she truly earned on her own. Her vision broadened and she could picture herself in the airline pilot uniform. She hoped to fly as soon as she reached India. She needed another 60 hours of flying to fulfil the total number of hours required for an Indian CPL. For this, her family suggested she should go back to her uncle's place and complete the requirement from Albany Flying Club as it now offered a good flying experience.

So, her last leg of flying happened in Albany. It was fun; with the CPL in hand, she could fly without any issue or restriction whatsoever. Every day, she would open her Jeppesen Airway Manual, close her eyes, move her pencil to mark one place, and then take off to head there. It could be flying over the Hudson one day, over some small town another day, spotting malls, Macy stores, anyplace. It was as if the sky had opened up for her and she could go anywhere she wished. *That* is the highlight of this profession; one can reach anywhere one wants to!

Another event she always remembers from those days was her flight to Buffalo, a town north of Albany, towards the Canadian border. It was a cold day but she hadn't imagined it would be snowing there. She encountered bad weather with ice all around; she could not maintain height as the wings got covered with ice and a Cessna does not have any anti-icing system. She contacted the ATC and asked for vectors to land. It was the first time she landed in an airfield covered with snow. She admitted that she was relieved once she was on ground that one time. One remembers these incidents clearly even though they happened more than thirty years ago, she reflects, as they have taught so many important lessons. As she puts it, 'It's your experience that helps in life; no textbook can teach you what experience can. Every experience you have had, no matter where, helps you grow as a person and in the profession.'

Having completed everything, she returned to Kolkata in February 1987. Once back, her first target was to convert her American CPL to an Indian CPL by submitting the required papers. She was lucky that by August 1987, everything was done. Shortly after, there was an advertisement for Indian Airlines' induction of trainee pilots. She still remembers sitting for the written exam on 26 August 1987. There were around 190 candidates in all, of which five were girls. She was the only girl who cleared the written exam. By 6 September, the group discussion and interview process were concluded and everyone waited patiently for the results. Not knowing what was in store for her, she stopped thinking about it. Then she heard that her friend Dharamraj had received a telegram informing him of his selection; she waited for a day or so but since she did not get any, she asked Dharamraj to check with his father (who was in the airlines) about her. It was common knowledge that the airline would induct one girl and she was the only girl who had cleared the written round. She was thus very curious to know why she had not received any information from them. While her friend's father was still checking, she received a letter from Indian Airlines asking her to proceed to the Central Training Establishment (CTE) in Hyderabad for her training which was to start on 4 January 1988. It was such a relief, she had really worked very hard; it would have been a great disappointment for her and her family had she not been selected.

Thrilled with this opportunity for a new lease of life opening up, her eyes would now only look up to the skies with a sense of satisfaction. She knew she was ready to face any adversity along the way. Their batch had 20 candidates – 19 boys and one girl. They also had seven Air Force candidates who were flying the VVIPS and were sent to their batch for a Boeing endorsement. As they started training, she told herself she had chosen to be in a male-dominated profession; the sooner she got herself to accept that, the better it would be to get into the system and be part of the batch. By now, she knew about the other lady captains in the airline. The number was small, but they had made their presence felt by their performance. By now, Capt. Saudamini was flying in command too. So Sangita felt her acceptance would not be a problem. She also knew she was here to be a pilot, nothing less, nothing more. Her determined nature and seriousness about her passion for flying made her batchmates accept her as one among them, and they all enjoyed working together as a team!

However, the training was not without some hitches since some seniors had a closed mind about women pilots. For the most part, though, it was smooth. Soon, she had successfully completed her training and was ready for her final release aircraft check for First Officer. This was a memorable experience in her life, she narrated. 'Capt. M.V.V. Rao was to do the release; the sector was Chennai–Madurai–Cochin and back to Chennai. She was to do two sectors and another batchmate was to do the other two. Cochin was the old runway, the Air Force one that we used to operate earlier. That itself was a challenging airfield but none of us had a choice, and with Capt. Rao, no one could say anything. He did all the F/O releases and each of us knew how strict he was till his last days in the CTE. How terrified we all used to be of him! We were waiting for him in flight dispatch. As he came, even before we could wish him, he looked at me and said, "Male or female, we don't bother. We want a competent F/O sitting in that aircraft, so don't expect any leniency." Those were his words, in his stern tone. So I nodded and geared up, telling myself to stay calm and concentrate on the flight.

'I walked ahead to the aircraft to perform my co-pilot duties.

I walked up the stairs and before I could reach the flight deck, the senior-most cabin crew member just pushed me into the cockpit and shut the cockpit door. I thought to myself how rude she was and wondered if they treated all First Officers like this or if it was because I was a woman; all kinds of thoughts were coming to me. I was still settling in my seat when the crew member came inside the cockpit and said, "Captain, I am sorry I had to push you in. You must be aware that yesterday, one of our Boeings went down in Ahmedabad. Passengers are very concerned and seeing you, a girl, that too so short, they will panic more. Moreover, you have come first and no other captain has come to the cockpit. Passengers may get scared that a woman is flying this plane, especially after what has happened to one of our aircraft."

She thought to herself at that moment, *what a start to my journey.* She was getting ready to be released as a co-pilot to fly regular passenger flights, and then to hear about the same aircraft involved in an accident. She also felt that people's mindsets had not changed in spite of a few girls flying in the airline, but seeing even the cabin crew expressing the same doubts surprised her. 'Those were the days, and we had to handle all kinds of situations,' she recalls. Back in the cockpit, her mind registered that this was her first flight on the B-737, and it was the first time she was sitting independently in the seat as a qualified First Officer ready to be released. She resolved to start with a positive thought and did not let a single negative thought or word bother her. She also knew that Capt. Rao would not spare them if they made even the slightest of errors. Steeling herself to focus, she prepared for the flight.

She readied the cockpit and they took off to the first destination. She did her sectors, and her batchmate did his. After the final destination, Capt. Rao asked them for their forms. It was such a great feeling when he handed back the form and said, 'Congratulations, you are released as First Officers.' Those words sounded like magic! They had been working on this one goal for years, and wanted to jump and shout to celebrate. All the hectic training and checks after checks were finally behind them! She breathed a sigh of relief. That's the story of her first flight, one she cannot forget till date.

She got posted to Kolkata and started flying from there. It was a good start. The captains were very friendly and willing to teach students everything required to make them confident as pilots. According to Capt. Sangita, base captains were the ones who taught them real flying. From Kolkata, the airline operated mostly to the eastern sectors where half the airfields did not even have Distance Measuring Equipment (DME); they would teach and show them visual cues that could determine approximate distance and help one judge and calculate to plan the descent. These experiences could not be compared with bookish knowledge. Those were the days, she reminisces. Today, pilots rely mainly on instruments; visual clues are now a thing of the past. In those times, captains knew it all; be it navigation, weather or aircraft manoeuvring, they could handle everything with minimum aids. She and her batchmates learnt a lot from all these captains, and they imbibed much more while flying on their routes. It was the best thing they could have asked for as co-pilots. They knew they should be ready to handle the aircraft, the weather, especially when flying out of Kolkata, a city known for vicious weather. She wanted to learn and experience as much as possible before she became a commander.

By 1991, she was moved from the Boeing to the Airbus A-320, the aircraft with the new fly-by-wire technology. In 1995, she co-piloted the all-women crew flight with Capt. Saudamini as the commander on the A-320 from Mumbai to Chennai and back. This flight is marked as the first all-women crew on A-320, in Asia and probably across the world. Finally, her turn came and she was sent for command training on the A-320. She was the second girl after Capt. Saudamini to get command on this aircraft. All eyes were on them, more so because of the new concept-based aircraft. Hard work brought good results and she was released as a commander, getting her command endorsement on the A-320 on 26 August 1996. It was the best feeling, one she finds hard to express in words even now. Till date, her first flight as a commander remains etched in her mind. It was like achieving one's ultimate mission in life. As she says, there is no greater joy in this profession than when one gets their command. Man or woman, the feelings are the same!

She happily recounts the experience. The date was 15 September 1996. She was still wearing her three stripes as her command grade had not come (four stripes indicated that one was a commander) but as her licence was endorsed, she was operating the flight in command from Mumbai. The engineer came to the cockpit and gave the book to the co-pilot in spite of seeing her in the command seat. She was unperturbed. Finally, when the co-pilot said, 'Ma'am is the commander; please give the book to her,' the engineer looked at her and reluctantly handed over the book which had to be checked for aircraft status by commanders. Such was the state of affairs women dealt with; they constantly had to prove themselves whereas men rarely faced such situations, notwithstanding the fact that all pilots go through the same training and checks before eventually reaching this seat. She recollects, 'I thought to myself, let them think whatever; I will do what I am supposed to and there is no looking back. It is interesting to state here that I started enjoying doing flights to Sharjah as all the security guards there would go on saying, "Look, look! A lady captain!"' It was a good feeling, a sense of achievement. Nevertheless, Capt. Sangita feels that gender should not hold any importance as everyone works hard to reach their goals. She thanks her stars for enabling her to reach the skies.

She strongly feels she was in the right place at the right time and worked hard to make it work for her.

'As commanders, we do face many situations but we are fully trained to perform and bring aircraft safely on the ground,' she adds. In her opinion, sometimes, interference from non-professional bodies hampers the work in a space that belongs only to trained personnel. For her, it is important that people learn and understand that. She recalls an interesting incident. She was at Nagpur Airport, getting ready to go back to Mumbai. Passengers had boarded, but no commercial staff was coming with the trim sheet (the final paper sign-off before the closing of the aircraft door). She kept asking for the staff but no one turned up. Finally, after persisting, the duty manager came and told her, 'Captain, we are waiting for one last passenger.' She checked the time; it was close to departure time. Her first question to him was, 'Does the passenger have any check-in baggage?' He said, 'No.' Immediately, she asked him to offload the passenger and revise the trim sheet with a listing of final passengers on board, so that they could depart. He quickly replied, 'No, no, captain, please don't do this, he is a VIP and if I let the aircraft go, I will be in trouble.' As the commander, she was not ready to accept this. She told him: 'I have 145 passengers on board and I will not wait past departure time for anyone. This is the captain's decision.'

She then picked up the mic and made an in-flight announcement. 'Ladies and gentlemen, I have just been informed we are holding for one passenger, but since it is past boarding time and close to departure time, we will depart shortly.'

After that, the commercial staffer had no choice. He knew that if the passenger came along now, people would look at him with annoyance, so he did as she had announced. Just as she was starting the left engine, she and her co-pilot saw a person running from the terminal to the aircraft. The engineer asked her if she could open the door for the passenger. She got a bit angry. How could the engineer ask such an irresponsible question when the engine was running! Keeping her cool, she told him that she could open the door if he took responsibility for the door opening with the engine running. All this was being recorded as per norm on the Cockpit Voice Recorder (CVR). His response, of course, was, 'No, Captain.' She started the second engine and then taxied. But as they reached the taxi holding point near the runway for departure, two Air Force aircraft came and they had to wait for about 5–7 minutes before take-off. The VIP was watching and she learnt that he had apparently told the commercial staffer, 'She can wait near the runway but not for me. I will have her removed from her job.' Sure enough, she was issued a letter asking her to explain why she had left the passenger in Nagpur. She was put off flying and her CVR was removed and checked for all recordings. 'We often face these issues from time to time for doing our job diligently,' she observes. 'These incidents do interfere in our work and sometimes become more strenuous than flying and handling the aircraft.'

Despite having put in more than thirty years of flying, even today one sees different reactions from people when they see a woman pilot. She talks about how strange it felt sometimes, when she stood at the cockpit door to see passengers deplane and someone would come and ask her if they could meet the captain of the plane. When she told them that she was the captain, they would say, 'No, no, the real pilot, meaning the commander.' Then the cabin crew would tell them she is the captain, pilot, the commander who has flown this aircraft and got them here. Some would go down with a smile; others had a worried look despite having reached safely.

Public perception has not changed much even though there are a number of women commanders now. Capt. Sangita feels the media can play a better role in upholding the profession more effectively by getting proper information and facts rather than creating hype, especially if there is a woman pilot involved. Women pilots continue to be discussed and scrutinised much more than their male counterparts. They still have to put in extra effort relative to their male colleagues. Her own upgradation from check pilot to instructor to examiner got delayed because of her gender.

Nevertheless, ignoring the gender angle, it has been a very fruitful journey, she feels. From flying school to a flying start with Indian Airlines, from flying Cessnas to the Boeing 737 and the Airbus 319/320/321, from co-pilot to commander to check pilot, instructor to examiner, it is a profession where the learning never stops. A profession full of challenges where every day, every flight on the same airfield can turn out differently due to multiple reasons, be it weather, gust or fog. This is one job that never gets monotonous. One may start out as a pessimist, but all actions bring about positive results. In a nutshell, Capt. Sangita can boast about her office being high up in the air where no two days are the same and where one never carries their work home—where else would one get this luxury!

After years of working hard as a captain, Capt. Sangita is all smiles as she is now an instructor and examiner on the Airbus 320.

Enjoying a relaxed moment at an activity organised by the Indian Women Pilot's Association, Mumbai

Off to an adventurous start – Indira Sharma participating at the shooting range for an NCC activity during her college days

Thrilled after winning the gold medal at a gliding competition

Welcoming Prime Minister Rajiv Gandhi at Garrison Ground in 1985, for the mini Republic Day parade

Eleven

Flying to Make the World One

Indira Sharma Mitra

She has always imagined the whole world as one. More so, as a pilot, she sees no boundaries. She sees herself as a citizen of the world and hopes everyone around the world sees themselves the same way. According to her, there is enough in this world for everyone, and those who don't believe that suffer and make others suffer. In her own words, 'I am a combination of the East and the West. I am a disciplined and reliable person; if I commit to anything, I will go to any extent to make it happen.' She is Indira Sharma Mitra, born on 30 January to Brij Mohan Sharma and Monika Sharma. Her father is Indian and her mother German, so to her, the whole world is one family!

She was one year old when her parents moved from Germany to Ghaziabad, India. The oldest among four children, she studied in Ghaziabad till Class 10, then moved to Modern School, Delhi, for classes 11 and 12. Even as a child, she remembers sitting in class and looking up at the blue sky and wondering what lies beyond. Ever the dreamer, she imagined herself soaring through the air.

It was at Indraprastha (IP) College in Delhi that she first came across the NCC, which was instrumental in helping her achieve her dream of reaching the skies. Having always been interested in sports, she remembers that even in college, she would be out either swimming or hanging out in the sports field. One day, while in college, she heard a loud noise. Curious, she followed the sound and spotted some uniformed girls lying on their stomach and firing guns in a makeshift shooting range. The sight instantly appealed to her. It was only then that she learned that the uniform was that of the NCC. She asked the girls if she could also try firing. One of the cadets agreed to let her try her hand at it, and she remembers lying on her stomach like the others and firing. To her and the others' surprise, she did well. Seeing her performance, one of the girls asked her if she wanted to join the NCC. The cadet added that it would be a great opportunity as well as a great experience. So, she complied and joined the NCC in her first year of college in 1983.

As part of the NCC, she started to learn shooting. It was fun and she enjoyed the sport. Life fell into a steady routine till, one day, she saw a notice that had been put up on her college notice board asking girls interested in aeromodelling to report at a particular place. She noted the time and date of reporting, and made sure to reach well before time on the appointed day, so as not to miss this new opportunity. She saw some army vehicles and at least 300 girls lined up, all ready to get onto the vehicle. The army vehicle took them all to Safdarjung Airport.

Smiling, she narrates the episode. 'It was something out of my dream... as a child, I used to force my dad to take us to

Safdarjung Airport because I loved watching the runway and observing the aircraft coming in to land.' At the airport, the girls were told that 20 of them would be selected for aeromodelling. Indira's eyes lit up when she saw a glider waiting there. She thought to herself, there are so many girls waiting to try aeromodelling, why shouldn't I try gliding instead? She saw a man standing nearby and went up to him. Pointing to the glider, she asked, 'Who flies this?' He replied, 'Our sir flies it. He's in his office now.' She got even more excited and asked if she could meet him. To her surprise, he allowed her. She entered the office – she still remembers the name, Sqdn Ldr Verma – and, after wishing him, she told him that she was from the NCC of IP College and wanted to learn how to fly the glider. He looked at her and asked her the reason for the NCC's visit, to which she replied that they were there for the aeromodelling class. He told her that if she wanted to start gliding, she would first have to become a part of the Air Wing of the NCC. Then, there would be a separate selection process for gliding, and mostly boys were selected. She asked him if she could try. Perhaps on seeing her enthusiasm, he explained that selection would be through a competition to be held amongst the Air Wing candidates a few days later. It would include a race of around 5–6 km across Safdarjung Airport. If she qualified, they could think about her induction. He may have thought that this would make her rethink it, but she decided she would at least give it a shot.

On the said day, she got there promptly on time and saw that she was the only girl among 30 participants. The race started and everyone thought she would give up, if not at the beginning, then surely halfway through. To their surprise, she not only completed the race, but was among the first five to finish. The Air Wing authorities were left with a complicated decision on their hands. Here was Indira, the only girl, but who had qualified fair and square. She was selected to be part of the First Air Wing Squadron. It was here that she believes her professional journey began. She was one among the boys, ready and gliding, touching the sky, just as she had always dreamt it – part of the Air Wing of the NCC, wearing the blue uniform and cap – she loved every moment of it then and, till date, loves her uniform!

As part of the Air Wing, they went to various camps, and by the second year, they were gliding more regularly. The best part for her was going to the Vayu Sena Camp. She won a medal for best cadet and, henceforth, her gliding lessons grew more frequent and advanced. Of course, this did not please her colleagues; they started saying that her father must be a big shot either in the Indian Air Force or the Navy. Then they learned that he was a businessman, not connected to the armed forces in any way. Indira did her best, and it was her dedicated toil that helped her. She took part in several competitions and won more medals. After winning the gold medal in a gliding competition in Jaipur, she was selected for the Republic Day Parade, a great honour for cadets. She was also awarded the 'Best Girl Cadet of India' in 1985. Since she had won both these awards, she was chosen to glide over Garrison Ground, where the then prime minister Mr Rajiv Gandhi was to be the chief guest of the mini Republic Day Parade. As Indira was gliding, handling it beautifully and coming close to the chief guest as he arrived, all eyes were turned towards the sky, watching the glider swoop down like a bird onto Garrison Ground. She remembers the moment of honour fondly, when she garlanded the PM who was accompanied by his wife, Mrs Sonia Gandhi, and the then army chief, General A.S. Vaidya, who even introduced her by name as the best girl cadet. Because of her achievements in the NCC and its Air Wing, she was given a scholarship to fly and acquire a Private Pilot Licence (PPL). And so, in 1985, she moved from one side of Safdarjung Airport (where her gliding lessons took place) to the other side, Delhi Flying Club, where her flying started.

For her, transitioning from the powerless glider to the powered aircraft was an amazing feeling. She had always loved being up in the sky, and this simply added to the exhilaration. Flying gave her a feeling of absolute achievement, a deep sense of satisfaction she had dreamt about for long. As her flying progressed, she grew more and more zealous about the sport. The greatest moment in her flying journey came sometime in March 1985. She reached the flying club as usual, and started her routine flying accompanied by her instructor for the regular sorties of circuit and land. She had often heard her colleagues talk about the joy of flying solo and had wondered when it would be her turn. The instructors never told them when they could anticipate a solo sortie, so they simply had to focus on improving their flying. Indira was flying perfectly that day and enjoying the feel of handling the small Pushpak, managing everything without any input from her instructor. They finished one circuit, took off for another, and after they landed, while the aircraft was on the runway, lined up for the third circuit, the instructor simply got off the aircraft and told her, 'Go, go take off. Enjoy your solo.' She looked at him as he got off the aircraft, a bit dazed by this sudden development. It was as though he had read her mind! She was left to do her bit. She asked the ATC for take-off clearance, informing that the pilot in command is Indira Sharma, solo; and off she went, up into the air. The aircraft felt much lighter, and she focused on her circuit pattern so as not to make any mistakes; before long, she was on the final track for landing. Only after landing did it sink in that this had been her first solo. It felt like clearing a major exam. She felt more confident and everyone started looking at her in a new light. She was considered one among the group now and the boys regarded her with respect. She felt the difference; till then she had not been taken seriously, but after the solo flight, everyone started giving her tips and information to improve and fly better and with more confidence. By 1986, she had cleared all exams and met all the flying requirements to get her PPL.

Having earned her PPL, she started dreaming of becoming a pilot, but there were financial constraints. Till then, she had been flying on a scholarship and did not know how she would be able to afford the training necessary to earn a Commercial Pilot Licence (CPL). She was not sure if her parents would take flying seriously as a profession and help her with funds. On the flipside, she did not know where to apply for another scholarship.

Indira decided she did not want to give up on flying and continued researching scholarships she could apply to. She got lucky while attending a friend's wedding. She feels her name, Indira, helped her. The wedding was of a close family friend and she attended it with her parents. One of the family members was part of the PM's security team, and the PM was expected to drop in to wish the bride and groom. Being close to the bride, she was standing next to the couple when PM Rajiv Gandhi arrived. He wished the newlyweds, and just as he was leaving, looked at her and said, 'Aren't you Indira, the glider?' She was overjoyed that the PM had remembered her name. She replied, 'Yes, Sir!' and took the opportunity to tell him that she had got her PPL on a scholarship from the NCC, and since she wanted to become a pilot, she needed some financial aid. Since Delhi was a union territory, there was no flying scholarship unlike in the states. To this, he simply asked, 'You want a scholarship?' She nodded. That was it; with that, he left. She assumed nothing would happen, that she would have to find some other means for a scholarship. However, two days later, when she was in the college hostel, there was a call for her from the Prime Minister's

Office (PMO), asking her to visit them. She was taken aback. She was a young teenager, still in college, and did not even know where the PMO was. She asked around and took a bus to her destination. She met his secretary, Sarla Grewal, who told her that the PM had granted her a scholarship for flying from the PM's Fund and wanted to know which flying school she would like to join. She had already been selected by the newly established flying academy, the Indira Gandhi Rashtriya Uran Akademi (IGRUA) at Fursatganj in Raebareli district of Uttar Pradesh, but had not paid the fees. On mentioning this, she was granted a 50 per cent scholarship. Armed with a cheque for ₹30,000, she went straight to Capt. Darwar's office in Delhi (he was in charge of the IGRUA at the time) and handed over the cheque. Thus, she was able to join the first batch at the IGRUA, in the year 1986. They were 19 trainees, alongside 18 boys, she was the only girl in the first batch of the new academy!

Fursatganj, a small town in Raebareli, was where this academy was started. It was the highlight of the town, and since this was the first batch of the flying school opened by the PM, all attention was on the progress of the trainees. They were made to work hard from the very beginning. Indira found it tough but fun. They slogged day and night, and when their training was about to be completed, Capt. Darwar approached her and asked if she would like to join Air India. Air India and Indian Airlines were paying part of the training cost at the IGRUA at that time, and so after the training was complete and the trainees got their CPLs, the teams from Air India and Indian Airlines would recruit them as trainee pilots in their respective airlines. They would join one or the other, based on seniority and a brief interview, but a job in one of them was guaranteed. The IGRUA still trains students who want to become pilots, but without the job guarantee. The aim was to showcase the academy and its first batch as well as the first girl in the academy, and she believes that because Air India had not recruited a woman yet, they wanted the academy to be the first in having trained the woman who could join Air India.

The thought was so welcoming that, initially, she got carried away with this idea of being a 'first', but she did not want to make any hasty decisions. She did her research and spoke to more experienced hands in the industry. A few captains presented a realistic picture. They said that surely she would get her 15 minutes of fame, but she should first decide on what would be better for her career. In those days, Air India had long layovers and flew only wide-bodied aircraft. She was told that she would do one landing in 15 days, and those landings would not even be done by her. Indian Airlines flew more routes in the domestic sector, where, every hour, there was a landing. Moreover, there were about five girls in Indian Airlines, so she would be accepted relatively easily, whereas in Air India there were no girls, and no one knew if they were ready to accept a woman in the cockpit. In terms of family life as well, Indian Airlines made more sense; in Air India, one would be away from home for 15 days, whereas in Indian Airlines, one would be back the same day or the next day. Keeping this in mind, she told Capt. Darwar that she would only be interested in joining Indian Airlines. Capt. Darwar was not happy with her decision; he wanted the academy's first female student to become Air India's first female pilot. But she stood her ground and joined Indian Airlines, and sincerely believes that it gave her career a head start. It is common knowledge in aviation circles as to what happened to the first few girls who joined Air India as it was not ready to accept women in the cockpit. It was only in the mid to late '90s that Air India inducted the first woman pilot. Capt. Indira joined Indian Airlines around February/March 1988, as part of Batch No. 38. There were 32 trainees, a mixed batch of pilots from the IGRUA and other flying schools who had passed the entrance test. Capt. Indira was the only girl in the batch, as per the prevailing trend.

They were to be trained for the Boeing 737-200 series, as the airline's fleet mostly comprised Boeings. Boeing was and remains an amazing aircraft, especially for trainees who joined the airline straight from flying school, having only flown the Cessna and the Pushpak. They could not dream of asking for anything better; the fact that they were going to fly big jets was all that mattered. The training phase in the Central Training Establishment (CTE) was challenging. The girls before Capt. Indira had already paved the way for the women, so she did not face any discrimination. However, the CTE was very competitive, and she had a daunting task at hand, being the only girl in a batch of 32 trainees. She was perceived as studious and serious, which in itself was a stumbling block when managing a good relationship with one's colleagues. However, she focused on doing well and working hard, knowing that it was the only thing that ultimately mattered. There was no bias against her for being a woman, but the training was very harsh, and the instructor took no heed when dealing with a girl. She clearly remembers the day when she did not perform well in one of her bookings, under training on the B-737 aircraft, the instructor shouted at her and gave her hell. He even said, 'You all come here to waste the money and time of the airline. If you do not perform well, you have no business staying here!' Since Capt. Indira had had a taste of this at the NCC, she remained calm and decided to learn from her mistakes. She worked towards performing better in her next sortie, successfully did so and moved on.

Speaking of experience, she flew Boeings till 1990. By 1992, she was trained on flying the A-320, but then there was a strike in Indian Airlines. During that time, by sheer chance, she met a Sri Lankan Chief Pilot in Chennai, who told her about Sri Lankan Airlines and the opportunities there. She was convinced and decided to join them in 1994 on a three-year contract. Aware that there would always be challenges in this profession, she took up this job. After her tenure with them, she returned to India and joined Alliance Air in 1997 (which had started operations around 1996). While in Alliance Air, she started flying Boeings again. It was also here that she got her first command, on the Boeing 737 aircraft in 1998.

She describes the feeling of finally earning this position as extraordinary and out of the world. She remembers the command training was even tougher than before, but that was a small, insignificant problem, compared to commanding a flight and facing real emergencies. This she felt was the actual solo – *a flight in your command*! 'As a commander,' she says, 'you see this profession as more challenging every day, every minute.'

She shares an experience from the time she had been in command for barely a year. This was in 1999 and she was operating from Vizag (Visakhapatnam). They had just taken off from Vizag Airport when they got a high engine oil temperature warning. Even before the co-pilot could announce the warning, Capt. Indira's eyes were on the readings. Along with handling the aircraft and following the departure procedure of a critical airfield, she was preparing for the next action. Just then, she noticed that the engine oil temperature was increasing rapidly and slipping into the red band. Before the co-pilot could give the mandatory call-out, her hand moved to pull the thrust lever of the affected engine to idle, simultaneously announcing her action so that the co-pilot was aware of her intentions. Within 13 seconds of the occurrence, she had shut down the engine. She remembered that there had been a circular stating that if the oil temperature rises beyond the acceptable limit, the engine has to be shut down within 15 seconds. Capt. Indira then informed the ATC about the nature of the emergency and asked for permission to return with all assistance on arrival.

Performing their checklist, they returned with a single engine, overweight, and dealing with cross-wind on the short runway of Vizag for a safe landing. That landing experience has stayed with her to this day.

It was a real-life version of what they had practised on the simulator as part of their training, but handling an actual aircraft with passengers made it a uniquely stressful situation. She was later appreciated for her prompt and appropriate action, which saved the company the expense of removing the engine for major repair work.

Capt. Indira loves this profession, which she says is full of adventure coupled with responsibilities, where no two days are the same, and where, at times, one sees wide-ranging shifts even within the same day. One may have taken off smoothly from an airfield, but on returning, may face severe weather, fog, or the runway being closed. Anything is possible and every minute holds something new!

She is probably one of the few lady captains who has carried out more than 800 landings in the Port Blair airfield in different conditions, be it monsoon or cyclone, operating both the Boeing and the Airbus. For her, being a pilot is a mix of everything – high risk, adventure, responsibility – along with a lot of travel. As she says, 'It's not easy but we are all performers!' Today, after thirty or so years in the profession, she has evolved a lot and continues to do so. She feels that with the kind of lifestyle she leads, there is a need to focus on inner peace and spirituality. For this, she loves visiting an ashram in South India.

As a mother, she wants to make sure her child grows up in the best possible environment filled with peace, harmony, and parental love and affection. It is also important for her to instil values in her son and teach him to appreciate what he has and give back to society by helping others. In fact, she feels that even adults need to learn this. On her part, she volunteers with a women-run group called Voice of the People, in Chennai, where she lives. She teaches English to classes 6–8. She says, 'It's fun for me and the kids.' These children have not been exposed to the fun learning style that she uses in the classroom. She tries to ensure that slow learners also enjoy themselves and benefit from her classes. Initially, she did not understand why some kids avoided her. Then she learned that they were never loved or shown affection; this made her change her approach, and she understood that a simple hug and talking nicely to children made all the difference. Slowly, they all started loving her and her classes. They call her their 'Pilot Ma'am'. She says that it is very satisfying when children open up to you and enjoy your company. They show and express selfless love, which she thinks is fading away from our society today. She hopes to be able to continue in this new endeavour, while balancing the time needed for her profession.

Now flying A-320s for Indigo Airlines, she believes that flying is what made her who she is today – '*a complete person*'!

Capt. Indira flew the Airbus 320 for Sri Lankan Airlines

Be it any airline or aircraft, Capt. Indira's first love will always be flying.

From cabin...

...to cockpit

Capt. Laxmi Malhotra Nagrath's journey created a record and features in the Limca Books of Records

Soaring to Success (The Early 1990s)

Twelve

From Cabin to Cockpit

Laxmi Malhotra Nagrath

The minute she is airborne, it feels as if all her problems have been left behind on the ground, and she is relaxed and happy. As a child, whenever she asked her mother about fairies, she would point to the clouds in the sky. Today, as a pilot, when she flies through cloudy, overcast skies, she wishes she could step outside the cockpit and find those fairies beyond the clouds!

Born in Delhi on 4 November to Shri Daya Nand Malhotra and Suraj Kanta Malhotra, Laxmi Malhotra Nagrath was featured in the *Limca Book of Records* in 2012 for being the first air hostess in the country to reach the cockpit, having joined as an air hostess in 1986 and then re-joined the same airline (Indian Airlines) as a trainee pilot in May 1989. Becoming First Officer on a B-737 in 1992, Capt. Laxmi Malhotra Nagrath's journey from the cabin to the cockpit was not only one of a kind at the time, but also inspired others to follow in her footsteps. Many cabin crew members later took up the challenge and qualified to enter the cockpit.

As a teenager, way back in 1986, her life was full of fun. Being the youngest child, she was everyone's favourite and popular amongst all friends and family. It was during that phase where once at a party with her cousins, someone threw her a challenge. She still remembers the exact sequence of events and narrates it with a smile.

'There was this guy who looked at me and said, "If you consider yourself smart, this is an advertisement of British Airways for cabin crew. Let's see if you can get through this."'

She took it seriously, and without telling her family, applied for the job. There was a written exam, which she managed to clear, followed by a group discussion and an interview. She did well in all the rounds and soon got a letter of selection, notifying her that London would be her base. She was extremely excited – it seemed so glamorous – at the kind of pay package she was being offered and the thrilling prospect of living in London. As a teenager, one could not have possibly asked for anything better! She wanted to join right away and make it her profession. But when she told her family, her father refused point blank. She thinks the reason was the government job he held, which, being of a sensitive nature, did not permit family members to take up foreign postings at that time. Laxmi was shattered. What had started as a joke had turned into a fond dream; the glamour of becoming an air hostess with British Airways appealed to her so much, she desperately wished to take up the offer. Her older brother saw how upset she was and wanted to help her. As he knew their father would not let her get into British Airways, he showed her a paper cutting carrying a recruitment ad for Indian Airlines and said, 'Why don't you apply here?' This raised another set of anxious questions: what if she worked hard and got through and their father again did not allow her to take it up? To this, her brother said that he would convince their father, but added that she could work there for two to three years to enjoy herself, after which she must quit. Buoyed by this hope and reassurance, Laxmi agreed and decided to apply. Sure enough, she got in, and with the support of her mother and brother, she convinced her father to let her join. Eventually, he did, but not without warning her first: 'It's not something that you would like, as this job does not go with your personality.'

At the outset, it had all seemed very attractive to her, but within six months, she was fed up and realised that this was indeed not the job for her; there was no growth in this sector. The only good thing that happened at the airline was that she learnt about other options in aviation. She felt inexorably drawn to the challenging work of pilots, and found herself thinking about becoming one. There the journey truly began, as she started doing research on how to train to become a pilot. And with support from senior captains and permission from the airline, she finally made it from the cabin to the cockpit.

When she announced to her family that she intended to become a pilot, she was surprised to find her father fully supportive and happy with her choice. Even though it was not common for women to take up this profession in the 1980s, she plunged right in. Having taken the step, she understood it was not easy, and flying wasn't as simple as some made it sound. To start with, the exams were tough, but she was prepared to battle through. Being from Delhi, she joined the Delhi Flying Club in 1987. The club provided the initial boost for her new journey; she can still remember her most memorable experience, her first solo flight. It was 8 August 1987, and she was doing a normal 'touch and go' exercise. After a couple of sorties, her instructor told her that this would be a full-stop landing. So, as instructed, after touchdown, she stopped the aircraft and prepared to ask for taxi instructions from the ATC. Just then, the instructor opened the door, looked at her and said, 'Go on, all yours.' Taken aback, she looked around before asking the ATC for permission for circuit and landing, informing a solo flight. She started rolling her yellow tail dragger, Pushpak. While lifting off, she felt a bit anxious being alone, but turning downwind, she was more at ease and started telling herself, 'Wow, I can do it!' What a feeling! She turned base-leg and to the finals for landing. As she taxied out of the runway to park, she saw her instructor waiting for her, looking excited! She was ecstatic herself, basking in the feeling and the moment every flyer waits for – the first solo, the experience that stays with them forever! There was no looking back after that.

Unfortunately, flying was very slow in the Delhi Flying Club with many restrictions since it was in the vicinity of a VIP area. Laxmi had barely managed to complete 50 hours of flying when she decided to leave and join the Bhopal Flying Club instead. There she acquired her Private Pilot Licence (PPL). Next, she wanted to advance to the Commercial Pilot Licence (CPL), so she applied for leave from the airline and joined the Ludhiana Flying Club in 1988.

Unlike the Delhi Flying Club, where there were several restrictions on flying, the Ludhiana Flying Club had none, and the skies were open to all. It was an uncontrolled airspace, so they could fly anytime. This was a welcome change for Laxmi. Here is where she feels her real flying began. They had an ex-Air Force instructor, a wing commander, Capt. Bakshish Singh. She recalls how mind-blowing his lessons were. One of her favourite memories of that time is when he literally took her for a 'spin' on the Cessna-152-A. As they climbed to 9,000 ft, he made the aircraft go into spin mode, and it took her a while to realise what was going on. They kept going till he smoothly recovered, at around 2,000 ft. It was a completely different feeling. When he looked at her, before he could say anything, she asked him if she could try. To her surprise, he agreed, but she told him she would like to recover earlier than he had done. So, they climbed to 10,000 ft and, under his guidance, she pushed the aircraft into a spin. The aircraft started to plunge and she began the recovery at around 5,000 ft, but was only able to do so by 2,000 ft. This was all with her tutor's instructions, but he let her handle it, which made her confidence and morale soar.

There was another instructor who took them to Patiala for night flying and even made them do loops. Laxmi quips that the instructors from Punjab were quite daring and great flyers, and that the trainees learned a lot from them. They gave the pilots the boost they needed, so that they felt ready for any eventuality. Laxmi faced one such challenge on a Pushpak, during her solo cross-country flight. Barely 20 miles short of Ludhiana on her return sector, her aircraft started getting out of control. Initially, she could not understand what was going on, but soon sensed that there was some severe weather (wx) phenomenon going on—strong winds buffeted the aircraft. The ATC at Ludhiana were desperately trying to get in touch with her; they wanted her to land as soon as possible because of the wx warning they had received. When she did connect with them, they gave her a heading to steer, trying to bring her on the final track to land as early as possible. Somehow or the other, she handled the aircraft, which was now shaking with the winds growing increasingly turbulent, and tried to land as early as possible in line with instructions from the ATC. She felt relieved when she saw the airfield straight ahead, yet the winds were getting increasingly stronger and were even changing direction. The ATC advised her to continue her approach. With great difficulty, she managed to touchdown with one wheel first and then another, somehow succeeding in getting the Pushpak down. But the aircraft began moving in all directions. She was shaken but successfully prevented the aircraft from going off the runway. She wasn't sure how she would taxi. Just then, she saw a jeep, and the ATC told her to shut the engine. The staff from the jeep then tied the aircraft with rope, so that it could not move. When she exited the aircraft, her legs were trembling and she threw up. The wx had been that rough. Although anyone in her place would have been shaken, she reported the next day for flying as though nothing had happened. She believes, after that day, her male colleagues in the flying club changed their perception of her. They realised she could and would take on any and every challenge when it came to flying, and started treating her as an equal. That was the day she knew she had broken the glass ceiling and had been accepted as a pilot.

By 1988, she and her colleagues earned their CPL. Everyone knew they would have to struggle to get into either Indian Airlines or Air India (Air India was, however, not encouraging or hiring woman), but as Laxmi was on leave from Indian Airlines, they thought it would be easier for her to get a job as a pilot. However, she had to appear for the exam like everyone else and go through the same selection procedure. Soon, a recruitment ad for trainee pilots was advertised by Indian Airlines (the only domestic airline at that time). They were all going to apply; the competition would be tough, but they had no choice.

Till date, those who were selected count it as a blessing; many who could not join had to give up and opt for some other profession. When Laxmi was selected after clearing the written exam, group discussion and interview, it was as if the world had opened up. Here she was, joining the same airline where she had been an air hostess for a year, and within two years, she was going to be in the cockpit. Her family was thrilled, and she was on top of the world! Even after getting the telegram notifying her that she would join as a trainee pilot in Batch No. 43, she had to pinch herself to be convinced that she wasn't dreaming!

The batch of 24 trainees comprised 23 boys and one girl, which was common those days. Thanks to the girls who came before her, at least one was selected per batch. This was sometime in late 1989. As the airline had inducted many trainee pilots in a short span of three to four months, the training was slow. Their batch was in the Central Training Establishment (CTE) for two years before they were released as First Officers (F/Os) in 1992.

Given the long duration of training, the training centre came to be like a home and they all became buddies. The boys accepted Laxmi as one of them and often, they would all hang out together. She really felt like a queen surrounded by 23 boys. It was here that she met her future husband, Krishnavir Nagrath, one of her batchmates. They got married during the training period and when they were released as qualified F/Os, they got a posting to Mumbai, where he lived with his family.

Now as a co-pilot on the B-737, she felt differently. Her work had changed and so had she. Exciting was too mild a word for what she was doing now; her enthusiasm made her prepare thoroughly even for her supernumerary flights. The Jeppesens was properly marked and procedures and limitations were brushed up on every day. It was the beginning of a new life, one that continues to give her a sense of deep satisfaction.

Laxmi felt that flying as a co-pilot may be a bit more relaxed than flying as a commander. But it surely teaches many things that are useful as one progresses towards earning command. Talking about those days brings a smile to her face, and she remembers a particular incident. She was in Hyderabad for her simulator training and, after the session, she caught the flight back to base, Mumbai. On landing, she was seated in the aircraft, waiting like everyone else for the aircraft door to open. Just then, the senior-most cabin crew member approached her and said that the captain wanted to see her in the cockpit. As a co-pilot, she could not question the cabin crew member about the captain's intentions, so she went to the cockpit. The captain told her that the aircraft in the adjacent bay had passengers on board but there was no co-pilot. She was required to operate that flight; it was going to Nagpur. She looked at him first, then at herself, as she was not in uniform. As if reading her mind, he said that permission had been granted for her to operate in civvies. She was told to take the flight bag and go immediately, leaving her night kit behind, as this flight was a domestic one. Her night kit would reach the Transport Department, where she could pick it up on arrival. Left with no choice, she took her flight bag and entered the cockpit of the other aircraft, which was ready to leave as soon as she sat down. The commander, who had already prepared the flight, announced the closing of the doors as soon as she stepped into the cockpit. She asked the ATC for permission for start-up and soon they were taxiing to the runway for departure. They reached Nagpur, and the captain told her that she could fly the next sector. She prepared the flight accordingly. Start-up was taken and after engine start, the commander took permission for taxiing, and as they started to move, the senior-most cabin crew member's voice sounded on the intercom, informing the captain that there was a man with a gun. He was standing in the middle of the aisle and walking towards the cockpit. Crisply, she said, 'Captain, we have been hijacked.' The relaxed atmosphere in the cockpit changed. The captain asked Laxmi to stop the aircraft, and simultaneously locking the cockpit door, they slipped into action mode. They changed the squawk code to one indicating that the aircraft had been hijacked. Then they informed the ATC, and talking to the cabin crew, gave them instructions to keep the passengers calm. The ordeal went on for a few hours. The cabin crew were pressured by the hijackers and this was communicated to the cockpit by them.

The pressure kept building, until much later, when none seemed to be relenting, the ATC informed them that this was a mock drill and that they could now open the door and ask for start-up permission once again, after the real passengers boarded! Laxmi was tired and stressed and she could see that the commander too was annoyed. Mustering courage, she asked him, 'Why didn't you tell me that this was a mock drill?' She knew that commanders were to be informed about the drill schedule. In an irritated tone, he replied that he too had been pulled out for this flight and was not aware of the mock drill. They finally left Nagpur more than three hours late and reached Mumbai at midnight, exhausted. She learnt that day that the nature of this job demanded that one must always be prepared. In short, expect the most unexpected!

All pilots look forward to making the transition from co-pilot to commander, and this was true for Laxmi's batch as well. Their batch got command after seven to eight years of flying as co-pilots, so they were not only very eager but also felt entirely ready, having gathered a lot of flying experience by then. The training was not so much about flying itself, but more about making decisions for a safe flight, being prepared for any exigency, safety of the aircraft, its cabin, weather, and so on. The baton was handed to them and they had to keep all forces together for a safe flight; it was ultimately a lesson of humility that she learnt. The final upgrade from co-pilot to commander happened sometime around 2002.

Every commander has their share of experiences which teach them real-life lessons. Laxmi says that although she has seen many episodes of bad weather and passenger misbehaviour, one of her recent experiences on the latest aircraft that she is flying now is worth sharing. Having flown the Boeings (737) and then the Airbus (320), where she got her first command, she is currently flying the B-787.

According to Laxmi, this incident remains fresh in her mind because it has led her to think about the role of destiny in her life. The flight was from Delhi to a foreign destination. They departed from Delhi on time; it was a nice clear day and the flight was smooth and comfortable. All was going well, they were about an hour and fifteen minutes from the destination, and Laxmi was mentally planning what she would do once she reached the destination, when suddenly she saw a message on the aircraft display from the company saying, 'There is a bomb suspected on your aircraft, and the bomb explosion time given is...' It further stated 'FYI & NA' (For Your Information & Necessary Action). She stared at the message for some time, then looked at the co-pilot, who was also staring at the message. They saw that their landing time was about 7 minutes after the expected bomb explosion time as per the message. There was no time to waste. Capt. Laxmi sprang into action at once, instructing the co-pilot to pull out the 'Bomb on Board' checklist and briefing the senior-most cabin crew on the situation. She asked the cabin crew to try and locate any suspicious item on board, and inform her about it without touching it. Then, she contacted the destination approach stating, 'Pan, Pan, Pan', apprising them on the nature of the emergency. She increased the speed of the aircraft to the maximum permissible limit to reduce the time to landing, and took permission from the ATC to maintain high speed till landing. She asked for direct routing and a short vector for landing and prepared the cockpit and cabin for early descent. Due to her efforts, the landing time was advanced to a good 10 minutes before the time given for the bomb explosion. She informed the company that they would land 10 minutes before the expected explosion, and that they must in turn inform all concerned parties on the ground to assist with step ladders ready for all doors. The flight was full, there were elderly passengers, children and pregnant women, and Capt. Laxmi's priority was to ensure that everyone deplaned safely.

When they were in descent, she instructed the senior cabin crew that only on her command should she evacuate the passengers. When she was on final approach for about 6 miles, she made a passenger announcement stating that, on landing, everyone must follow the instructions from the cockpit or cabin properly. This was for their safety. She made this last-minute announcement because she knew there could be chaos and tension in the cabin, but by the time the passengers realised what kind of announcement it was, the aircraft was already touching down. Laxmi vacated the runway on the high-speed taxi track, where she could see the 'Follow Me' vehicle ready for them. She was suddenly asked by the ATC to shut the engines, which she did. She then asked the ATC for step ladders, but there were none that she could see. She kept asking for them, keeping a watch on time running out swiftly. She told herself, 'I landed a good 10 minutes ahead. There should be no mistake now, and passengers should be safely evacuated from the aircraft.' But when the step ladders did not reach within the few minutes, she announced for evacuation from all exits, as per laid-down procedure. The chutes were deployed and all passengers were evacuated. It was a stressful experience, but the entire crew performed their duties well, right from the efficient co-pilot to every member of the cabin crew. Thankfully, they were all out safe and away from the aircraft in the coaches heading towards the terminal. The crew was never informed about what happened with the bomb. The necessary security agents with dogs were deployed to search the aircraft. Although Capt. Laxmi was appreciated for bringing the aircraft down safely and getting the passengers out in time, she has a graphic memory of that crucial 1 hour and 15 minutes. The responsibility of ensuring the safety of all passengers and the pressure of the ticking clock through that last leg of the flight has stayed with her. That was no simulator; the stakes were very real. A good pilot understands what the profession requires; every minute here is different and valuable.

Today, Capt. Laxmi feels blessed about where she is. Having transformed from an air hostess to a commander, she is grateful for this magic! Flying the Boeings when she joined, moving on to the Airbus that she first commanded and now flying the 787s, she says it's the same feeling, the 36-year journey has been great and one of complete fulfilment. She admits that she owes a lot to Indian Airlines (now Air India) for having given her a life-changing opportunity. She believes that she owes the company everything – from her life partner, to who she is today. Thanks to this profession, she is calm and patient, has learned to be humble, and to respect the environment, especially weather. She says, 'I went from being no one to becoming someone who is very blessed today.' Flying the Dreamliner, she is still a dreamer. Being in the cockpit, 40,000 ft high, is what makes her life feel complete and magical. She can ask for nothing more, she says, for no money can buy what she has!

Capt. Laxmi is happy flying the Boeing 787 Dreamliner today

A photo taken right after Capt. Sapna G. Patel got her dream job as First Officer with Indian Airlines

From the flying school days at the Indira Gandhi Rashtriya Uran Akademi

Commanding an all-women flight on International Women's Day

Thirteen

Breaking the Shackles

Sapna G. Patel

As she steadily notches up power for take-off, she feels a sense of freedom, peace and calm. She is pleased to be exactly where she is – in the pilot's seat. People look for avenues to de-stress; for her, flying is the answer. The magnificent beauty she experiences in the cockpit is enough, there is no need to seek it anywhere else. Even after having flown for nearly thirty years, she remains in awe of the sunrises and sunsets she has the chance to witness. Capt. Sapna G. Patel is one of the few women pilots in India who made it to the cockpit in the early '90s. Born on 21 January 1969 to G. Patel and Hemlata Patel in a conservative Gujarati family in Gwalior, she was barely one year old when they moved to Mumbai in the quest for better opportunities.

She took her first flying lesson when she was only seventeen at the Baroda Flying Club in Gujarat. This experience changed her life! The exhilaration of being up in the air was enough to make her passionate about flying. She still remembers that day – 21 October 1986 – and the path that led her to this flying school.

She was studying commerce at Narsee Monjee College, Mumbai, but she did not like the subjects and would constantly gaze out of the class window. One day, she noticed a small yellow aircraft flying overhead (the college is located opposite Juhu Airport). Mesmerised by these little planes going up and down, she was determined to find out about them. She felt lucky on learning that one of her seniors in college frequently travelled to Baroda for flying lessons and decided to approach him to get more information on her newfound fascination. She was glad when he talked to her about flying and about how much he enjoyed practising it every day. Her interest piqued, she told her mother about this new field she had discovered. As luck would have it, she had relatives in Baroda, and her mother agreed to send her to her cousins' house there to try her hand at flying.

She still recalls her first experience in the flying club. 'I never realised that my first flight experience would give me such excitement that I would not stop talking about this and be poised to pursue flying professionally.' At first, her mother was not sure if this was a viable career option, but she agreed on condition that Sapna would continue going to college and earn her degree alongside attending flying school.

Being allowed to fly was enough to make her agree to everything else, and she joined the Baroda Flying Club sometime in late October 1986. She attended college during the week, boarded the train to Baroda from Mumbai every Friday night, took flying lessons on Saturday and Sunday morning, and caught the Sunday night train (general compartment) to Mumbai to be back at college on Monday. She stuck to this schedule for nearly nine months until she earned her Private Pilot Licence (PPL). It was exhausting, but her heart was set on her dreams. In fact, family and friends would question her mother for sending her seventeen-year-old daughter on a night train to Baroda, that too to learn flying. Flying was an unheard-of career at that time. Sapna narrates, 'My mother was as ambitious as I was, so she ignored these relatives and supported my dream of becoming a pilot.' Her mother's encouragement helped her complete her first phase of flying training when she got her PPL. Then came the big question: *What next*? She knew a PPL alone would get her nowhere; she needed to go on and get a Commercial Pilot Licence (CPL) to be able to enter the industry. Yet, she had no idea how to go about it. Sapna remembers, 'When I was about to finish my PPL training, my mother decided to visit me in the flying club. This worked out rather well for me.' Her mother met her instructor, Capt. Mistry, who told her that a PPL would not take her daughter very far, that she would have to continue flying and get a CPL in order to get a job. He also told her that there was a new academy in Raebareli district of Uttar Pradesh, the Indira Gandhi Rashtriya Uran Akademi (IGRUA), which admitted girls. The entrance exam for the academy was scheduled to be held the following month, and Capt. Mistry suggested that Sapna take the exam. He promised to make sure she completed all the training requirements so that she would not miss the exam. Once that was done, to ensure Sapna's licence was issued on time, her mother decided to accompany her to Delhi. They took the train to Delhi to personally submit the papers to get the PPL. Everything seemed to be falling into place. On her part, she made no mistakes and cleared the IGRUA entrance written test, which took her a step closer towards her dream.

But at the final interview before selection, she saw that several candidates were from pilots' families. She got a bit worried but decided she would do her best, then leave the rest to destiny to determine her fate. She walked into the room with her head held high. There were six interviewers on the panel and all eyes were on her. Here was this petite eighteen-year-old, who could hardly be associated with flying. The first question they asked her was, 'Do you know how an aircraft flies?' She was handed a paper to draw and explain her answer. She promptly drew the four forces of flight – thrust, drag, lift and weight – elaborating on how these forces help an aircraft fly. When she finished, they simply said, 'You may go now.' She was taken aback, as she knew everyone before her had spent nearly 10–15 minutes in the interview room. If she left at that point, she would likely miss her only chance to fly professionally, so she decided to at least speak up. And the next thing she knew, she was saying, 'Sir, I want to ask all of you something: is this one question going to decide my entire life? I have journeyed through a curfew-hit area, travelled in an unreserved compartment, and stood in a queue all day in the DGCA along with my mother, a single parent, to get my licence, and you want to judge me based on my response to just one question? How can you justify making a decision based on one question?' She said this without a thought about the impact it might have. The panellists were shocked, and there was total silence for a while. Then, one of the judges asked her to sit down, and to her surprise, her interview went on for nearly 30 minutes more! They asked her many questions and she was able to answer about 75 per cent of them. When the results were declared, she was thrilled that she had been selected alongside another girl (Rachna Suri). She had been anxious after the interview. *Had she said too much? Would it ruin her chances at selection*? But Capt. Sapna firmly believes that her courage and spirit got her to where she is today. She was selected to be part of the third batch at the IGRUA; they were 25 students in all (including 2 girls) and their course started in August 1987.

Moving from Mumbai and Baroda to Fursatganj, where the academy was located, was a complete change. There was nothing to do in Fursatganj except fly, attend ground classes and study. Women were a minority; there were about 40 boys and 4 girls at that time. There was far greater pressure on the girls to prove themselves; even if they were above average, they would be considered average. In those days, the academy was biased towards boys, and girls struggled to gain recognition. But all the hard work paid off when Sapna finished her flying, earned her CPL, and was inducted into Indian Airlines.

Talking about the academy being in a remote location, she felt it helped her to become independent and tough, preparing her for any challenge. According to her, there can be no doubt that it is a wonderful academy for people who are serious about this profession. Till today, she is grateful to former Prime Minister Mr Rajiv Gandhi for conceptualising this institute. If it weren't for him, the IGRUA wouldn't exist.

In late 1989, Capt. Sapna joined Batch No. 44 in Indian Airlines. She felt like the whole world had opened up; she had progressed from flying a Pushpak to a Cessna, to finally becoming a trainee pilot to fly the B-737. She confesses that she had never thought she would ever fly such a big aircraft. Even during her flying school days, whenever she saw a Boeing land at Baroda Airport, she had never imagined she would be sitting in its cockpit in just a few years' time. She had started flying in 1986; it was now 1991. One of her favourite memories is sitting in the cockpit of a Boeing 737, preparing to be released as a First Officer. It was the happiest moment of her life, and she has only gone from strength to strength ever since!

As the airline was phasing out Boeings, she moved to the

A-320. This created an opportunity for her to be trained on the new 'fly-by-wire' technology. They finished their training and got their endorsement by 1994. In December 2003, she qualified for command training on the A-320.

This was yet another experience that presented unique difficulties for her as a woman. In her words, 'I had just returned to flying after my daughter Afrah was born, which was in March 2002. The training got even more tough; balancing family needs and training was very challenging. Honestly, men in aviation do not realise what women have to go through, especially when they have a family. Men also have families, but they are not grounded for nearly a year when they have children, which is true for us women. And once we report back, we require medical clearance, without which we cannot start training. We need to get our weight in check to meet the airline's fitness requirements. Then, we need to go through the entire training procedure, including ground classes, the extended refresher course, full simulator training, and CA40 checks. Men don't have to go through any breaks of this kind! First, you are grounded for a year and, then, it takes nearly another year to return to the cockpit. The stressful training, long hours, and challenges of handling a small child are difficult to mediate. But we have managed and have proved that we can and we will. Most of us were promoted to command after having our babies, and none of us have quit for this reason. It just shows we keep our chin up and slog to get back where we belong – the cockpit!'

All pilots dream of commanding their own flight from the time they start flying. In a way, commanding an aircraft is the real solo flight! Commanding an A-320 or any jet aircraft comes with a lot of responsibility. The safety of the passengers, the entire crew, the aircraft and the image of the airlines – all of it depends on the commander. In flying school, you are only responsible for yourself. In a much bigger aircraft, the passengers literally trust the pilot with their lives. The sheer weight of that responsibility ensures that every pilot puts in 100 per cent on every flight. Everything else takes a backseat when commanding a flight. They may miss important family moments, especially with their children, when they are in the air, because unlike in a desk job, they cannot get in touch with them till they are back on the ground. However, all that hard work adds up when your family feels proud of you and then everything is forgotten – the stress, the difficult moments, the sacrifice of family time.

Every captain, male or female, has faced challenges that have made them tougher as pilots. Capt. Sapna too has had her share. She recounts one such experience. 'One of the challenges of flying is that you have to handle the interference of those who have little or no knowledge of this profession, which can be very demanding. I recall, some two to three years ago, at the peak of the monsoon season, I had to command a flight from Hyderabad to Delhi. The flight was full of parliamentarians, even a minister. At Delhi, we encountered a severe thunderstorm with strong winds that were constantly changing in intensity and direction. I was preparing to land. The ATC was constantly updating me about the weather, and I continued my approach. The winds became gusty when I was just a few miles from touchdown, and I had to do a go-around. By the time I climbed to a safe altitude in the go-around procedure, the runway was also changed due to the winds. I started my second approach, and informed the passengers (but the cabin crew later told me the passenger address system was not working properly) and despite some difficult handling, I made a safe landing. I heard later that a parliamentarian had filed a complaint through the ministry, writing, "There was an engine fault, the captain went down first, then went up. The engine sound changed, but no announcement was made about this. Then, the captain came back and landed on a different side of the runway." I was sent this complaint and was asked to explain myself. I was angry with my operational department for indulging the complaint, but I gave my reply to them in the form of two weather bulletins for that day. They realised how bad the weather had been, and I was not called for further explaining. In fact, I think they (the parliamentarian) should have appreciated that the flight landed safely, seeing how the weather was wreaking havoc. This is really an unfortunate situation that many of us have experienced in some form; people sitting in the cabin only want to complain rather than appreciate a safe flight!'

Another major issue in our country, Capt. Sapna opines, is the 'VIP culture'. Once, in early January, they had landed in Tirupati and were told to expedite their departure to Hyderabad as the prime minister was expected to arrive that day. Once the PM's aircraft landed, the runway would be closed for operation till he left. A science exhibition was to be held, for which some 200 scientists had already arrived in the city. Capt. Sapna and her crew expedited their departure and were ready for take-off when the PM's aircraft was in the vicinity of the field. After they took off, the PM's aircraft landed. But after take-off, they encountered a snag – the landing gear (wheels of the aircraft) was not going up. Capt. Sapna informed the ATC about the nature of the emergency and requested permission to return. To this, the ATC replied, 'Due to VIP movement, the runway is closed, you can go to Chennai.' She informed the ATC that since they were hardly any distance away from Tirupati and as per the checklist and company policy, she would have to request permission to land there. Moreover, with the gear (wheels) hanging down, they could not divert elsewhere since the fuel consumption increases by 180 per cent with the landing gear down. But even after this, they were not given permission to return. It seemed absurd that they were hanging in the air facing an emergency, and instead of getting support to bring the aircraft down safely, Capt. Sapna was having to argue for permission to land. Given the circumstances, she took a stand and firmly informed the ATC of their decision to return and to make the runway available for them, ignoring the VIP closure. The controller probably realised the gravity of the situation and finally conceded. They landed safely, but chaos unfolded soon after; commandos surrounded the aircraft, and when the aircraft door opened, engineers and the airport manager entered the cockpit and begged Capt. Sapna to somehow take the flight to Hyderabad. She remained calm and simply picked up the defect report book and noted down the snag. She handed over the book to the engineer and told them that they would talk once the snag had been rectified. It took more than an hour to rectify it, but the engineer was unwilling to certify that the flight was fit to fly, as it had to be checked on a test flight. To her disbelief, they requested her to carry out the test flight, so that the flight could be certified and subsequently leave the airport. That particular day, she had already flown from Hyderabad to Delhi in the morning, landed making the CAT-3 approach (fog condition) in Delhi, returned to Hyderabad in gusty weather, flown to Tirupati, and then had to return after take-off due to a fault. If she did a test flight, it would be her fifth landing of the day! But instead of understanding her predicament, they continued to request her to do it, saying that since the VIP aircraft was parked in the airport, no other aircraft could be permitted to be parked there. After much thought, she told them that she would do a test flight only if the DGCA gave permission. So, special permission was obtained from the DGCA to do the test flight. The passengers were offloaded into a coach with the cabin crew, and Capt. Sapna and her co-pilot took off. They performed the check list to check if the landing gear operation was normal by moving the lever up and down a few times. Satisfied, they returned, and the passengers were reboarded. After requesting the DGCA for extension of Flight Duty Time Limitation (FDTL), Capt. Sapna and her co-pilot operated the last leg of the flight, landing safely in Hyderabad. She claims that this remains one of her most tiring and stressful flights to this day, all because of the VIP closure. But the most rewarding outcome of her efforts was the appreciation expressed by passengers after the flight as also later on the Air India website. Passengers kept sending her their thanks and appreciation, which was heart-warming. Even the then CMD Mr Ashwini Lohani passed on a word of appreciation through the Tirupati staff. But she still wishes the company had given her an appreciation letter for that extraordinary day.

Later on, she was promoted from her role of Instructor to Examiner, after having undergone a complete upgradation course and checks. This is the ultimate dream for any pilot. Today, she is the second woman examiner on the A-320 in Air India.

The number of women pilots in India has gone up and they are better accepted today, but they still face many ups and downs. According to Capt. Sapna, regardless of the challenges, it gives her immense joy and pleasure to do her job which keeps her so close to nature and closer still to spirituality. She describes flying as a world of adventure and mystery, where each day is different, each sunrise and sunset feels special, where clouds and rainbows still enchant her, where one is constantly learning something new. The greatest satisfaction of her life is seeing people look on in awe wherever she goes, especially when they learn that she has been flying for more than twenty-nine years. She feels humble and at the same time proud of who she is!

Being in a profession that makes her feel relaxed, Capt. Sapna is always ready with a smile and at ease, for any flight, any time.

Capt. Nequita Reynolds, ready to fly the Airbus 320

Nothing brings her more joy than flying aircraft

Fourteen

Masterstroke: Sisters of Cockpit and Cabin

Nequita Reynolds Gupta

Two sisters, one an airhostess and the other a pilot, worked in the same airline for the first time when Nequita Reynolds Gupta joined Indian Airlines (sometime in late 1989), where her older sister Noleta Reynolds Athayde was already employed as an airhostess. They came to be known as the 'First Sisters' in the same airline, one in the cabin and the other in the cockpit, both operating from Mumbai. Nequita says with a smile, 'Captains knew her and me differently. Her friends had to formally greet me in the cockpit, as was the protocol, while at home they would treat me like a little sister. In the aircraft, they had to address me as Ma'am or Captain. But we both accepted this as part of our lives as professionals, and so did our family. They would see one of us getting ready in the pilot's uniform and the other in the cabin crew uniform and that was fun!'

Nequita grew up in a house where everything around her was taken apart and put back together, from sewing machines to cars. Being the youngest among four brothers and a sister, she would act as their helper, fetching screwdrivers or anything else they needed. Her father and brothers believed that learning was best done by opening up and examining things. She too learned to understand systems by breaking them down into their physical components. So, it was natural for her to take an interest in machines from a very young age.

She was born on 10 November in Mumbai, where she has lived all her life. Her father, an aeronautical engineer, was an aircraft maintenance engineer with Indian Airlines. As a child, they would often travel by the airline together. Whenever they entered an aircraft, she would peep into the cockpit and would be invited in by captains who knew her father well. The cockpit always fascinated her. She says, 'I was thrilled every time I visited captains in the cockpit, and even as a kid, I thought this would be the profession I would love to pursue. I would often ask my father if I could be one of them, pointing to the pilots, and fly these machines.' Knowing the cost of embarking on this path, Nequita's father did not encourage her much, but he did not discourage her either. He was the only working member of their family at that time, and she understood his concerns. So, leaving behind this dream, she began to explore other career choices. She had a Plan B ready. She wanted to join college and become either a chartered accountant or a lawyer. Yet, the idea of becoming a pilot occupied her mind all the time.

She still recollects the time of her Higher Secondary School exams. She was preoccupied, mulling over what to do next. But things changed overnight. They lost their father all of a sudden, and it came as a big shock for the entire family. Her mother along with her siblings took charge of the family. As Nequita was the youngest, they didn't want her to feel that their father's loss would hamper her dreams. So, one day, her youngest brother, who was very close to her, asked her, 'Do you want to become a pilot?' It was precisely the motivation she needed to carry on and she jumped at the opportunity, not knowing how he was going to manage the cost of her training. She could only promise him hard work and dedication. Although, in the late '80s, nobody knew what the future of women in this field would be, deep down Nequita knew that focus, dedication and hard work would lead her to the cockpit just as she had dreamt!

Her sister, who was already working with Indian Airlines, had mentioned that there were a few women flying as captains. Encouraged by this, Nequita's brother decided to let her try her luck in this field. He knew it would not be easy, but she could at least make an attempt. The very next day, he decided to visit the Juhu Flying Club in Mumbai to find out how to become a pilot. Today, it is easy to get this information online, but in those days, one had to physically visit a flying school. He did the spade work and gathered all the information available, so that Nequita would not face any hurdles in starting her flying. The first thing he got her to do was clear the medical round as required for flying (second class medical) and informed her about getting the Student Pilot Licence (SPL) for her to start flying. She prepared herself, got her SPL, and joined the Juhu Flying Club.

There were very few women at the flying school and they were not taken seriously. She was disappointed but not affected by this. She learnt about the DGCA exams and took classes for these written exams, while preparing simultaneously for the RT (Radio Telephony) exam. The Chief Flying Instructor (CFI) at that time promised the students that whoever cleared the exams could start their flying. Nequita managed to clear all the exams, but the CFI did not keep his word. She was very upset and spoke to her brother about it. He had given some engineering exams in the USA and knew of a flying school where she could complete her flying to get a Commercial Pilot Licence (CPL). She also knew many students from the flying club were going abroad to finish their flying. She was delighted when her brother got all the paperwork done for her to enrol with a flying school in the USA.

As she had cleared her papers in India for converting the American CPL to an Indian one, now her target was to finish her flying lessons and get the CPL at the earliest. She knew she would be ready to apply for a job in Indian Airlines on her return. To her dismay, the first school she joined in the USA was very slow and wasted a lot of her time. She decided to change schools, found out about the Skywings Flight Training Academy in Dallas–Fort Worth, Meacham Field Airport, and signed up there in mid-1988.

The flying club in USA was totally different from the Indian one. There were facilities that were unheard of in India. The schools were well-equipped with a number of aircraft and instructors. There was no restriction on flying hours or runway closures; you had to perform to have your lessons sped up. The target was to progress to solo flights so that you could log in hours quicker. Despite all these positives, Nequita noticed there were hardly any local women who wished to pursue this profession and join a commercial airline. While she did not see any American women, she met another Indian woman from small-town Bhopal, who had mostly finished her training when Nequita joined. But they met briefly and Nequita learned that she too was there to finish her training faster and was hoping to work with Indian Airlines, the only airline hiring women as pilots in India.

Nequita did not let anything bother her; she was happy to be able to fly regularly, which helped her finish much earlier than she would have managed in India. Of course, she had to work hard and clear the exams. Keen on completing the course at the earliest, she concentrated on her training and rested only after getting her CPL.

In those days, Indian Airlines needed pilots, and new pilots were inducted nearly every 3 to 4 months. Missing those slots would have closed the option of joining the commercial airline. Indian Airlines was the only domestic airline in the country at that time; it was also the only airline that gave women the chance to be a part of the cockpit and fly shoulder-to-shoulder with male colleagues. Among Air India, Indian Airlines and Vayudoot, Indian Airlines was the most preferred choice for women. During this period, there were talks that Air India was planning to induct their first female pilot. This was around late 1989–90. On the other hand, since 1980, nearly every year, one girl had been inducted into Indian Airlines, and there were nearly 10 to 11 women pilots flying with the airline. They had been accepted and had proved themselves in the cockpit.

When Nequita returned from the USA with her CPL, coincidentally, an advertisement by Indian Airlines for trainee pilots was published in the newspaper just a few days after. Her older sister, Noleta, was working in Indian Airlines as an air hostess. She was happy that Nequita was applying as a pilot. People were gossiping, but they both knew that their families were happy and open to the fact that they may both work in the same airline, one as a pilot and the other as an air hostess. Everyone knew what these jobs were like. The sisters had distinctive personalities and both enjoyed their respective work, neither wanting to switch from what they were doing. Nequita got selected after the written exam, group discussion and interview. Her entire family was overjoyed when the telegram arrived, informing her about her selection as a trainee pilot in Indian Airlines.

Selected in Batch No. 45, she reached the training centre in Hyderabad sometime in late 1989. They were 29 recruits in all, of which, as was the trend those days, Nequita was the only girl. The trainees were so excited about being part of the airline and being inducted into training for the Boeing 737. They knew that the endorsement usually took about a year, but as the airline had inducted many batches at short intervals, their training took more than two years. That did not bother them though, because they knew they would finally become First Officers and fly a big jet! Their batch was released as First Officers on the B-737 in 1992.

Capt. Nequita recalls the training period. 'When I started my training on the B-737, I faced strange comments from a few senior commanders.' As she was slim, small-built and not very tall, these captains would bluntly tell her that she would not be able to fly the Boeing 737 and handle all emergencies such as single-engine, hydraulic, etc. She would listen calmly and say to herself, 'The airline has inducted me. They must have seen my height and how I look. Then why do these people, senior captains, only think and talk negatively?' When she started her simulator training after completing the Boeing technical DGCA papers, she picked up the courage to talk to her instructor about it. To this day, she remembers how he looked at her, smiled and said, 'Pay no attention to these idiots, they don't know how to fly this aircraft. Don't worry, you'll do well as you don't need brawn to fly these jets, you just need brains.' For Capt. Nequita, these words of encouragement coming from her instructor at the start of her career were greatly comforting and reassuring. Of course, from then on, it only got better. She had the same training as the others; there were no special or extra benefits given to women. She and her simulator partner faced the same emergencies, be it hydraulic, single-engine or electrical failure, and they had to perform to clear their checks. She was trained and released as First Officer on 31 March 1992. She relives the feeling of sitting as a co-pilot on a B-737 and can still visualise that day!

As there were only a few women pilots those days, they were noticed and scrutinised. While the men got away with being average, women had to be above average to be accepted. Nevertheless, these fearless women survived, performed, and proved their value several times over. She thinks this survival instinct of theirs, to do what it takes, is what has resulted in their acceptance among colleagues over the years. They have witnessed the change in the cockpit and in their attitude towards 'the women pilots'.

Capt. Nequita's batch barely had 500 hours on the B-737 when they were moved from the Boeing to the A-300, a wide-body aircraft, given a tremendous shortage of co-pilots on the A-300. Here, again, there were some captains who told Capt. Nequita that she would not be able to handle the A-300. She would just listen, smile and attend her training, remembering the words of her first Boeing instructor. She loved flying this aircraft as much she did the Boeing, and she flew the A-300 for years. Later, their batch was moved to the A-320 (as Boeings were phased out), and they eventually earned their commander position on the A-320, which she flies till today as a commander.

The transition from co-pilot to captain happened in late 2002–03. Recollecting the years as co-pilot, she recounts that they were much more relaxed and happy-go-lucky, and everything seemed to happen without much hassle. But being in command is a bigger challenge; you are the sole person in charge of the entire aircraft, be it cabin or cockpit. Capt. Nequita realised how a captain's thinking changes in this situation – they cannot take anything lightly and must inspect every detail themselves. It's their flight and their responsibility to ensure a safe flight from Point A to Point B. No matter how good the staff is or how good a friend the engineer is, one cannot take anything for granted. As she puts it, 'The buck stops with us, and we are the ones the passengers have placed their trust in; it is our duty to make sure the flight is safe, smooth and comfortable.' Captains have to be authoritative when the need arises and draw a line between personal and professional relationships. Another thing being in command teaches you is that learning in this profession never stops; in fact, learning from others' experiences is also important, as no book can teach you everything. These experiences not only teach you how to handle difficult situations but prepare you to accept them. Capt. Nequita's close friend and colleague from the airline went through an accident early in her career. After this, she remembers how they both sat down with the Boeing manuals and read every word in there, as, during the discussion with the fact-finding committee, the lawyers did not understand the technical aspects of flying and everything had to be explained to them clearly. Though Capt. Nequita did not go through the trauma of any accident, it was a learning experience for her; this learning has stayed with her till date.

Everyone, whether male or female, faces professional challenges and learns to take them in their stride. But one thing that men don't have to face as much as women do is challenges in handling family demands, especially with kids. Marriage becomes a tough part of a woman's professional life, and more so in this profession. When you are expecting a child, you are grounded and, after the birth of your child, it takes nearly a year for you to return to active flying. In the bargain, you give up endorsements, instructorship and, sometimes, even seniority in your batch. In a nutshell, your profession takes a backseat, whereas your male colleagues don't have to face any such setbacks.

Capt. Nequita got married to her batchmate, and although he knew the profession and its demands, she says that, after having children, it got tough for both of them. Even though the increased workload was a shared responsibility, she points out that children's demands and expectations from their mother is different from that of their father. They have four children, two of their own and two nieces (Noleta's daughters), as Noleta's husband had passed away in an accident and, after a few years, Noleta too had succumbed to a life-threatening disease. She had entrusted Capt. Nequita with the responsibility of taking care of her daughters and made her their legal guardian. The sisters shared a very strong bond and were very close to each other. Capt. Nequita loved her little nieces very much, so she and her husband were happy to bring them up as their own. Yet, bringing up four children was not easy. Balancing this became a veritable part of Capt. Nequita's life, and with everyone's support, she learned to manage this difficult phase. Today, they are all grown-up; her nieces are working, her son is in college, while her daughter is in high school. It is true that no women pilot has quit her job because of family duties, and Capt. Nequita says it has been a blessing that the airline understood their extra needs and gave them time accordingly.

Today, commanding the Airbus family aircraft – the 319s, 320s and 321s – Capt. Nequita finds immense satisfaction in her work. Having become a check pilot, she still puts in maximum effort to give her trainees the best. There are no shortcuts or leniency in the job. Work cannot be taken for granted, and a person who does not perform cannot be given clearance, be it male or female.

Pilots go through a range of experiences when airborne. They could be aircraft with snags, passengers who become unruly causing safety hazards, different weather scenarios. After flying for more than two decades, Capt. Nequita and her colleagues have realised that there has been a tremendous change in the environment, due to which they face greater weather hazards today. The storms, wind gusts and heavy rainfall they face reflect how we have neglected our environment. The weather today is becoming difficult to penetrate, which was very different from how it was in the past. Pilots are getting used to these phenomena, but Capt. Nequita says that it is definitely changing every year. She shared an interesting experience during one such weather-stricken flight that well describes how difficult the situation can become. This happened quite recently.

'We were entering Mumbai during the monsoon season. I had a co-pilot who was new, with barely a few hours of experience. We were approaching the airfield and the weather was getting bad. In some of our A-320s, we have some new wx radars fitted; on these radars, thunderstorms, lightning, etc., can be seen. The co-pilot was completely glued to the wx radar, which displayed severe weather around Mumbai. I kept telling him to give the standard call-outs and do the R/T (Radio Communication to the ATC), but he seemed lost looking at the radar picture and was barely responding to my calls.' She knew she had to make her approach, which she had already planned. She had also noted where she would be discontinuing and doing a go-around if required. But she needed her co-pilot to be mentally present in the cockpit and give his full attention. She knew she had to somehow make him relax. She saw that the selection on his side was for a longer range and was also very bright, so she told him to change the range and reduce the brightness. The moment he did that, he saw the wx within the range of their approach to the runway, relaxed, and immediately responded, 'The wx is not that bad.' She got his attention and told him to give her all the call-outs and maintain visuals with the field. As a training captain, Capt. Nequita understood the need to change her co-pilot's focus and the importance of understanding the psychology of a fresher who has had practically no experience in severe weather. It's not always a technical problem that a captain has to handle, but with every situation, one has to make their move quickly and correctly. They landed safely, and Capt. Nequita gave him a de-brief of what she did and why. It was a learning experience for him, and she feels that such experiences would help him handle a similar situation better the next time.

The learning curve never stops, especially in this profession. You have to be open to keep learning. The minute you think you are perfect, you could compromise on safety and actually be one step closer to disaster. Even today, Capt. Nequita feels that she learns every day, from the flights, her co-pilots, engineers, cabin crew, dispatchers, and even loaders. All of this has helped her evolve as a pilot and become a better person! Every experience serves as learning, and after parking the aircraft, she is grateful for what she learned that day. It is this love of learning and flying that gives her the confidence to face every challenge that she encounters, be it professional or personal. She believes there is no other job that can teach you so much. Her work continues to enrich her life; nothing can replace the joy of flying and witnessing the most incredible sunrises, sunsets, rainbows, and all the beauty of nature from high up in the sky. To sum up, she says, indeed this job is the most amazing thing she could have dreamt of doing. She feels truly blessed to be who she is – a pilot, flying like a bird; any other profession would be unthinkable for her!

Capt. Nequita (second from right) enjoying a relaxed moment with her mother, brothers and sister, Nolita (second from left).

Capt. Avantika Rastogi (R) during her co-pilot days on the Airbus 300, with Capt. Indraani Singh (L).

Capt. Avantika Rastogi being welcomed after successfully completing an all-women flight on International Women's Day

Different Flaps of the Wing (The Mid- to Late-1990s)

Fifteen

Making Her Hobby a Profession

Avantika Rastogi

Born on 19 August in the small town of Meerut, Avantika Rastogi wonders what inspired her to become who she is today – an airline pilot – as she comes from a family that consists primarily of doctors. In 1987, when she finished school, popular career options were medicine, engineering and, perhaps, teaching. Her parents, J.K. Mittal and Leela Mittal, were quite sure she would either appear for the All-India Pre-Medical Test (PMT) and go on to become a doctor, or become an engineer. But destiny had different plans for her, and being the youngest of the siblings, she chose otherwise. After the school exams in March, and before beginning college in July, she told her parents she wanted to do something unusual and exciting, something she had heard her classmates talk about. She was talking about the NCC Air Wing, where students learned to fly small planes. She wanted to venture into this arena but knew it would be difficult to convince her family, for such an adventurous activity would sound bizarre to them. Nevertheless, she managed to cajole them into allowing her to have a little fun during her holidays and experience flying as a hobby.

Little did Avantika know that one day she would be an airline pilot. She owes this to the two scholarships awarded to her by the Government of Uttar Pradesh, which led her to think that she was cut out for a career in aviation and also gave her parents the confidence to let her pursue it seriously.

Coming back to 1987, on finishing her schooling, Avantika and her parents went to the Delhi Flying Club. To her disappointment, she was informed that due to its proximity to the VIP area, flying was no longer permitted. It was a setback, but she was not ready to give up. In her words, 'I contacted several people, trying to find some way to fly. Finally, I met one Capt. Ajit Singh, a flying instructor from Lucknow, whose name I still remember even after all these years because meeting him is what led me to become who I am today. He told my parents about a good flying school in Lucknow, which many children from surrounding areas attended. As luck would have it, my mother is from UP, and we have several relatives in Lucknow whom we visited during our holidays. I persuaded my parents to take me to Lucknow since I was already on a holiday. At my maternal grandparents' home in Lucknow, I convinced my maternal uncle to help me find out more about the flying school. My family in Lucknow was very supportive; they were as excited as I was, if not more, because they had never been exposed to such adventures. Flying sounded totally new to them, and they wondered what it would be like. It might sound funny, but when we decided to visit the flying school, my entire family, comprising my uncles, aunts and cousins, accompanied my mother and me to the school because they also wanted to see what these small aircraft looked like and wondered if girls would be allowed to fly!'

When they reached Lucknow Airport, after they located the way to the Flying Training Centre, Avantika started to enquire about the enrolment and training procedure. She was handed two forms to fill out, and asked to pay ₹11. Imagine her utter delight when she was told that with this nominal payment of just ₹11, she had become a member of the flying club!

Soon, they met an instructor who, in addition to providing information on the school, assured them that girls too were taking flying lessons. He also told them about a government scholarship for flying. Not wasting any time, Avantika applied for it and considers herself lucky to have won this scholarship. Though it only subsidised her flying fee, it did provide an impetus for her parents to allow her to learn flying and later make it a full-fledged career. Leaving Avantika behind with her cousins, her mother returned to Meerut.

The very next day, Avantika went to the flying club and was assigned the instructor whom she had met. She observed that her flying would not be an everyday affair; there was a lot of waiting time given the number of students enrolled there. Moreover, being in the minority, girls were not given much encouragement or importance. She did finally manage to get her slot and started off. Narrating her first flight experience, to this day, her voice has the same passion in it. 'It felt like being out of this world, like a bird, I was looking down at the streets, houses, moving cars, all of which seemed like little toys.' Steadily, her skills improved as she picked up the art of flying; it felt amazing to control the Piper Cub, the small training aircraft in which she was learning, with her instructor's guidance of course. She was glad she was not in the classroom studying for the PMT and preparing to be a doctor. This was definitely far more exciting!

Avantika worked diligently and performed better each day. It certainly didn't seem like a hobby to her anymore; she was serious about learning more and honing her skills. In order to advance, she found out that if she cleared her written exams for the Private Pilot Licence (PPL), she would be flying every day without fail. So, she studied hard, took the required exams, and managed to clear them all.

Now, she was able to fly nearly every day, building hours and experience, eagerly waiting for her solo sortie. She remembers that day with a smile. 'I came to the school as usual and my instructor and I went for circuit and landing as per routine. I was imagining when my instructor would let me fly the little Piper Cub alone when, suddenly, after a few good sorties, he asked me, "Ready to go on your own?"' She looked at him, not knowing what to say. Even before she could reply, he opened his door and said, 'Go on and let yourself fly.' Till date, she recalls that moment when she asked the ATC for permission for circuit and landing, informing them about the solo flight and giving her name as the pilot in command. That day was a turning point. Flying soon became a passion, and she considered herself lucky to have the opportunity to soar through the skies like a bird!

On earning her PPL, she was both happy and sad. She did not want to give up flying, it was no longer just a hobby; she was already looking for opportunities that would allow her to continue flying. She learned that the government of Uttar Pradesh was offering more scholarships, including some for Commercial Pilot Licences (CPLs). Once again, she applied immediately. She also learnt that women were flying as pilots in Indian Airlines, and this reinforced her belief in her dream. She felt her parents may now understand and let her take up flying professionally after she tells them about the women pilots who were employed in the airline.

After writing the exam for the CPL scholarship, she informed her parents about the achievement of earning the PPL. Then she asked them if she could pursue flying as a career if she got a scholarship for further flying. At first, they were taken aback.

Her mother said, 'You were only trying this as a hobby. You need to study and earn a graduate degree.' Her parents were also concerned that she would not be able to find a job as a pilot. Naturally, they had many questions. After all, back in 1988, who had heard of women being employed as pilots? Meanwhile, Avantika won the CPL scholarship and found the confidence to convince her parents to let her chase her ultimate dream. It was difficult, but she persisted. Soon enough, they gave in, and although she continued training for the CPL in Lucknow, she also joined a BSc course in a college in Meerut, keeping the promise she had made to her parents.

She was more motivated now than before, when she started flying for her CPL. But to her misfortune, the flying at the club slowed down further. She had acquired the PPL around mid-1988, and had re-joined within a few months for flying towards getting a CPL, but instead of putting in more hours, she could barely manage one hour of flying in a week. She grew restless and worried about how long it would take her to finish her training to acquire the CPL and whether she would ever find a job afterwards. She also suspected that, sooner or later, her parents would lose patience and object. So, she scouted around for other options. She learned from some of the boys in the club that after obtaining their PPLs, they aimed to go abroad to train for the CPL. She began thinking along those lines, wondering whether her parents would agree to bear the costs involved. The cost of flying training was one thing, but whether they would agree to her travelling abroad was another question mark.

As she was also pursuing an undergraduate degree, she spent time shuttling between Lucknow and Meerut. At home in Meerut, one day, she mustered the courage to talk to her parents about going abroad to fly. There was a lot of resentment initially, but when she told them about many of her colleagues from the flying club doing the same, including girls, they decided to give it a thought.

Perking up, she started thinking and planning ahead, choosing to remain positive and anticipating being able to go abroad and pursue flying, which had become her first love now. She also knew that since they had cousins in the USA, her parents were likely to acquiesce.

Finally, in 1989, she left for the USA and landed at her cousin's place in Connecticut. A few weeks later, she started discussing her flying plans with her family there, and with their help and support, shortlisted a flying school in Harwinton. Her cousins saw how passionate she was about it, how she had made up her mind to work hard to finish the flying training required to get her CPL.

The very next day, she reached Harwinton Flying School to sign up. She felt a familiar excitement at seeing the small planes flying, similar to what she had felt back in Lucknow. It seemed like a dream come true! She hadn't been certain that she would be able to fly and thanked her stars for this new beginning and the opportunity to achieve her dream—the CPL.

In this small private school, she was overjoyed to see the new Cessnas; back in Lucknow, they still had the older Piper Cub. Since she had already logged about 70–80 hours, she worked towards flying solo as soon as possible, aware that after that, she would be able to fly nonstop and meet her training requirements at the earliest. She managed to clock the mandated hours and, armed with the CPL, returned to India more excited than before, ready for new opportunities.

Without any delay, she wrote the exams to convert her FAA CPL to an Indian one. Meanwhile, Indian Airlines advertised for recruitment of trainee pilots. Luckily, Avantika could clear the exams and convert her licence. After submitting her papers to the DGCA, she was allowed to apply for this vacancy; had she missed that slot, she probably would not be where she is today, because after that advertisement, there was a gap of nearly ten years before a new induction. (Although the airline did induct one internal batch and another from the Indira Gandhi Rashtriya Uran Akademi (IGRUA) at Fursatganj in Raebareli district of Uttar Pradesh, there were no advertisements for outside candidates.) She counts her blessings even today; surely she had been at the right place at the right time, and the rest is history.

Following the written entrance exam for the position at Indian Airlines, there was a group discussion followed by an interview for final selection. It was tough competition; there were about 300 candidates at the written exam of which only 30 had passed, and they knew only 25 would finally be selected. She was thrilled when she received the telegram instructing her to proceed to the Central Training Establishment (CTE) in Hyderabad, to join Batch No. 46 as a trainee pilot. Her batch was the first to include more than one girl; it consisted of 3 girls and 22 boys. One of the girls, Manjeet, was an internal candidate, who was moving from the position of cabin crew to trainee pilot; the other, Renu, was a senior captain's daughter, forming the first father-daughter pair to work in the same airline. Thanks to the performance, dedication and hard work of earlier women pilots, space for women in the industry was steadily expanding.

Avantika and her peers began training in December 1989. At the training centre, they realised there were many batches that had not yet completed their training. It was a college-like atmosphere, with so many of them inducted within a few months of each other. The training dragged on; preceding batches were yet to graduate, so they knew they would be in the training centre for a year or even more. They didn't mind because they knew they were already in the airline, and that was a big consolation. Their batch took nearly three years to complete the training before they were released as First Officers.

It was 1993 by the time they became First Officers on the B-737. 'It felt like a big achievement,' Capt. Avantika recounts.

'It gave us pride to be sitting in the cockpit and also instilled in us a new sense of responsibility. From Day One, we were told First Officers are considered second-in-command; and when the need arises, we should be able to act as leaders to take decisions. It marked the beginning to the learning process and we knew one day we will be commanding flights on our own!'

As co-pilots, she and her colleagues were learning about the jet aircraft, its different systems, the flaps, thrust reversers; hydraulics, etc. It all seemed new and not as simple as the Cessna that they had flown thus far. Each of them was trying to learn and improve their skills and acquire a better understanding of the duties required of them in the cockpit. They needed to put in a lot of effort to master everything, but they worked relentlessly and enjoyed every moment of the learning curve.

They had flown Boeings for barely a year or two when their batch was moved to other aircraft. Some went on to fly A-300s, and others A-320s. They were quite disappointed when just as they were beginning to feel comfortable flying the Boeings and were in the process of mastering it, they were moved to another aircraft. Moreover, their batch got split during training for these two aircraft. However, as the airline was slowly phasing out Boeings, they had no choice. Capt. Avantika first went for training on the A-300, a wide-bodied aircraft, a twin-engine jet airliner. There were a couple of innovations that made this plane special. The wide body and raised cabin floor meant it could carry passengers and cargo, allowing airlines to increase profitability. It could carry 270 passengers and was designed to serve the short to medium haul market. She was ready for learning on another new aircraft and channelled all her energy towards it. She soon got her endorsement and flew the A-300 as a co-pilot for years, enjoying the wide-body experience. Later, she was made to train on the A-320. The Airbus 320 had its own charms; it was the latest 'fly-by-wire' new technology aircraft, instead of having a central control column. It was a glass cockpit, the systems being controlled by dedicated computers. All flight controls were operated by electronic signals. It was a different challenge to be trained on these aircraft, but once she mastered the knack of flying them, there was no looking back. She loved flying the Airbuses as much as the Boeings. However, the real change in the flying experience and personality, the ultimate point of pride, unfolded when she began her command training, sometime around 2003–04.

Command made a world of difference. Commanding a flight is every pilot's dream – the pinnacle of satisfaction for all the hard work they put in from the time they take to the skies. Commanding a flight is not just about status or control, but comes with big responsibilities. One cannot be promoted to commander if they cannot handle the aircraft or perform emergency drills. However, as commander, a pilot becomes the sole authority, handling aircraft snags, unruly passengers, cabin crew, and other issues. A commander is also expected to handle everything with ease and calm. According to Capt. Avantika, the profession makes pilots calmer, as it teaches them how to negotiate various challenges while ensuring that flights are safe and comfortable.

Every flight presents a different situation. Sometimes, a commander has to resolve issues between the cockpit and the cabin, whereas at other times, they might have to deal with an older co-pilot with a bad attitude. In her words, 'It was something that I had to handle quite early in my command days, I was doing a flight with a co-pilot much older than me. He had not been promoted as a commander, so because he was older than me and still a co-pilot or because he was male, whatever the reason, he seemed unhappy to see me in the commander seat. He was not responding well to the cockpit preparation that I was discussing while still on the ground. I knew I needed a competent person who would be available in an emergency, so in a subtle manner, by changing my tone and with utter diplomacy, I started a conversation in a manner that would get him involved in the cockpit. I realised that, as a commander, you are responsible for creating a healthy atmosphere in the cockpit. But I experienced the real weight of my responsibility as a commander when I had to reject a take-off from Bangalore Airport. I can still recall that flight and that moment, even after so many years.

'I was at the take-off point at old Bangalore Airport. The flight was bound for Delhi, with a full load of passengers. We took the ATC's permission, entered the runway and, as I started the take-off roll, and opened the throttle (power) for take-off, the aircraft started to gather speed, crossing 100 knots. All operations were normal, the speed started building up, and we were now in a high-speed segment. Just then, I noticed a flock of birds to the left – not one or two, but about a dozen or so, headed right towards the engine, about to hit it. The aircraft was close to V1 (the speed beyond which rejecting the take-off is not permitted). As the co-pilot had not yet announced V1, and I knew that at that high speed every second would matter, I immediately took the decision to reject the take-off, loudly announcing 'Stop', and simultaneously took the action for stop/reject, following the SOP. It was a critical moment; later, I learned that three birds had hit the engine, and seven blades had been damaged. I stopped the aircraft on the runway using all possible braking mechanisms and then taxied the aircraft to the parking bay, even though I was anticipating a tyre burst due to the high-speed reject and was mentally preparing for an evacuation on the runway. Although the brake temperatures shot up and we got a high-temperature warning, there was no tyre burst; so I taxied to the bay and asked for the stepladder so that the passengers could disembark safely. I knew that the trauma of the high-speed reject must have shaken them already.'

She said she did exactly what they practise in the simulator on every licence renewal check. She can laugh about the incident today, but she alone knows what she really experienced in those few crucial seconds. She didn't even have the time to see how her co-pilot reacted. In fact, she realised the impact of her decision only much later; she also understood the importance of her training, the habitual use of checklists, and the shouting any pilot is given for not calling 'Stop' before a reject. It was her loud call to stop that alerted the co-pilot, who then was ready to carry out the seat-oriented checklist (SOP) that is followed in all emergencies. She was glad that the simulator training is tough, and that SOPs are taken seriously. Though she was unnerved, she set aside her own feelings for the moment; the safety of the aircraft and its passengers was her primary concern. That day, had she lost even two seconds, she would have had to get airborne, and since the engine had been damaged badly, it would have caught fire. In other words, she and her co-pilot had averted a major accident.

Another thing that helped that day, the absence of which could have caused some injury, was the possibility of taxiing to the bay. Even though Capt. Avantika was mentally prepared for a tyre burst, an evacuation on the runway would have been difficult, the passengers would have been frightened, and confusion and chaos would surely have followed, especially since passengers rarely follow safety instructions properly.

'As pilots,' she explains, 'we are taught to respond quickly in any eventuality, as every second counts. Flying teaches us to take split-second decisions. Every experience makes us confident and disciplined, and it teaches us to respect our work and follow checklists.'

Over the years, the number of female pilots has risen and they have come to be more widely accepted. However, people outside the aviation industry continue to disbelieve that women can fly as commanders. Capt. Avantika is still asked questions such as 'Are you the real pilot or someone who just helps?' Presumably because of her gender. Most people cannot digest the fact that she has commanded flights, as the 'main' pilot, for more than seventeen years. Others assume that she must have quit the job as she is married and has children. They have to be told that women don't simply quit because of marriage or children but choose instead to balance all aspects of their lives. Of course, family support goes a long way in dealing with this highly stressful job.

Today, Capt. Avantika is on deputation to the DGCA as Senior Flight Operation Inspector (SFOI), one of the few women in this position. Her role requires ensuring regulatory requirements are met by all schedule and non-schedule operators. Some other responsibilities of an SFOI encompass carrying out various inspections, including that of the cockpit, special operations, training facilities, and making sure training standards are maintained. They also carry out investigation of incidents and conduct oral viva for issuance of Airline Transport Pilot (ALTP) licences, and so on. She feels lucky to have moved here in 2014. It has helped change her perspective greatly, and has taught her more about aviation and how vast this field is. She feels, sitting in the cockpit, one does not always see the world outside; being in the DGCA has helped unlock new horizons for her.

For Capt. Avantika, as with many of her colleagues, the journey has been arduous but fruitful. She feels Indian Airlines has been an excellent place to work and is thankful to the airline for giving her this opportunity. She truly loves flying and feels it has made her a positive-minded soul, teaching her to accept all of life's challenges. Even after twenty-five years in the profession, whenever she sits in the cockpit to take off, she enjoys every moment of it and can talk endlessly about the beauty of flying. She feels quite strongly that this is a profession one has to be in for the love of flying.

For Capt. Avantika, what started as a hobby, turned into a profession that she loves.

Sonica Verma (third from right) at the flying academy with her colleagues

Capt. Sonica Verma's solo sortie experience – joyful and thrilling.

Sixteen

Entering the Open Skies

Sonica Verma

In 1992, Indian aviation touched a new milestone. The government's Open Sky Policy was the springboard for the setting up of new airlines in India. She recalls that East West Airlines was one of the first, and since she lived in Mumbai, she went to their office to apply for a job. The immediate reaction of the staff was to direct her to the person in charge of cabin crew recruitment. When she told them she was there to apply for the position of pilot, they were perplexed. After much persuasion, they permitted her to submit her application. At the interview, she was asked only personal questions and nothing regarding her qualifications or skills. She could not believe it when they said, 'We cannot hire you because we are too new an airline to hire women pilots and we don't know how the fliers will react.' She was disappointed at being rejected on grounds of gender, but in a way, she was also relieved that she did not have to work with people of that mindset. With patience, perseverance and some good luck, doors finally opened for her when she saw the advertisement for another new airline – Jet Airways.

In contrast, the interviewers here were very fair and professional. They grilled her on technical and operational knowledge. Not one allusion to gender was made.

In May 1993, Jet Airways took to the skies, and in its very first batch of pilots was one woman – Capt. Sonica Verma Chhabra. The only girl in the group of thirty-two pilots who joined Jet Airways in December 1992, when the airline was incorporated. And thus, she became the first woman pilot in a private airline in India.

Born on 24 March in Chandigarh, to Capt. Ashok Verma and Nirmal Verma, she grew up in Mumbai. Her father, an ex-Air Force pilot, had retired from the armed forces to join Air India. Sonica grew up in an Air India society, surrounded by pilots, engineers, navigators and flight attendants. She was the second of three children, with an older sister and a younger brother. In fact, it was her brother who, from a very early age, would constantly talk about becoming a pilot, but destiny had different plans for him. Sonica, on the other hand, had never thought of becoming a pilot and believes it happened by sheer accident. Being a tomboy, she spent most of her time with the boys in her building, most of them sons of pilots who would often talk about aircraft and flying. She would listen with avid interest and then do her own research to verify what they said. She recalls, 'My friends were mostly boys, pilots' sons, and they always talked about aircraft and flying techniques. I would listen to them and later ask my dad if what they were saying was correct, as in, did he use flaps for take-off and landing, and many such questions relating to flying. He was confused as to why I was asking, but he always sat down and answered all my questions patiently.'

After her schooling at Jamnabai Narsee School, Sonica joined Narsee Monjee College in Mumbai. She was enrolled in the commerce programme but found her classes very boring. It was at this time that one of her classmates, who was her neighbour, began his flight training at the Baroda Flying Club. Whenever he was in Mumbai, he would go over to her house to catch up on the classes he had missed in college. After helping him with studies, she would ask him about his adventures at the club. His stories enthralled her, and that's when her interest in flying took seed. Day and night, she would think only about flying, so she decided to speak to her father for permission to give it a shot herself.

Picking up guts one day, she told her father about her interest. She had a slight eye power number and wore spectacles. She knew that perfect eyesight was a mandatory requirement for a commercial pilot, so she settled for flying as a hobby. But hobby flying was just not possible in India as it was too expensive and there weren't enough flying clubs around.

Sonica began exploring options to see where she could fly. America looked like a good alternative; many of her friends had gone there, particularly to Texas, to learn the skill. As it happened, Capt. Verma went for his regular medical check-up to New Delhi. He mentioned to the eye specialist that his daughter was showing a lot of interest in flying. Unfortunately, one needed perfect eyesight to pursue it, and she wore spectacles. That's when the doctor told him that the rules had changed and one could now become a commercial pilot as long as the number was within the range of plus/minus 3 and correctable to 6/6.

Capt. Verma came home and gave Sonica this news. Ecstatic, she applied for and cleared her medical exam at the Air Force Central Medical Establishment (AFCME), New Delhi. A decision was taken to go to the US in the summer holidays and learn the basics of flying, to see whether it was all that she had imagined it to be. She quickly got down to gathering information about the flight school options and settled on Hal Aviation in Malden, Missouri.

Sonica still remembers her first day when, in May 1988, accompanied by her father, she reached the flying school. The Cessnas looked so different from the big aeroplanes she was used to seeing, the ones her father flew. It made her even more gung-ho about what she was there to do – actually fly these planes! Her father enrolled her at the school, and the very next day, ground classes began. A few days later, she sat for the exam and passed. Now she was all set to start flying.

The instructor took her to the hangar, to the aircraft they were to fly. He explained everything about the aeroplane, from the engine and propellers to the inside of the cockpit, the flight controls and the instrument panel.

Next, they refuelled the aircraft. Then Sonica had to take the weather by making a phone call to the Weather Station. They did not have an ATC at Malden but used a Unicom frequency instead. This is a non-government communication facility which may provide airport information at certain airports. Locations and frequencies of Unicom are normally shown on aeronautical charts and publications. She had to hear it a few times as the words and accent were new.

Once ready, they started taxiing towards the runway. The movement of the little Cessna felt strange to her. She tried to keep calm and enjoy her first experience, but she was too excited! Soon they were rolling, and within seconds, they were airborne. That feeling of elation has stayed with her forever after. Her father eagerly awaited her return. When he asked her about her experience, she had only one word to say: 'Magical!' She knew then that this was what she wanted to do. Being a pilot, he understood how she felt. Probably remembering his own early flying days, he smiled and nodded.

Her lessons began. She revelled in not only the flying but also the sense of freedom it gave her. Only a flyer can really understand the freedom of flying. The greatest joy lies in flying all by yourself. Sonica too waited eagerly for her first solo flight. The day is so fresh in her mind even now. After a few circuit-landings, her instructor got off the aircraft and said to her, 'You're ready. Go on, fly your solo.' It was most unexpected and that moment has stayed with her ever since. She felt a sense of thrilling disbelief having to handle the aircraft by herself. Still, with ease and full confidence, she carried out her first solo, wholly certain that this is what she wanted to do for the rest of her life. She thoroughly looked forward to her flying lessons and solo flights. Flying was a fantastic thing, and she learnt many skills and techniques. There were new experiences every day, new mistakes made and new lessons learnt, all part of the joy of flying!

One truly memorable experience Capt. Sonica cherishes from her ab initio days was the time she went solo to practise her manoeuvres, a few days before her Private Pilot check-ride. She set course in her Cessna towards the eastern sector for her practice. While practising, she heard the school authorities call all aircraft back to the airfield. She wondered why but acknowledged it and turned her plane back towards the airport. She could see nothing but grey clouds engulfing her little plane as it started bobbing about. She was suddenly in bad weather – a frontal thunderstorm had come in quite unexpectedly and nothing was visible. She thought to herself, 'No problem, I'll just follow my instruments and reach the airport.' But her instruments were showing her a different direction from the one they should have been in. She got a little confused momentarily but decided to follow her compass nevertheless and started tracking to the station. In the meantime, she could hear her instructor repeatedly call out her aircraft's call sign. She answered that she had heard him and was returning. But he didn't stop calling. That's when it struck her that they could not hear her! She had a transmitter failure. He probably realised it at the same time as he asked her to click her PTT (Push To Talk switch) once for a yes and twice for a no. It was a quick fix alternate way of communicating, and it worked! He asked, 'Did you hear my instructions?' One click. 'Are you returning to base?' One click again. 'Do you know your position?' A delayed click.

So while navigating and manually flying her little plane, getting thrown around because of the thunderstorm, Sonica had to communicate in this most unconventional manner. Putting all her training to test by first following her instruments, she followed the local lost procedure, which was to fly low near the water tower of the nearest town and read its name. As she broke clouds, she came close enough to the water tank to read: M-A-L-D-E-N! How could that be? Malden had a water tank near the airport, and she was surely not in the vicinity of the airport. She noticed a railway line, which was not there between the eastern sector and the flight school. Instead, she remembered crossing one while driving south of the airport a few weeks ago and, yes, she had seen a water tank there as well! And she realised that, due to the strong winds, she had probably drifted away and was south of the airport. Even her compass, which was telling her to fly northwest, made sense. She flew back confidently and sure enough, she saw the airfield right in front of her. It was around 11 a.m., yet dark as night. The school had put on all the runway lights and cleared her to land on any of the five runways she preferred. She came in and made a perfectly smooth landing despite the strong, gusty winds. Taxiing into the apron, she saw all her colleagues standing in front of the school building, watching her anxiously. She parked the plane and walked into the building to a hero's welcome! She had not realised the seriousness of the situation, which was evident from the relief on everyone's faces now that she had landed safely. She had stayed calm and simply concentrated on flying her plane back to the airport.

After finishing her PPL, Sonica wished to continue her flying lessons in the US to obtain her Commercial Pilot Licence (CPL), but her father suggested that she return to India and apply to the Indira Gandhi Rashtriya Uran Akademi (IGRUA) at Fursatganj in Raebareli district of Uttar Pradesh, if she wanted to take up flying as a profession. Even though she wanted to stay on, she felt her parents had been incredibly supportive and this was the least she could do in return. She needed to log additional hours since the requirement for admission to the IGRUA was a Private Pilot Licence (PPL) with 30 hours solo. She had flown 15 hours solo as per American requirements. One of her friends who was flying with her also faced the same requirement. They rented a four-seater plane, a Piper Cherokee, for a week and planned a long cross country, almost along the length of the continent. They spent quite some time planning it, meticulously taking all the necessary clearances and permissions. Two friends went along as passengers. The day Sonica cleared her Private Pilot's check-ride, they set course.

They flew from Malden to Meigs Airport, Chicago, making a couple of refuelling stops on the way. They were in Chicago on 4 July and celebrated the occasion on the banks of Lake Michigan. From there, they flew to Teterboro, New Jersey, as they could not get permission to land at JFK (John F. Kennedy International Airport). They took a bus to New York City and stayed at Times Square, exploring the city over the next couple of days. They were on a shoestring budget and were lucky to find accommodation at the YMCA. Sonica knew that her father, who was a Boeing 747 captain with Air India, was expected to be in New York on a flight pattern over the next few days from the time they were there. Much as she would have loved to meet him there, they could not stay that long as it would upset their schedule and budget. So she went to the hotel her father would be staying at and left a note for him with the concierge. Later, when she spoke with her father, he said he was amazed at how soon she had flown to New York whereas it had taken him thirty years to get there!

From New York they were to fly to Houston, Texas, but discovered that they had miscalculated a bit and had more flying hours remaining. While they were discussing this, the owner of the pilot shop overheard their conversation and asked if any of them had been to New Orleans. When they said no, he strongly recommended the place, adding that they were in luck as he had all the navigation charts needed to get there. Re-routing their way, off they went. New Orleans was as lively and exciting a place as promised. They had a wonderful time before heading back to Malden via Memphis after seeing Elvis Presley's home, Graceland. After this fantastic experience of flying across America as just teenagers, it was time to return home. Sonica packed her bags and said, 'See you later' to her friends as she had heard it was difficult to clear the IGRUA entrance exam. She thought she would give it a shot, more than once if necessary, but told them she would certainly be back.

On returning to India, she started preparing for the conversion of her US licence to an Indian PPL. Soon, there was an advertisement for the IGRUA and she began studying for it. She cleared the written exam conducted in New Delhi and did well in the interview that followed. All this happened quickly and before she knew it, she was set to join the IGRUA in a month's time.

She was among the 32 trainee pilots selected to join the fifth course, which had a total of five girls including her, a large number in those days. The IGRUA was a phenomenal experience where all aspects of the training were par excellence. She made friends for life while there and even met her life partner, Vivek Chhabra, who was one batch senior to her.

Air India and Indian Airlines had subsidised the training costs of the cadets at the IGRUA with an assurance that the pilots would be given employment with the two national airlines. They were also part of the selection process as the pilots were being trained primarily for these airlines. The training was to have been completed in eighteen months but actually took twenty-seven months. The main reason for the delay was that neither airline had a vacancy.

Sonica and her batch graduated in January 1991 from the academy, but they were still without jobs. Around August 1991, Air India came out with an advertisement for pilots from the IGRUA and Vayudoot (a government-owned airline which was downsizing). She applied immediately, because, firstly, working with Air India had been her dream and, secondly, there were no other jobs available in the foreseeable future. Vivek, who was already in Air India, was not sure if this was the right decision. He felt that if she joined the company, it would hinder their family life, especially once they had children. Sonica told him that it was up to them to make it work and assured him she would do her best to make sure that their personal life would not suffer. She went ahead with her application with the firm conviction that she must at least make an attempt to fulfil her long-standing dream to work with the national airline.

She studied hard for the written exam, but destiny decided otherwise. She failed the exam *by one mark*. Everyone was shocked as she had always performed well at school and the academy, and had never failed at anything before! More than anyone else, Sonica was devastated. That's when her mother consoled her with the wise words, 'Whatever happens, happens for the best.' But Sonica was so miserable at the time, that she could not see the silver lining in the dark clouds.

The director of the academy too was taken aback at the news. He immediately offered her a job at the institute. She thanked him, and asking for a little time before she joined, she went on a short vacation to clear her head. Accepting her fate and reclaiming her positive outlook, she returned to the academy, where she became a simulator instructor and taught the cadets instrument flying. The director offered her the opportunity to become a flying instructor. For that she had to sign a bond, clear the next level of aviation exams for the Senior Commercial Pilots Licence, and train to become an instructor. She asked permission to clear the exams first and said she would consider the bond later. He was agreeable. Sonica prepared studiously and cleared all three papers even as she conducted simulator sessions. She had been at the academy for over six months and was feeling homesick, so she requested the director if she could go back home. This was in February 1992. Thanks to the Open Skies Policy, a few private airlines were just commencing operations. Again, destiny intervened, making Sonica return to Mumbai when she did, which is when she saw the advertisement for Jet Airways in May. She applied for the position of First Officer, and the rest, as we know, is history.

Jet Airways was a young, dynamic airline with a fair-minded, vibrant and progressive work culture. They started operations by leasing four Boeing 737-300 aircraft from Ansett Airlines in Australia. Sonica did her Boeing 737 First Officer endorsement in Melbourne. Her training at the IGRUA held her in good stead and she did well in her endorsement training with Ansett. Since they did not have any trainers of their own then, they flew with Australians initially, and then as the airline leased two Boeing 737-400 aircraft from Malaysian Airlines, they trained with Malaysian pilots as well. This international exposure at an early stage helped all the pilots at Jet Airways gain a sense of professionalism and widened perspective.

In 1994, Vivek and Sonica tied the knot. She would fly six days a week, four sectors a day while Vivek, who was also a First Officer on the Airbus 310 in Air India, would fly around five–six days in a month! Her hours piled up soon and she cleared her Airline Transport Pilot Licence (ATPL) exams as well. The airline was growing, and they found her suitable for command, so she was sent for her training, precisely three years after being released as a First Officer. She got her command in February 1997. She took a break from flying to welcome her firstborn, a son, in March 1999. Her daughter was born in 2002. In the interim, she had become a Check Pilot and had also been cleared to fly to Leh in 2001 when Jet Airways started operations to Ladakh. In 2006, she upgraded to the post of instructor and in 2008, she became an examiner. Thus, Sonica became the first woman examiner in India. Recognising her achievement, the Ministry of Civil Aviation bestowed upon her an award for significant contribution to Indian Civil Aviation in March 2011. She was also the first woman captain from any airline to operate to the critical fields of Leh and Thoise, both located in the mountainous regions of Ladakh, the most critical airfields in the country. The high terrain and the fact that these airfields are situated above 10,000 ft with barely any navigation aids are extremely challenging for any pilot. Therefore, each pilot must be trained to the highest level of proficiency.

When her children were young, Capt. Sonica preferred to remain on the B-737 as she operated domestic flights and conducted simulator training, which brought her home most days. She felt she had the best of both worlds – she would get her daily thrill of flying and still have ample time at home with the children. Those were the good old days of more turnaround flights and fewer layovers. Even if she flew four sectors a day, she was usually back home after that. She feels happy that she never missed a single school event, be it their Sports Day, assemblies or parent-teacher meetings. Her husband has always been an extremely hands-on father and has more than shared duties in their upbringing.

She feels having family support has been her greatest blessing. Firstly, her parents exhorted her to follow her dreams, then her husband always encouraged her to take up new challenges, and her parents-in-law provided the best possible support system. Living in a joint family, she could leave her children at home with her mind at ease. Capt. Sonica's father-in-law is also a retired Air Force pilot and, interestingly, both he and her father flew extensively in Ladakh. Many a dinner table conversation would revolve around comparing experiences of flying there.

When the children were older, when her son was ready to go to college and her daughter was a high-schooler, she decided to transition to the Boeing 777 aircraft. It was a good decision because by then flying on the narrow-bodied aircraft had changed drastically, with too many layovers and night flights. She loves flying the 777, a beautiful aircraft which would take her to London, Paris, Amsterdam, Singapore, and to Toronto as well where her son is studying.

In April 2019, due to financial troubles, Jet Airways temporarily stopped operations; in June, it went into liquidation. Many employees moved on to different airlines, nationally and internationally. Capt. Sonica could not bring herself to leave the airline that had given her so much: a job when she had none, equal opportunities throughout her career, a great working environment and the best of colleagues. She is waiting for a final resolution to come through for her beloved airline and hopes to touch the skies again in her beautiful blue, white and yellow bird.

A smile of complete satisfaction – one that follows many successful flights around the world!

At the Leh Airport, with the crew, after completing a challenging yet wonderful flight to Leh

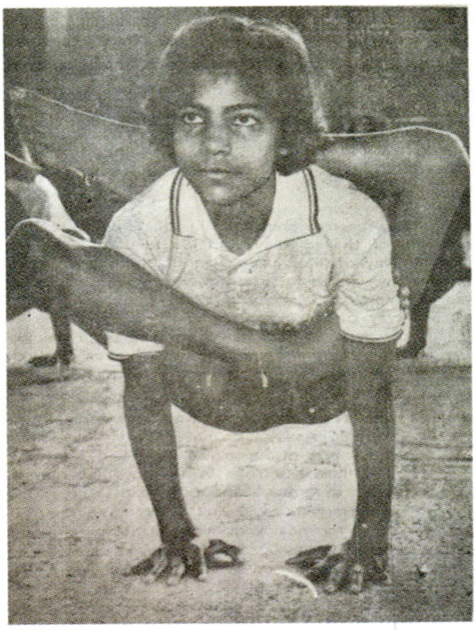

Nine-year-old Sunita performing yoga

A picture of Capt. Sunita Nirula practising yoga at her Mumbai home. Yoga remains an integral part of her life even today.

Being felicitated in San Francisco as the commander of the first all-women flight that create the world record of 'round the world' direct flight in 2017

Seventeen

From Yoga Mat to the Cockpit

Sunita Nirula

While growing up, meditation and yoga were integral to Sunita Narula's life. She hails from small-town Karnal on the outskirts of Delhi, where she studied at a government-aided school. From being a national yoga champion to a commander on the B-777, the second woman to join Air India as a pilot in 1994, Capt. Sunita's journey is not only amazing and inspiring but also an exemplary story of one individual's steely determination and persistence in overcoming challenges. No hurdle, however big, could obstruct her dreams from being fulfilled. Indeed, she believes that fate brought her to where she is today.

Sunita was born on 12 April in Karnal to Rajinder Lal Narula and Santosh Narula. She credits her parents, her mother in particular, as being an influential force in her formative years.

Her mother was a teacher in Guru Nanak Girls' School, which Sunita attended. She always motivated her children to aim high. In Sunita's words, 'My mother was a very ambitious lady, and as we were growing up (my siblings and myself), she used to tell us stories of great personalities and their inspiring work, so that we too would be motivated to accomplish big things.' Every day, she would pick one great personality and educate her children about their achievements and the struggles they had faced in reaching their goals. The stories were a catalyst for young Sunita who would yearn to do something similar in her own life. Their mother taught them several life lessons to prepare them to face challenges; she was brave and bold herself, and hoped her children would be the same. One of the highlights of Sunita's career – her world record flight (an all-women crew on the direct Delhi–San Francisco–Delhi flight, which circumnavigated the earth in 2017) – owes entirely to her mother who instilled in her since childhood, the belief that anything is possible.

Sunita's interest in flying started after she finished her B.Com studies in Karnal. In those days, she was an avid sportsperson – she played hockey at the state level, was a state champion in high jump, a national-level athlete and a four-time national champion in yoga. Besides sports, she was always engaged in activities that kept her highly motivated and dynamic. She decided to learn to ride a scooter. Happy to become an expert at it in no time, she wanted to now try something that would be more challenging. As they lived close to the Karnal Flying Club, she would often watch the yellow Pushpak aircraft fly over her house. This aroused her curiosity, and she wanted to find out how and what she could do to try this. She would often point at the small aircraft overhead and ask her mother whether she could fly them too and soar through the sky 'like a bird'!

Her mother encouraged her, did some research, and found that she knew of a clerk in the flying club through an acquaintance, and the very next day, she took her daughter to the club, where she met Capt. Gurney, an ex-Air Force Wing Commander who was the instructor in-charge at the club. A strict disciplinarian, he wasted no time and shot a series of questions at Sunita, all in English. In response, Sunita just stared at him blankly; having studied in a Hindi-medium school, she could not understand the questions. But bravely enough, she asked him to give her some time to prepare. She feels that seeing her so calm with no sign of nervousness is what made him give her a chance.

He handed her some papers and told her to come back after reading them, so that he could test her. She knew that she had to perform well on this first test, so on returning home, she got right down to mastering everything she had been given to read. Within a few days, she returned to Capt. Gurney for the test. Without checking the papers, he started asking questions, such as, 'What is a nautical mile?', 'Describe the different types of clouds?', and more. She fell silent again, as these topics had not been covered in the notes she had been asked to study. Before she could say so, Capt. Gurney shouted at her, saying that she was wasting his time, and was not serious at all. Marshalling all her courage and whatever English she knew, she told him, 'Sir, this information is not in the papers you gave me to read.' He took the papers from her and realised that they were technical notes on the Pushpak. Then, he posed a few questions about the Pushpak in a calmer fashion, each of which she answered correctly. There were some flying students nearby whom he asked a couple of questions, but even their answers were not as accurate as hers. Pleased with her grasp of all she had learnt, he invited her to join the flying club. He also gave her information about Haryana government's scholarship scheme for flying meant for girls, which Sunita promptly applied for. She feels very lucky to have won that scholarship for the Private Pilot Licence (PPL).

Buoyed by her achievement, she went to the flying club the following day to embark on this wonderful new adventure. But each day passed and she did nothing. Indeed, she felt totally lost as nobody bothered to talk to her or even acknowledge her. Coming as she did from a lower middle-class family, having a petite frame, wearing a salwar-kurta, her hair in two braids, unable to speak English fluently, she was aware she was a misfit among the smart, affluent women there from Chandigarh and Delhi. She was demoralised, but did not give up. She tried to network with people, and in doing so, she found a familiar face – Urmil Yadav, who had been with her in her yoga days.

Listening to her story, Urmil understood her situation. Sunita still remembers what her friend told her that day: 'Sunita, if you really want to fly, the only way you can make them notice you is if you pass the PPL/CPL exams.' Urmil helped her register for the exams and even gave her some books and notes to study. Sunita did as she was told, slogged through her B.Ed classes, and eventually wrote all the PPL papers and two CPL ones. She was as surprised as the rest of the flying club members to find that *she was the only one who had passed all the exams*! This was a pivotal moment. Overnight, Sunita became widely known in the club. This was the first time that people started taking her name; suddenly everyone was discussing a certain Sunita Narula who had cleared all the papers. This was the beginning of her ascent into the sky. Capt. Gurney became her flying instructor, and the very next day, she started her flying journey.

Her days at the Karnal Flying Club became gratifying. She was being noticed, everyone was talking about her, and many wanted to know how she had managed to pass the exams. Not only did she enjoy the novel experience of being noticed but sitting inside those 'yellow birds' was a fantastic feeling! Slowly but surely, she was learning and getting the hang of flying. One of the challenges in those days was to keep the little aircraft straight on the runway. Pushpak being a tail-wheel aircraft, most flyers initially had trouble keeping it straight, both for take-off and during landing. Sometimes she managed, but at other times, she needed help from her instructor. Her instructor never discouraged her, but he explained how every pilot has a different set of problems when they first start to fly. Sunita worked very hard and soon came to master the technique of flying. She was now eagerly awaiting her next big moment – 'to get her first solo'.

She has a smile as she recalls the sequence of events. 'It was a clear day, there was not much wind, and we were practising as usual, when my instructor told me that if my performance remained consistent, he would consider letting me fly solo the following day. I got excited and asked if I could fly solo the same day. As it was getting dark, my instructor wanted to wait for the next day. I thought to myself, I am performing well today, why wait for tomorrow, when anything could happen? So, I told my instructor, "Sir, I can see everything clearly, it's not dark yet, can I fly solo today?" I believe my persistence made Capt. Gurney eventually leave me on the runway and say, "Go, enjoy your solo."'

She had been ready for that moment, and in no time, she was up in the air, all by herself, thrilled to bits. When she landed the aircraft, parked, and came out, her instructor was waiting for her, equally happy. Although he is no more today, till his last days, he would tell students about her and how she had snatched her solo from him. Sunita approached her career in a similar fashion – head-on, without a moment to lose – and never let herself feel dejected.

The solo gave her and her instructor confidence in her flying abilities, and from that moment onwards, her career accelerated. She completed her PPL shortly after, and since her flying scholarship only extended up to the PPL, she stopped going to the flying club. Her parents could not afford to pay for further flying, and she could not risk being unemployed. So, she enrolled herself in a college for higher studies. One day, however, things changed. Capt. Gurney came to her house to meet her father, and told him, 'I see that Sunita is a bright and deserving student. She would do well in this profession. You must let her fly.' He also told her father about the flying academy, the Indira Gandhi Rashtriya Uran Akademi (IGRUA) at Fursatganj in Raebareli district of Uttar Pradesh, and convinced him to allow her to take the entrance exam. He assured her father that if Sunita got selected in the academy, the PM's Fund could sponsor 75 per cent of her fees; her parents would only need to fund the remaining 25 per cent. Her father was convinced and encouraged her to apply and to think of flying as a profession.

Sunita applied to the IGRUA while she attended B.Ed classes. The exam was tough but she passed. After the written test, there was an interview, following which Sunita was selected to be part of the sixth batch of the IGRUA, commencing in February 1989. She and her family were in high spirits about this new beginning.

Delighted, she went to Raebareli to join the academy. Once there, reality hit hard. She felt as if her life had turned into a nightmare. She felt absolutely out of place among the affluent students and flying instructors, given her Hindi-medium schooling. She could not speak English well and, although understanding her lessons was not a problem, answering her instructors confidently in English was an issue. Her batchmates, including the other women, did not interact much with her at first. Practically alone, she was left wondering where she had landed. At one point, she even thought of leaving, but reminded herself how hard her parents had worked to arrange for the remaining fees at the academy to make her dream come true. Several people were counting on her to become a pilot, and she could not let them down. So, she forced herself to face it all undaunted and complete the flying course.

The change, however, came when her batch took the first internal exam – the 'Air Regulation' paper. When the results were declared, everyone saw their marks and asked around as to who had scored the highest marks. Nobody bothered to ask Sunita how she had done, and she did not tell anyone. On request from one male student, the instructor announced everyone's marks. Sunita had the highest marks, and the next highest scorer was a whole 10 per cent lower! Everyone was stunned, and for the first time, her batchmates paid attention to her and learned her name. At this point, she knew she was there to stay. She did well in all subsequent exams, completed her training and got her CPL in 1991. She also secured an M.Com degree from Himachal University on correspondence basis.

Now they keenly awaited being inducted by the airline as the norm went. But things suddenly changed during their training. Academy students were now no longer automatically joining Air India or Indian Airlines as expected, and Sunita and her batchmates were sent home as there was no job vacancy. The period following her training was tough. People told her parents that she was unemployed because she must have not performed well. They even went so far as to say that she must have failed at the academy. Unkind comments followed that the money spent on a flying school could have been used to get her married instead. Sunita was already feeling low because she did not have a job and these insensitive people added to her misery. However, since she had an M.Com and a B.Ed degree, she took up a post of junior lecturer to avoid the negative people around her. She also sat for several competitive exams that she came across in newspapers, for employment in banks, the police force, SSB (Services Selection Board), cabin crew in Air India and SSC (Staff Selection Commission). She passed them all and continued to believe that life had better things in store for her.

Having cleared the SSB for the Indian Air Force (IAF) induction, she took the decision to join the Forces. The uniform had always fascinated her, and although, of course, flying was her first choice, without a job, the Air Force was the next best option. She was happy to be selected in the accounts branch of the Indian Air Force and was asked to proceed to Hyderabad, in January 1994. Within a month of joining, however, Air India came out with an ad to hire pilots. Knowing about her passion, her parents immediately informed her of this. She took a chance and applied for the job, though she did not know whether she would get time off from her Air Force job to go to Mumbai for the exam.

She remained optimistic, and to her good luck, some well-wishers like Sqdn Ldr Ashok Kumar and AVM Nirmal Thussu understood her situation, and she was granted leave for three days. She took the overnight train to reach Mumbai for the exam. Here she was overwhelmed by the number of candidates present. Half of them were sons of pilots, and all of them appeared to be from wealthy families. Nevertheless, she reminded herself that, having come this far, nothing should deter her. They gave the exam and the results were declared the very next morning. Sunita's name was among the candidates who had passed. Before she realised it, the interview was also conducted the same day. Despite tough grilling by the interview panellist, she managed to answer most of the questions. While leaving, she decided to mention her selection at the Indian Air Force to add weight to her candidature. Now she was mentally preparing to return to Hyderabad, but the very next day, the results were declared and, to her surprise, she found she had been selected! It was the happiest moment of her life. She resigned from the Air Force and joined Air India in 1994, as the airline's second woman trainee pilot (Capt. Rashmi K. Miranda being the first).

Being the second woman pilot for Air India was a huge accomplishment. However, when you are a woman in a male-dominated profession, sometimes even basic needs prove to be an uphill task. Describing this, she said, 'When they started simulator training, the bookings were programmed at odd hours. During late evening and night bookings, I experienced that there were no women's washrooms in the simulator complex.' She remembers having to ask her male simulator partner to check that nobody was in the washroom and to stand guard outside while she used it. Women really had to make their own way in order to survive. Then there would be talks among trainers about whether she would need extra bookings, as they doubted her competency as a woman. But to their surprise, nothing of that sort ever happened, and her training proceeded with a minimum number of sessions. Eventually, she learnt to ignore these unwelcome comments from others.

Her first endorsement was on the A-310 as a First Officer. Next, she moved to the B-747 as F/O, and then returned to command the A-310 before moving on to the B-777. Today, she is a commander on the B-777.

As an F/O, Sunita encountered another roadblock by virtue of being a woman in the field. As compared to her batchmates who were entrusted with greater responsibilities, she hardly got a chance to handle take-offs and landings. Then, in 2004, when it was her turn to undergo command training, she had barely 2,650 hours of flying time under her belt. She had handled about four landings on the B-747 and very few on the A-310, notching up a total of only 10–15 landings. She was not underconfident, but slightly concerned as she had to take command training on a wide-bodied aircraft (A-310) without having much of a feel of it beforehand. However, that did not change her mind.

She began command training as scheduled. Once the simulator

training was done, the command LOFT began. One day, after landing in Chennai, on the way to Singapore, she spoke to her instructor, Capt. S. Balasubramanian, about her apprehensions. She recounts his response: 'I do not feel the same way, Sunita. I have seen two or three of your flights, and your handling is good.'

This changed her outlook. It gave her the confidence she needed to progress smoothly as a commander on the A-310.

Flying as a commander included such experiences as handling stall warnings, weather diversions, even a go-around on short finals in Hong Kong because of a jeep on the runway. But her most memorable incident occurred a few months into flying as a commander. She can still visualise that flight clearly. 'It was a flight from Mumbai to Cochin and onwards to Kuwait. Everything seemed fine as we started from Mumbai, but as we got airborne, my flight instruments, except for the artificial horizon, went blank. Nothing was working. Soon, my co-pilot's instruments also went blank. I climbed to the minimum safe altitude (MSA) to analyse the problem and take corrective action. As we levelled off, my co-pilot's instruments started working again. So, we followed the prescribed checklist, comparing the co-pilot's working instruments with the artificial horizon. Everything appeared to be working fine. I was told to climb further and to inform the ATC, before taking the call of whether to return to Mumbai or to continue on to Cochin. Once we climbed to 7,000 ft, my instruments began working. Still, I wanted to be sure before taking the final decision, so I maintained level for some time. As all the instruments appeared to be working and operations seemed normal, I made the decision to proceed to Cochin and started climbing to cruising level. But as we climbed and moved away from Mumbai, the instruments started misbehaving again. Sometimes mine would go blank, and sometimes my co-pilot's. It was a stressful flight. We were kept on our toes, but I remained cool. I handled the flight with whatever aids were available, navigating through rainy June weather. During my approach in Cochin, I requested a radar vector to land, as I did not want to rely on the faulty instruments. We finally landed safely in Cochin, but my legs kept shaking even after we landed.' To this day, she feels this was one of her toughest flights, more so being a new commander having flown for just a few months in command.

Capt. Sunita did not want to simply record the snag in the defect book. She waited to inform the engineer personally about the whole flight and how the instruments had blanked out. Sure enough, the aircraft was grounded immediately. Later, she learned that, a week before the flight, there had been heavy rainfall in Mumbai, and the aircraft had been parked outside. Water had entered the avionics compartment, which somehow did not get completely treated before the flight, and this caused the malfunction. This was a big learning experience for Capt. Sunita. She believes comprehensive training, coordination among crew members and presence of mind prepare pilots to handle situations in the air and ensure safe landings.

In 2008, Capt. Sunita became commander of the B-777, the long-range aircraft. Counted among the world's largest and most powerful twin-engine commercial jets, the B-777 is also the second-largest aircraft in the world. On 8 March 2010, she piloted Air India's long-range, nonstop flight (Mumbai–JFK) to celebrate International Women's Day, making her mark as one of the commanders of the first all-woman Ultra Long Range (ULR) flight.

Capt. Sunita's career trajectory success owes to her dedication and hard work. In 2015, she became an LTC (Line Training Captain) – the first Indian woman to do so – on the B-777. Then, in 2017, she commanded the Del–SFO (Delhi–San Francisco) flight, which circumnavigated the earth with an all-women crew, making a world record. In 2019, she became a Type Rated Instructor (TRI) on the B-777.

Capt. Sunita allowed nothing to come in the way of her dreams – not her humble beginnings in a small town, nor her handicap with spoken English, nor any problem of resources and mentors. She worked diligently and won against all odds to get where she is today. She considers her bird's eye view of the world – from 30,000 ft in the air, enjoying and witnessing several sunrises, the famous Northern Lights, active volcanoes, the snow-covered Alps – all of which fills her with exhilaration, a blessing she is grateful for!

She does not consider flying as just a job, but a heartfelt passion that she nurtures, which keeps her constantly motivated. She would love to recommend this path to everyone, and would certainly love it if her teenaged daughter followed in her footsteps.

In 2020, Capt. Sunita became a CRM (Crew Resource Management) facilitator.

She has operated flights to bring PPEs (Personal Protection Equipment) and other valuable medical equipment from Shanghai, and, under the Vande Bharat Mission, to repatriate Indians back to their homes during the Covid–19 lockdown last year.

Happy and content as a captain and instructor on the Boeing 777

Celebrating India's independence day with the crew in New York

Capt. Trisha Mohan – India's first...

...and only woman commander of the massive Boeing 747, the Jumbo Jet, also known as 'The Palace in the Sky'

Eighteen

Flying the Jumbo Jets: Commanding the Boeing 747

Trisha Mohan

Tall and strong, intelligent and talented, Capt. Trisha Mohan surprises people when she tells them she has been a pilot for twenty-five years. She makes a statement with her statuesque presence, in the smart flight crew uniform accentuated by four stripes. And if that isn't enough to impress you, she also happens to be India's first and only woman commander of the massive Boeing 747-400, the Jumbo Jet, affectionately known as the Queen of the Skies.

Born on 19 November in Bangalore while her father, Sqdn Ldr Satish Chander Mohan V.M., was posted in Yelahanka, Trisha's world was all about aviation. He flew the AN-12 transport aircraft in the Air Force and later joined Air India as a captain. Trisha, along with her two sisters, grew up in Bombay in an

Air India community, surrounded by pilots and flight crew.

All three daughters enjoyed accompanying their father on his flights, but the one whose face lit up the most with excitement the moment she stepped on an aeroplane was Trisha. As luck would have it, her father flew the B-747 Classic, and she would be captivated while climbing the stairs to the upper deck cockpit. The lights and switches, the chatter of the ATC on the radio, the sheer exuberance of this massive beast of an aeroplane breaking through the clouds and soaring into the infinite blue sky left her feeling elated and incredibly lucky to witness this spectacle.

The cockpit mesmerised her, and she just knew that she must fulfil her calling of flying a plane. Flying was in her genes and, coming from a long line of decorated military war heroes, a fierce sense of patriotism directed her passion towards becoming an Air Force fighter pilot to serve her country.

However, in the early '90s, the Air Force hadn't yet opened its doors to women. Women aviators had to wait for a very long time, with the first women fighter pilots being commissioned only in 2015. Not one to be dissuaded, Trisha redirected her vision to what surely must be every pilot's dream: to fly the magnificent Jumbo, the grandest aeroplane built at that time, the very same aircraft her father piloted!

Having set her mind on it, she spoke to her parents. Her father warned her about the hardships she would face as an international pilot, the long flights and strenuous medical exams it would entail, that it would undoubtedly be tougher for a woman. He suggested considering other options, especially since she excelled in academics and sports as well. But Trisha remained resolute about flying the big jets. Her mother, Nalini, without batting an eyelid, asked her, 'When do you want to start?' Trisha was overjoyed. Seeing her determination, her father too supported her wholeheartedly and ensured that she got the best guidance and training available in the field of his expertise.

Thirty years ago, it was her mother's hearty encouragement and confidence in her that kept her going, unfazed, even when many warned her that women would not last long in a male bastion like this. Trisha's mother was her inspiration, the towering force that helped her break all barriers and boldly forge ahead. In fact, to this day, her mother continues to be her greatest pillar of strength, along with the unflinching support of her two sisters, Anjini and Ishika.

Trisha started training for her Private Pilot Licence (PPL) in 1988 at a flying school in Missouri, USA. Her father, after the initial apprehension of sending his seventeen-year-old daughter halfway across the world, saw her performing beautifully amongst the '10 girls and 500 boys give or take', and this further validated his faith in her. The joke back home was that she received her PPL to fly, (even a Jumbo), even before she could qualify for her driving licence!

While completing her PPL in the USA, she got to know about the Indira Gandhi Rashtriya Uran Akademi (IGRUA) at Fursatganj in Raebareli district of Uttar Pradesh. The academy was founded by the Government of India, and aided by our national carriers Air India and the erstwhile Indian Airlines, and was the only dedicated flying academy in the country at that time with state-of-the-art infrastructure and a faculty team comprising the best ground and flight instructors. Trisha considered both options for her Commercial Pilot Licence (CPL), and decided that undergoing the more rigorous training at the IGRUA was better than the expedited training in the USA.

At the end of 1988, she returned to India, and, subsequently, in March 1989, she cleared the entrance exam and tough selection process to join the IGRUA's sixth batch.

It was a highly competitive environment at the academy. She realised that if she wanted that airline job, she had to work harder than ever. Having grown up in Bombay, this sudden transportation to the heartland of Uttar Pradesh, where she was just one of a handful of girls, was extremely difficult and she felt homesick for a while. The outlook towards girls in UP was very different from Bombay where she had been raised very liberally, and she suddenly found herself immersed in a far more conservative society. In the local village, where, till date, women's faces are behind the *ghunghat*, Trisha and her friends would get glared at for wearing jeans.

But the training in the academy was glorious, she says, and thanks to the founder Capt. N.K. Dawar, everything was conducted professionally, upholding the highest standards. He himself would instruct pupils on the coveted twin-engine, turboprop King Air (C90A) and demand the highest level of proficiency from them. It is a matter of personal pride that she obtained her solo within two hours under his instructional training. In that period, she forged lifelong bonds with her batchmates, amongst them her future husband, Arup.

Her greatest memories of life at the IGRUA are of the winter months when the dense fog would prohibit flying for days at a time. She and her batchmates would immediately head for the train station, hop onto the iconic Kashi Vishvanath Express and travel unreserved to Delhi – sitting on the floor, legs dangling off the footboard, singing songs for most of the fifteen-odd hour journey.

Just when Trisha and her batchmates graduated with their CPL in 1991, they were informed that Air India and Indian Airlines had changed their policy and were no longer hiring new pilots. This came as a massive setback as it was considered a natural progression for pilots graduating from the IGRUA to be inducted by either airline, since there weren't any other commercial airlines in the country at that time.

This was a very stressful time not only for her but also for the hundreds of potential pilots who had completed flying courses at various flying clubs in India and abroad. A significant amount of money had also been invested in their training. All this left her feeling very uncertain and nervous about the future.

Then in 1992, the government announced a new Open Skies Policy for domestic airlines. As a result, many private airlines such as East-West Airlines, Damania Airways and ModiLuft were founded. Trisha applied to all of them. Initially, the airlines were reluctant to accept a female applicant, but she persisted. She appeared for entrance tests conducted by every airline and cleared them all in flying colours. After one particularly long and gruelling interview, she was told that although she had excelled in her performance among hundreds of boys and girls, the company 'cannot create our airline with women as pilots as we need to consider the safety factor'. Trisha was appalled. It was like being lassoed back to ground zero. She knew it was definitely not a concern about safety, that it was the unjustified orthodox mindset of the times that sparked their resistance. She never imagined that being a woman could be a disadvantage in an equal job opportunity, and began to wonder if she would ever get a job.

As luck would have it, Air India started hiring pilots once again in 1993–94. Applying for that job and dedicating all her time and effort to it became Trisha's top priority. She knew that she would be competing against thousands of pilots across the country, all of whom were aiming to bag the same opportunity. Her efforts were rewarded when she sailed through the highly competitive and strenuous selection process, and finally joined Air India in 1994.

Trisha was catapulted into a whole new world. The entire organisation was everything she had dreamed about, and more. Starting with its top-of-the-line training department with the best faculty, ground classes, instructors and simulators going on to its wide-bodied aircraft fleet, with flights around the globe.

She was inducted into Air India's second-ever batch with pilots that included women, and along with her was her good friend,

Sunita Narula, her batchmate from the IGRUA. They received a lot of attention, especially in the context of their performance with the big jets. Moreover, these two women were fairly young, which was added to the reason why some of the senior pilots initially doubted their ability. On paper, men and women were equal, but in reality, women had to work tenfold as hard at every step to prove themselves.

Trisha recalls that if she got complimented, it was only in comparison to her male counterparts: 'You fly as well as your colleague (male pilot!).' It was almost as if that was the benchmark – to fly as well as a man. 'I never tried to put forth my case verbally, I preferred to let my work speak for itself,' she smiles.

Her work started on the wide-bodied Airbus A-310, the highlight being flying into the old Kai Tak Airport in Hong Kong. The one-of-a-kind Instrument Guidance System approach into Hong Kong was one of the most difficult in the world where the aircraft is guided over the populated city up to about 600 ft towards a red-and-white checkerboard on a hill, before turning a sharp right onto the runway, usually with strong gusty crosswinds. Possessing the required IGS special crew qualification, Trisha was thrilled at the opportunity to fly in Air India's last landmark flight into Kai Tak. They landed at Kai Tak and took off from the new Chek Lap Kok Airport the next day.

And then, a few years later, in a culmination of all her dreams and efforts, the day finally dawned when she underwent conversion to fly the iconic Boeing 747-400; the original source of her inspiration. Its tag line, Your Palace in the Sky, derived from its majestic, near-regal stature.

She couldn't ask for anything more. You should see her talking about her aircraft. Her face radiates with child-like effervescence and wonder. Ask her about her favourite time flying the aircraft and she talks about doing circuit training in Bombay. 'Sitting in the cockpit, having the whole aircraft to yourself, doing touch and go's, circuit landings in my hometown Bombay at 2,000 ft above ground level... the feeling was simply glorious! Opening thrust on all four engines, feeling the roar of the engines, the acceleration, rotation, soaring into the sky, final approach and landing, all on a Jumbo! Circuit after circuit. I could do that forever. It's bliss!

To this date, when I look at the sheer size of the aircraft, I wonder how this even flies... And though she cruises faster than the latest jets, at .86 Mach (86 per cent of the speed of sound), she's extremely stable through turbulent weather!'

Just as the long range and reach of the Jumbo spanned far and wide, Capt. Trisha's horizons broadened with exposure to these diverse places and their fascinating cultures. From the stylish European cities of Rome, Paris, London, steeped in history, to mystic Seoul and Tokyo, to modern New York, Chicago and Los Angeles, all the way to the expansive untamed beauty of Africa and Perth and Sydney in the southern hemisphere, she was eager to explore and learn from each of these experiences.

Apart from the thrill that comes with the job of flying a B-747, she has also witnessed some unforgettable incidents that have challenged and tapped into her very being as a pilot.

Once, while flying from Los Angeles to Frankfurt, she had to deal with a life-and-death situation on board. A young female passenger developed a case of severe appendicitis. A doctor on board advised that if emergency medical surgery was delayed, it could prove fatal for the girl. Chicago was the closest airport but visibility was marginal as it was snowing heavily and all runways were covered with ice. After quickly assessing all the pertinent factors, they decided to divert. They had to jettison fuel (to reduce the aircraft weight within permissible limits) and landed safely where the girl was then taken away by paramedics. Timely action and presence of mind saved a girl's life, while simultaneously being responsible for and looking after the safety of the rest of the 400-odd passengers.

Another instance was the time she had to depart from the tricky 'table-top' runway at Calicut Airport. In typical monsoon weather, she had to display extraordinary calmness and not succumb to pressure from the ATC and other agencies. The Boeing 747-400 has a body length of 231 ft. So, for engine start, the aircraft has to be pushed back onto the runway, thereby occupying it. While starting the engine, a fault warning occurred for which appropriate procedures had to be followed. The weather was rapidly deteriorating; other aircraft were holding overhead while one was about to divert as it was low on fuel. The ensuing delay led to tremendous pressure from the ATC to quickly start taxiing and get airborne. It was imperative to remain composed and make the right decision for the safety of her passengers and crew. The fault eventually turned out to be a 'No Go', so she took the right call to turn back to the bay for mandatory maintenance action.

Such lessons teach pilots much more than what they learn in the classroom or during training sessions. Being in command requires dealing with many people, resources and tremendous pressure all at once. As the final decision and responsibility of more than 400 lives rest with you as commander, you grow as a person very quickly.

She goes on to talk animatedly about the thrilling Canarsie approach for runway 13L into JFK Airport, New York. The Canarsie was a challenging, curving, non-precision approach with a low-altitude final turn to align with the runway. Executing that in one of the busiest airports in the world after a long Atlantic crossing is one of her all-time favourites.

Akin to these, there are many other magical moments everlastingly imprinted in her memory.

The image of the infinite expanse of stars on a clear moonless night while flying over the ocean would leave her with a feeling of being 'one with the universe'. The visual spectacle of the Northern Lights on an Atlantic Oceanic crossing at higher latitudes, or after a long and tiring night flight, experiencing the first hint of dawn that gradually glows and brightens into a glorious sunrise... she can go on and on about the magic of it all.

Today, being the first and only Lady Commander on the 747, (true Maharani of the skies), she feels it's a complete privilege and honour and wouldn't want to trade this cockpit for any other. 'It has to be a flight deck 33,000 ft high!' If you asked her what plane she would rather fly, you would get an expression that says, 'Are you seriously asking me that question?' As long as the B-747s are flying, so will she! In fact, as her career progressed, she opted out of moving to the B-787 Dreamliner, the latest and most advanced plane in the world. The latest machines do not interest her as much. She only has to see a Jumbo and her face lights up.

Many people are under the mistaken impression that women pilots find it difficult to get married and have a family. In fact, Capt. Trisha settled down with her childhood confidante, course-mate at the IGRUA and Air India colleague, Arup, who's currently a commander on the Boeing 777. Being a globe-trotting, jet-setting couple can be difficult, especially when it comes to raising a family. But it certainly helps that they both understand the demands of the profession. Arup is a terrific partner; they are now proud parents to two teenaged sons, Aarhan and Aeshan. And there is no greater feeling for her than flying her two sons, just as her father did with her and her sisters. Flying your kids around the world! Now that's a family tradition to beat!

She laughs and remembers the time she flew her parents and the cabin crew told them 'Your baby is flying the plane!' Her parents were thoroughly amused and proud of their 5'10" tall baby.

Unlike in other professions, pilots flying international routes cannot be in physical touch with their families when they are on a flight. There was a time when she spent quite a few month-long postings in Frankfurt. She missed her toddler son terribly, and with it, all the precious joys and landmark moments of that time. Leaving him before every trip was simply heart-breaking and she couldn't hold back the tears each time. Her only reassurance was that he was in his Nani's love and care, the kind that only Nanis can give...

The post-maternity period before returning to flying was difficult as well. Capt. Trisha had complicated pregnancies and had a tough time rebuilding her fitness levels and clearing the medicals. She then had to undergo a series of qualifications again with an extended refresher course, full simulator training and aircraft checks. The extensive retraining periods post-delivery are lengthier and more arduous for women pilots than in other professions.

Moreover, on returning from long-haul flights, jet lag and exhaustion catch up with them. So, although they are back home, it is tough for them to take care of their families. Capt. Trisha has become adept at juggling work and family life. Her friend, whose husband is also a pilot with Air India, once asked her, 'How do you deal with jet lag? I always see you with your boys, playing with them, doing activities with them, picking them up and dropping them off at school even after your long flights! But my husband sleeps incessantly and is no help at home, let alone spend time with the kids.' Capt. Trisha told her, 'I am passionate about what I do, and I have always wanted to be a pilot. But as soon as I am home, I have no time for jet lag! I love being there for my kids.'

Flying, home, kids – she does it all with panache! Swimming, yoga, running on the beach helps her keep fit. She also has her own team of schoolmates, called the MisFits, who play throwball together in tournaments across the city. 'It's great fun playing together and bonding with like-minded sporty people, and, of course, winning a trophy or two along the way helps,' she grins. She combines her love for children and passion for football by organising football tournaments for both boys and girls every year, especially encouraging the young girls and the lesser privileged children. Whenever she's in Bombay, she also loves contributing her time and energy to her alma mater and her children's school, Jamnabai Narsee School, where she has been an active member of the Parent Teachers' Association for many years.

Today, she's immensely grateful to all those who have been an integral part of her journey and have played influential roles, whether big or small, at various stages of her life. She is especially grateful to Air India, the entire organisation, for all the opportunities given to her and for having brought her to this stage in both professional and personal life. 'It truly is like being part of a family, one that looks after, nurtures, encourages and supports one of their own, and I wouldn't dream of being anywhere else!'

Air India has given her continuous and unflinching support in all her endeavours and they have worked productively together to initiate and promote several causes she firmly believes in. Such as the Air India Pilots Welfare Society (AIPWS), which looks after the overall welfare of the pilot community, both retired and serving, as well as the Air India Pilots Welfare & Solidarity Society (APWSS), which extends support and solidarity to fellow pilots.

She is on the committee of the Indian Women's Pilots Association & International Women Professionals in Aviation and Aerospace (IWPA), Mumbai Chapter. Created by stalwarts of the earlier generation, she uses this platform to encourage and motivate other women in the field of aviation. Here, she was recently felicitated for being the vanguard and the first and only woman commander in India on the Boeing 747-400.

Having been a pioneering lady pilot in Air India, she is eager to empower and assist the now continuous stream of an increasing number of women pilots entering Air India trying to navigate their way. She is constantly addressing the inclusion of women's issues – maternity leave, adoption, single parenting, to name a few.

Back when she started out at Air India, the uniforms presented an amusing hurdle. In 1994, it was assumed that all pilots were male. So even their uniform was masculine, with baggy trousers and oversized men's shirts. Capt. Trisha boldly initiated the move to modify it and persevered together with various departments in Air India and new designers with new proposals, until subtle style changes to their uniform, which were decidedly feminine, were endorsed.

Ask her if it's still a male bastion, and she smiles. Even today, the ATC out of habit says, 'Roger that, *Sir*!'

Capt. Trisha and her ilk have unknowingly influenced the decisions of possibly an entire generation of women to get out there and follow their heart. She believes that it is important to show the girls of our country that they can be anything they want to be and that the sky is no limit.

Her hope is to inspire and let young girls know that if they set high ideals, with determination and resilience, they can accomplish and achieve them whatever their goals maybe.

When asked if she knew she would become a trailblazer, she laughs. 'That was never the plan. I just love flying and I had to do it. The feeling is unparalleled. I never wanted to be 'The First' or 'The Only'. I just wanted to do what every other young boy or girl wants to do: to live my dream. And I continue to do that – 40,000 ft in the sky. One nautical mile at a time.'

Completely at ease with herself and with the aircraft she loves to fly – the Jumbo Boeing 747

The first sister duo to become pilots

Generation-Next

Nineteen

Fearless Sisters

Deeksha and Aashna Sharan

The new generation, or generation-next, is testimony to the greatest advancement of technology and innovation in human history. Modern technology is a key word for the members of this generation. It has revolutionised all industries, and aviation is no exception. Crossing time zones in no time is a common event in people's lives. Aircraft have been upgraded with the latest technology in terms of speed, safety and comfort. Travelling is quicker, easier and cheaper than ever before. Time is a precious commodity, whereby the quantum of air travel has increased manifold. In turn, there is a spike in air traffic as well, leading to congested airways. However, there are many aids available to ensure continued smooth operations.

From the year 2000 onwards, we have seen a steep rise in the number of women opting for this profession, abandoning the age-old view that gender could be an obstacle. Airlines in India have opened their doors wide for them, making India the world leader in the number of women pilots employed. Fearless and daring, these women have made their own mark in this profession.

FEARLESS SISTERS

Sisters Deeksha and Aashna, daughters of Capt. Devi Sharan, were barely eleven and seven years old when IC-814 (a Kathmandu–Delhi flight on the A-300) was hijacked and rerouted to Kandahar, Afghanistan. Capt. Sharan was commanding the flight. Even though the girls were young, like their mother, they too were anxious, but they were confident that their father would return safely, along with all the passengers. Fearless as children, they could not think of any other profession that would better suit them than their father's, when they were older. So, it came as no surprise to the parents that the girls wanted to be pilots, just like their father. Apprehension and doubt never crossed their minds.

Deeksha was born on 9 April to Capt. Sharan and Navneet Kaur. A generation-next pilot, she flies in command for Air India on the Airbus.

Born and brought up in Delhi in the midst of pilots, the two sisters agree that their best memories are from their many family trips. They were lucky to travel a lot as their father was a pilot. They spent no holidays in Delhi, and visiting different destinations became the norm, a habit they still hold dear.

Capt. Deeksha remembers how, as a child, she was enamoured by her father's uniform and cap, which she would wear all the time. From early on, she would picture herself becoming a pilot once she grew up. She was in Class 6 when her father's plane was hijacked, and she and her sister can still accurately recount the traumatic series of events. However, even such a disturbing experience did not deter her from her ambition; her mind was quite made up.

She talks about the time when her family was in Hyderabad for a holiday, and they planned to leave for Dubai the following day. Capt. Sharan was on leave, and this was not a flight he was rostered to fly. He received a call from Delhi requesting him to return there to operate a flight to Kathmandu. Flying in and out of Kathmandu required special clearance, which Capt. Sharan had. As there was no other qualified captain available, he agreed to operate this one flight, after which he would proceed on his vacation. Capt. Deeksha remembers it was very early in the morning, and she was sleepy as she faintly overheard her parents talking. Her father told her mother that he was leaving for Delhi to operate just one flight due to an exigency and would return to Hyderabad later the same evening, and as planned, they would leave for Dubai the next day.

But this was not to be. On the way back from Kathmandu, the aircraft was hijacked by terrorists. Later that evening, Capt. Sharan's wife received a call from one of his colleagues, informing her that the flight had been diverted and had left the country. With a heavy heart, he told her that it had been hijacked. The colleague advised her to return to Delhi with her children, as the situation could take a while to resolve. No one knew at that time what the outcome would be, as no further information was available. Capt. Deeksha remembers the day vividly, and her mother telling them that their father's plane would not be landing in Delhi, that he had been asked to take it to some other place. She was probably preparing them to stay calm and doing the same herself as well. The next thing the girls knew, they were packing to leave for Delhi. Since they were young, Deeksha and her sister did not quite understand the gravity of the situation.

Back home in Delhi, a continuous stream of people visited the family. Although the girls knew about the hijacking, they did not really understand what it meant. Aashna, who was seven years old at the time, recalls there were many people crying and consoling their mother, and she wondered why they were crying when her mother or sister weren't. She was too young to understand the danger her father was in and the concern people had for him. Their mother remained in a positive frame of mind and encouraged her daughters to do the same. She was a pillar of strength and urged them to continue believing that he would be back soon. In fact, because of how she carried herself and handled media queries, she was invited by the then Prime Minister, Mr Atal Bihari Vajpayee, to address the family members of the passengers on that flight. The two sisters remember accompanying her to this event, where she told the people in the gathering, 'I know my husband, he will bring all his passengers back safely.' She even told the prime minister, 'My husband is a big fan of yours and I hope you prove him right.' Her sheer will and tenacity held them together, even as she too must have had a hard time keeping her emotions under control.

She stayed in touch with the Prime Minister's Office for more information on the status of the flight. Those eight uncertain days seemed to last forever. On 27 December, a relief flight was announced. However, the next day, this flight was cancelled. Finally, on 31 December, the flight was despatched. The operating captain had a satellite phone and, on reaching Kandahar, he connected Capt. Sharan with his family. They were all so emotional that they could barely say hello to him. But now at least they were certain he would be back home soon.

On the evening of 31 December 1999, when Capt. Sharan's wife and daughters reached the airport to pick him up, they were overwhelmed at the sight of passengers from the flight carrying him out of the airport, thanking him for being their saviour. That night, people poured into Capt. Sharan's house; it was a happy occasion, a good start to the new millennium, with more than one reason to celebrate. However, to keep the atmosphere happy, they decided never to speak about the incident again. Instead of dwelling on the past, they made sure to enjoy every moment together without taking one another for granted.

A few years later, when Deeksha was awaiting her Class 10 exam results, she told her parents about her desire to become a pilot. She knew they would support any career choice she made, regardless of any past incident. She had full support and encouragement from her mother. Her father, however, wanted her to consider other options, so he suggested waiting for the results before making a final decision. He told her that if she scored above 90 per cent, she could seriously consider flying. He believed that if she wanted a career in flying, she should fly while still in school (Classes 11 and 12). He reasoned that as there were vacancies in airlines, it would be relatively easy for her to land a job at that time and her exam results would indicate her ability to cope in school. Deeksha was quite confident that she would get 90 per cent, but when the results were announced, even she was surprised to find she had scored 95 per cent. Her father was so pleased that he suggested she go abroad for higher studies. Her heart was set on becoming a pilot, though. Eventually, he understood and agreed.

In 2005, Deeksha began her flying journey while studying in Class 11. Her classmates attended various extracurricular activities, so they thought that her mother, who would come to pick her up every day, was also taking her to some similar extracurricular class. Whereas, in fact, her mother would drive her every day to the Karnal Flying Club for flying classes. For Deeksha, flying was not simply an activity that she wished to add to her resume. She was serious about joining a commercial airline after getting her Commercial Pilot Licence (CPL).

Balancing school and flying was not easy. She had to pull off several late nights in order to keep up in school. Her mother was her shining beacon, making it a point to drive her to classes and helping her cope with all the pressure. Her presence and encouragement were like a bulwark of support. Even when she was exhausted, her mother would put her mind at ease, telling her not to worry as tomorrow would be a better day. Deeksha had to put in a lot of hard work and missed out on parties with her classmates, but she never gave up on her goal. She was happy to make sacrifices if it meant she could achieve something bigger! Her aim remained steadfast – completing her CPL before finishing Class 12.

Since she was flying while attending high school, her progress in flying was understandably slow. However, she got her first solo flight after completing barely 10 flying hours. That experience left her feeling on top of the world, singing and enjoying every bit of that flight! After the solo, her father suggested enrolling in other flying schools to speed up the training process. So, during the summer vacation after Class 11, when her classmates were preparing for Class 12, Deeksha went to Hyderabad and completed over 100 flying hours, thus making the most of the time available to her during the holidays.

The more she flew and amassed experience of different situations in the air, the more passionate she grew about flying. She was eager to finish training soon so that she would not miss a job vacancy. She was now dreaming of entering the cockpit of an Airbus. While preparing for the Class 12 exams, Deeksha also gave the DGCA exam for her CPL. Thinking back to those days, she remembers how difficult and strenuous it was to prepare for both sets of exams simultaneously. However, the pressure of the Class 12 exams felt easier simply because she was keener to pass the CPL papers. And as a result of her efforts and family support, she passed all the exams. It was such a huge relief when all her hard work finally paid off!

In 2007, Deeksha was eighteen years old and had just finished school, when she applied for a job with Indian Airlines. She was lucky to clear the entrance exam and the interview and was hired as a trainee pilot on the Airbus 320. She was one of 28 selected candidates, of which 5 were women. It was a new era with more airlines to choose from and more women pilots being accepted and inducted. But imagine a girl just out of school, mature enough to know what she wanted and working towards completing all requirements to reach her goal? It was Deeksha's level-headedness and dedication that allowed her to realise her dream of getting a job with a commercial airline as a pilot! She is truly an inspiration to school kids out there looking for a career in aviation!

She underwent training in Hyderabad, at the training centre for Indian Airlines. She was released as a First Officer (F/O) on the A-320 and was posted to Mumbai, where she currently resides with her husband and child. In 2015, Deeksha's turn for command came and she began her command training. It is a tough training but every pilot looks forward to upgrading their position and becoming a commander. Her dreams were no different. She admits that during her training, her thoughts did go back to the time her father's aircraft got hijacked. She always remembers that episode. These days, the threat of terrorism is constant, particularly to airlines. Therefore, there is immense security and many systems in place. Crew members undergo special training in order to deal with these potential threats. But for her it was an important concern, and she decided to talk to her dad and get his input on this. She asked him how he had handled the terrorist way back in 1999. Apart from vast experience, she realised that his calm demeanour was probably his biggest asset. Till date, he can adeptly handle and negotiate all manner of situations. Both sisters unanimously agree that he is a diplomatic person who solves issues most effectively. Therefore, being in the same profession is a plus point for them as they can reach out to him with any queries and rely on him for flying advice even though he flies the B-787 and they fly the A-320.

Capt. Deeksha has been flying for over eleven years, commanding flights since 2015. Since she became a pilot when still so young, she matured early. Becoming a commander changed her thinking completely and gave her a different perspective on many things. She believes she is now able to handle situations amicably and with ease. Being a naturally calm person, she recognises that wasting energy on petty matters is foolish. She narrates an incident from one of her flights.

'It was an early morning 2 a.m. flight from Mumbai to Goa. There were some unruly passengers (probably friends) who were hampering the cabin crew from rendering their services on this short flight. The crew informed me of their behaviour and, on my command, ignored their continuous calls. But after the flight landed, these people stood on the aerobridge and insisted that the cabin crew must apologise to them for not attending to them, and only then would they leave the aerobridge. This was hampering our boarding for the return sector. The commercial staff approached me to ask the concerned crew to apologise, so that the boarding could be announced. But as I was aware of the actual situation, I took my stand and decided that since they had misbehaved, the crew would not apologise. I suggested that the commercial staff could announce a gate change, put the step ladder and start boarding. This was done and we departed on schedule. It was only after the aircraft left that these people realised that standing on the aerobridge, they were wasting their own time and energy at 3 a.m. Hopefully, they learnt their lesson.'

Thanks to her work, she has matured enough to be able to handle situations in a poised, positive and effective manner. She feels truly blessed to be in a profession that she enjoys and looks forward to each day. Flying the beautiful Airbus is the most rewarding work she can ever do, she affirms. There is not a moment of regret and each flight brings joy and peace to her.

Four years younger than Deeksha, Aashna is not far behind.

Today, she flies as a commander of the A-320 for Indigo Airlines. She admits that she only thought about becoming a pilot after Class 10. She had finished her exams and was on holiday, when her sister Deeksha was leaving for Hyderabad to complete some flying hours. Aashna accompanied her. One day, Deeksha asked her if she wanted to come along for a joyride on a Cessna. She promptly agreed. Once they were airborne in this small aircraft, Aashna realised how wonderful it was! She was at once sold on the idea of becoming a pilot. It felt amazing and she could see how much Deeksha was enjoying it. Aashna even asked her sister if she could perhaps teach her about flying. From this point on, flying became her singular goal and consuming passion. She eagerly wanted to follow in the footsteps of her sister and father.

When they returned to Delhi, Aashna told her parents about her newfound love. They were taken by surprise, as they had thought she would follow some other path. A career in flying is risky, a fact Capt. Sharan was well aware of. He knew of the uncertainty that accompanies this profession, having himself been a pilot for years and having gone through many experiences. He knew all about the difficulties that this profession presented. Their elder daughter, Deeksha, had just become a pilot and had joined Indian Airlines, and now the younger one wanted to toe the same line! As a father, he was happy that in spite of their hijacking experience, his daughters were intrepid and confident, ready to take on any challenges that came their way. He and his courageous wife decided to fully support Aashna's aspirations. Like her sister, she joined the Karnal Flying Club while in Class 11. Her mother would pick her up from school and drive her to her flying lessons. Aashna managed to complete more hours than her sister had and to get her solo just as quickly. The sisters would often share their excitement about flying and discuss their solo flights. She was happy pursuing this new love, enjoying the direction her life had taken. In fact, both sisters realised they had grown closer because of this common passion. Deeksha guided her sister through flying school and was available to her as a mentor. There was always something to talk about, and they could not wait to swap anecdotes.

Aashna was eager to finish flying school as soon as possible, and like Deeksha, she too wanted to join a commercial airline. She would listen to her sister talk enthusiastically about work, including the Airbus endorsement, and would grow impatient. However, unfortunately for her, the DGCA published a new rule stating that the DGCA exams cannot be taken until completion of Class 12. Although she already had a Private Pilot Licence (PPL), she had to wait another year to appear for the CPL exams, and without clearing those exams, she would not be able to apply for a CPL. In this aspect, Aashna felt she was not as lucky as her sister, as she had to wait till the completion of Class 12 before she could continue her flying to get the CPL. After graduating from high school, she joined the Karnal Flying Club and, subsequently, the Patiala Flying Club to finish her hours faster. Once she got her CPL, she marched onward to get herself trained for A-320 type rating as there were no vacancies at Indian Airlines and, to apply for a job in private airlines, the A-320 type rating was a must for prospective pilots.

While waiting to secure a job, Aashna appeared for the Airline Transport Pilot Licence (ALTP) exams to enhance her resume. However, she had to wait for a few years to be able to apply to any airline. Finally, in 2014, she got selected and joined Indigo Airlines as a trainee pilot.

After completing training, she was ready to embark on a new challenging life as a co-pilot. Until this point, she had only heard her sister and father describe their own flying stories to encourage and inform her of what she was heading for. But now it was her turn, she was a co-pilot, sitting in her own seat and learning everything she could, and she wanted to garner her own lessons and experiences. On the other hand, she knew she could discuss her problems with her sister and father whenever she felt like.

She shares one of her most memorable experiences as a co-pilot, something she never thought could actually happen. This was a flight from Bagdogra to Mumbai in bad weather, and during the flight in cruise, her commander's windowpane cracked. It was a long flight and all through the route, they were anticipating bad weather. Her commander remained totally in control, calm and optimistic. He knew what had to be done under the circumstances. So he checked the MEL (Minimum Equipment List) and followed the procedures listed there to continue safely on this long flight to Mumbai. This was a great learning experience for her. That day, she saw and learned how her commander checked the MEL, took the decision, and continued the flight to Mumbai. The experience also taught her how wx can sometimes interfere with an aircraft, and how one must take decisions in such circumstances. She learned the number of calculations a commander needs to make to maintain safety. This incident taught her more than what any textbook ever could. It boosted her confidence as a co-pilot at the time. Today, as a commander, she commands flights with confidence and conviction. Also, every experience during her earlier days added to her learning, and that is why when she was upgraded for command with barely 3,000 flying hours, she was positive she could handle this responsibility well.

Indigo Airlines has many young commanders, including her, she reveals. However, the company ensures that they are mature, responsible and capable of effective decision-making before promoting them to the position of commander. Aashna has also learned from her father and sister that when things seem to be moving too fast, it is important to slow down and analyse the situation before making any decisions. This lesson helped her immensely, particularly when she became commander in May 2018.

She shares an incident that occurred when she was still a new commander and it reflects her unwavering belief in herself and in flying. She remembers that during her command training, she had experienced landing in the rain only in the simulator; the monsoons had not yet set in. She admitted to her father that since she had not landed in actual rain, she felt a bit uneasy, especially as she was now in command. He assured her that the examiner knew her capabilities, so she should fly with full confidence. Shortly after this conversation, she commanded a flight to Mumbai. The monsoon season was yet to begin in Mumbai, but just as they were approaching the city, it started raining. She continued her flight into Mumbai with total ease and kept her co-pilot informed by providing a full briefing of their approach and go-around. As they were landing, it started to pour. However, it was a smooth touchdown and she felt great landing in actual rain! Her clear thinking and self-confidence made her forget that she was landing in rain as a commander for the first time. It turned out to be a routine flight. She has always kept her father's words in mind: 'Take your flight with confidence, it really helps.'

Both sisters have had great journeys. Deeksha transitioned smoothly from high school and flying school to the airline when she was just nineteen years old. Aashna, although she began the same way, had to wait for nearly three years before she was hired as a pilot. Regardless of their struggles, these young commanders followed their dreams. They never took things for granted; they stayed focused and dedicated throughout. The cockpit is truly where they belong. They agree that they are totally at peace up in the sky, where they cannot be disturbed by anything, not even by their phones, a nuisance we all face these days. They believe their work is innately imbued with calm, peace and relaxation, and it's a journey worth every moment!

Capt. Aashna Sharan – commander, Airbus 320, with Indigo Airlines

Capt. Deeksha Sharan – commander, Airbus 320, with Air India

Conclusion

Twenty

Behind the Cockpit Door

Ever since the Wright Brothers flew their first flying machine in December 1903, people have been fascinated by the miracle of flight. The aviation industry has grown manifold, becoming a way of life for many. Its modernisation has made it possible for humans to reach impossibly far destinations in the shortest possible time. In addition, flying into space has also become a reality today.

People still love to look up at the sky when they hear the sound of an aircraft, spellbound, and perhaps even dreaming of taking flight themselves. I have often noticed passengers like to peep inside the cockpit as they board the aircraft; some even like to meet and shake hands with pilots, enraptured by their work. The array of panels, knobs and lights in the cockpit often make people exclaim, 'Wow, do you have to know every bit of this equipment? How do you monitor all these instruments?' Pilots smile and let them know that this is what they are trained to do; they are accustomed to the layout of the cockpit and its procedures and scans, so it is easy for them to monitor every panel. No job is easy, but flying big jets calls for more specific and intense training. It is a high-risk profession where every second matters. Decisions have to be correct, concise and quick as they affect the passengers on board. There are no shortcuts to procedures, no maybes in decision-making; it's either a 'yes' or a 'no', or in technical terms, a 'go' or a 'no go', and thinking in this way becomes second nature to pilots when faced with any situation.

As this book talks extensively about women as pilots, it would be apt to conclude with a description of what it takes to become a pilot and, more importantly, of how to maintain a career in flying.

To begin, flying is a non-degree professional course. The first step is joining a flying school, where there is intense flying training alongside ground classes for technical skills and performance of the aircraft. Students are required to pass technical and performance exams, based on their technical knowledge and performance, related to the aircraft they choose to fly. Other areas of examination are navigation, metrology and air regulations. These are specific exams conducted by the DGCA, the licence-issuing authority in India. They also undergo a medical examination by a DGCA-approved medical institute. Students receive a licence after successfully clearing the exams and proving their medical fitness, besides logging flying hours in dual, solo, cross-country, and day and night conditions. The training is considered complete only after a flying test is conducted by a DGCA-approved examiner. While this training and practical experience does not amount to a degree, pilots earn a CPL after meeting the requisite hours and clearing the exams. Most flyers therefore achieve degrees either via correspondence or by joining a university outside of their flying institute.

The next big challenge is gaining employment in an airline as a pilot. The selection procedure usually takes place after an airline advertises its requirement for pilots. If a candidate holds a valid CPL and meets the required medical fitness standards, both of which have specific periods of validity beyond which they require renewal, they apply to the airline and write the stipulated entrance exam. Such an exam typically tests candidates in technical knowledge and aptitude. On clearing the written round, a candidate faces a group discussion and personal interview. The interview, conducted by panellists from various segments of the aviation industry as well as a psychologist, is intense.

Those who make it often feel lucky and blessed, as only about 3 to 5 per cent of applicants are selected. They are then inducted as trainee pilots under probation and are only made permanent crew members after rigorous training, including flying and technical training on the aircraft they are inducted to fly. Even after being released as First Officers, they are placed under probation for one year. If a trainee fails any checks or exams at any stage, their services can be terminated.

An airline's training for specific aircraft can take anywhere between nine months to a year or more. It starts with technical and performance ground classes. A trainee learns about every system in the aircraft and then they face exams at the end of each module. Anything below 70 per cent is considered failing; one is given up to two chances to clear each test. Following these, one takes a consolidated technical exam. Besides learning about the technical aspects of the aircraft, one also needs to study extensively about its performance. The aircraft performance includes study material such as charts for day-to-day take-offs and landings, optimum weight for every flight, keeping in mind issues specific to the airfield, including wind, terrain, slope of the runway and elevation of the airport, all of which affect the performance of the aircraft. It also includes the ideal speeds for take-off and landing and during various other emergencies, such as gear-down flight and single-engine performance, among others.

Once a candidate passes these internal exams, they are permitted to take the DGCA technical and performance exams. The pass percentage remains the same. After the DGCA exams, one moves closer to flying, with simulator training based on the aircraft they intend to operate. This training comes close to the practical application of technical and performance knowledge. It includes navigation and weather handling, which a pilot experiences daily. Since the simulator replicates the actual feel of the aircraft, candidates train in complete uniform, even carrying flight bags that contain mandatory items such as the Quick Reference Handbook (QRH), airport let-down charts and en-route maps.

Simulator training also encompasses extensive emergency drills, such as reject take-offs, single-engine performance, hydraulic failure, pressurisation failure, fuel leaks and electric failure, etc. The bookings take place continuously for 4 hours, with the pilots taking turns to be commander and co-pilot for 2 hours each. Like any cockpit, the simulator also has two crew members, one flying commander and a non-flying co-pilot. On every flight, each captain performs their duties and checks lists – commonly referred to as seat-oriented tasks – and each trainee performs these same actions in the simulator. However, an instructor is present during simulator training. A trainee's performance is recorded in a log that contains all practice exercises. After the training is complete, a DGCA-approved examiner tests the trainee in flying, managing, handling and landing the aircraft in emergency situations, mostly with multiple emergencies. They also test the trainee on the limitations of the aircraft and their performance and technical knowledge. Next, the trainee moves on to an actual aircraft for a few hours and has to clear the day and night checks. After they clear all aircraft checks, their licence is finally sent to the DGCA, along with the results of the written exams, simulator checks and medical fitness test for endorsement for the aircraft for which they have undergone exhaustive training.

Receiving the licence with an endorsement for a particular aircraft is an exhilarating feeling for every pilot. It is a deep sense of achievement and a certification that you can fly the big jet!

After receiving their licence and before they are posted to their base, the new pilot goes through more checks – one Second Officer and three First Officer release checks with an examiner on a regular passenger flight. Finally, they begin to operate regular scheduled flights. But the journey of training does not end here. The young pilot now undergoes LOFT with an instructor, who monitors performance and provides route familiarisation before clearing them for a flight with any commander of the base. One's flying journey begins as a released co-pilot or First Officer only after being cleared by the instructor. The pilot has six-monthly route checks in the aircraft, simulator checks that include all emergency procedures and medical fitness exams. There are also yearly technical and performance exams and many upgradation training courses and checks.

Once they pass the DGCA exams and log a certain number of flying hours, a pilot climbs slowly to the rank of a captain; then, after more exams and still more hours, their licence is upgraded to an ALTP, and they graduate to the position of a commander. In a nutshell, they move from First Officer to Captain to Commander. The ladder of growth does not end at this point. A pilot may choose to work towards becoming a check pilot, an instructor, and finally, an examiner. Every step requires more exams, more checks and more training.

If a pilot is moved to another aircraft, say from a Boeing to an Airbus, they go through the full training procedure once again. Once they receive an endorsement for a particular aircraft, they fly only that aircraft; even if they are moved back to their first aircraft, they need to undergo training yet again.

Returning to work after 30 days' leave requires a route check before a pilot can fly. If for some reason they are grounded for more than 6 months, they go through complete endorsement training again, including ground classes, with all exams and checks. Medical fitness certificates have to be renewed every 6 months.

When a pilot is on the way to becoming a commander (provided they possess a valid ALTP licence and medical certificate), they first take command ground classes, then simulator command suitability checks and, lastly, command training. It is a completely new training, resembling an endorsement, but it is stringent with no leniency. The pilot once again goes through LOFT at base and then ten command route checks. There is no gender difference in training and every captain has to go through the same procedure, clearing multiple checks and exams. After this exhaustive training, during which a trainee can be laid off for any reason, they receive a licence for a PIC (Pilot-In-Command) endorsed for that particular aircraft. This is the ultimate achievement of a pilot's career. From flying school to First Officer to Captain, a pilot waits for the day they become a Commander. It is like being on top of the world!

To sum up, the next time you peep into a cockpit or look up into the skies to watch an awesome aircraft flying past, you can be sure it is in safe hands. A pilot's career is full of checks, exams and training that last till the day of retirement; even if they are due to retire in a day, they cannot fly without clearing their checks. A pilot only flies on a valid licence and a valid medical fitness certificate. Surely this is a profession where training, ground classes, checks and exams are part and parcel of the job. New aid, new equipment, airport upgradation and aircraft modification all require regular training.

Although pilotry is a stressful profession where one must handle emergencies single-handedly and make split-second decisions following SOPs at all times, it gives the pilot a powerful sense of achievement. It involves years of checks and exams that slowly become part of one's way of life.

A sneak-peek into a pilot's diary reveals the multiple checks and rounds of training they have undergone, besides the real-life lessons they have learned. In a nutshell, a pilot is always prepared for the unexpected. Yet, even the most challenging, high-risk situation that this profession entails does not take away the pleasure of operating these magnificent flying machines. A pilot is the epitome of sheer grit and determination, loving every moment of their chosen life!

Acknowledgements

Ideas don't necessarily transform into reality. You need someone who encourages you, understands your passion and pushes you to put down those thoughts on paper. I am grateful to my dear friend Chaya J. Nanawati and, more importantly, her sister Preeti Joshi who, while visiting me from the USA, gave me the seed that sowed to turn my passion into a book!

It all started as stories that people found interesting and inspiring. They were amazed at the fact that women in India have not only been dreaming to reach for the skies, but have worn the wings to fly since 1936.

I dedicate this book to all those amazing women around the world who have not only inspired me but many more like me in their passion to fly. This book would not have been possible without the support and information provided by all those who willingly agreed to be part of this work of compiling the lost history of women in aviation in India.

I extend my thanks to Manjul Balakrishnan (the elder daughter of Capt. Sarla Thukral) and her son Rahul.

Thanks to my sister-in-law, Mandira Mohan, whose maternal

uncle Mr Rakesh Jayal introduced me to Mr Rakesh Mathur (nephew of Capt. Prem Mathur) and his wife Vimi Mathur. I truly appreciate her generosity in welcoming me to their home and, along with her sister-in-law Nandini M. Chandraratnam (niece of Capt. Prem), providing me with all possible information, written notes and pictures of Capt. Prem. Vimi also introduced me to Mr Mahesh Sahai, another nephew of Capt. Prem, who readily took time out to interact with me and shared valuable information related to her childhood.

Thanks to Piali Ganguli, niece of Capt. Durba Banerjee, for her inputs, stories related to Capt. Durba on flying and for providing pictures of her aunt.

Special thanks to all my fellow captains flying in the airlines (Indian Airlines, Air India, Jet Airways, Indigo) for taking time out and sharing their stories to make this work possible.

Special thanks also to CMD of Air India, Mr Rajiv Bansal, for his invaluable words of encouragement with his foreword for the book.

My heartfelt gratitude to the brave Gunjan Saxena for having appreciated this work, finding the time to read the manuscript and considering our civil flying as important by giving such a lovely blurb.

A big thank you to Ankita and her team for the beautiful cover art. I highly appreciate the attention given to detail that has succeeded in bringing out succinctly what the book is all about.

A huge thank you to the editorial team at Amaryllis, for being as invested in the book as I am.

A real big thanks to Rashmi Menon who helped to get everything organised, and to Bidisha Srivastava, who was always available each time I had any query, and gave the final touch-up to the text.

And, finally, to my dearest family, daughters Taranee and Anchita, who were constantly available for any help I needed during the compilation stage, and also for helping me whenever I got stuck with technical issues on my laptop.

Last but not the least, my husband Deepak, for listening to the stories a number of times and patiently giving feedback. I really can't say if he enjoyed doing this, but he certainly gave his inputs as and when needed.

Abbreviations

AAI—Airport Authority of India
ADF—Automatic Direction Finders
AFCME—Air Force Central Medical Establishment
AIPWS—Air India Pilots Welfare Society
ALTP—Airline Transport Pilot's Licence
APWSS—Air India Pilots Welfare & Solidarity Society
ATC—Air Traffic Control
BFI—Bihar Flying Institute
CFI—Chief Flying Instructor
CPL—Commercial Pilot Licence
CRM—Crew Resource Management
CTE—Central Training Establishment
CVR—Cockpit Voice Recorder
DFDR—Digital Flight Data Recorder
DGCA—Director General Civil Aviation
DME—Distance Measuring Equipment
F/O—First Officer
FDTL—Flight Duty Time Limitation
FYI—For Your Information

IAF—Indian Air Force
IATA—International Air Transport Association
IGRUA—Indira Gandhi Rashtriya Uran Akademi
ILS—Instrument Landing System
IWPA—Indian Women Pilots' Association (now International Women Professionals in Aviation and Aerospace)
LOFT—Line Operating Flight Training
LTC—Line Training Captain
MEL—Minimum Equipment List
METAR—Meteorological Terminal Aviation Routine Weather Report
MSA—Minimum Safe Altitude
NDA—National Defence Academy
NDB—Non-Directional Beacons
PIC—Pilot In Command
PMO—Prime Minister's Office
PMT—Pre-Medical Test
PPE—Personal Protection Equipment
PPL—Private Pilot Licence
PTT—Push To Talk
QRH—Quick Reference Handbook
R/T—Radio Communication to the ATC
RT—Radio Telephony
SFOI—Senior Flight Operation Inspector
SOP—Standard Operating Procedure
SPL—Student Pilot Licence
SSB—Services Selection Board
SSC—Staff Selection Commission
TCAS—Traffic Alert and Collision Avoidance System
TRI—Type Rated Instructor
ULR—Ultra Long Range
UPSC—Union Public Service Commission
VOR—Very high frequency Omni-directional Range
WX—Weather